GREAT TRUE SPY ADVENTURES

GREAT TRUE SPY ADVENTURES

Selected and edited by

ALFRED PERLÈS

ARCO PUBLICATIONS LIMITED

LONDON

First Edition 1957
New Edition 1958

CONTENTS

v

ACKNOWLEDGMENTS

Acknowledgment is made to the following for permission to use material in this anthology:

Behind the Scenes of Espionage by Winfried Lüdecke.
   Published by George G. Harrap Limited.

The Dark Invader by Captain Von Rintelen.
   Published by Lovat Dickson Limited.

The Story of Louise de Bettignies by Antoine Redier.
   Published by Hutchinson & Co. Limited.

I Spied for France by Marthe Richer.
   Published by John Long Limited.

Russian Hazard by Dorian Blair & C. H. Dand.
   Published by Robert Hale Limited.

My Master Spy by Marthe McKenna.
   Published by Jarrolds Limited.

The Adventures of Sidney Reilly by Sidney Reilly.
   Published by Elkin Mathews & Marrot.

The Revolt by Menachem Begim.
   Published by W. H. Allen Limited.

Duel for the Northland by Kurt Singer.
   Published by Robert Hale.

The Eddie Chapman Story by Frank Owen.
   Published by Allan Wingate Limited.

No Dram of Mercy by Sybil Kathigasu.
   Published by Neville Spearman Limited.

Joey's Quiet War by Thomas M. Johnson.
   Published by the *Reader's Digest*.

Operation Cicero by L. C. Moyzisch.
   Published by Allan Wingate Limited.

The Idol of San Vittore by Indro Montanelli.
   Published by the *Reader's Digest*.

Odette by Jerrard Tickell.
   Published by Chapman & Hall Limited.

Specially Employed by Maurice Buckmaster.
   Published by the Batchworth Press.

Spy Catcher by Oreste Pinto.
    Published by T. Werner Laurie Limited.

The Crime of the Century by J. Edgar Hoover.
    Published by the *Reader's Digest*.

The Atom Spies by Oliver Pilat.
    Published by W. H. Allen Limited.

The Soviet Spies by Richard Hirsch.
    Published by Nicholas Kaye.

The Missing Diplomats by Cyril Connolly.
    Published by the Queen Anne Press,
    copyright *Sunday Times*, London.

The Petrov Story by Michael Bialoguski.
    Published by William Heinemann Limited.

Acknowledgments with thanks go to J. F. Bristow, E. V. Corbett, Anne Barret and Barbara Allanson, without whose enthusiastic research work into espionage literature this volume would not be complete as it is.

THE EDITOR.

PREFACE

THE tremendous fascination which the subject of espionage never fails to exert upon the imagination of man can be explained by a very good reason, or indeed several very good reasons.

For one thing, espionage is as old as the world. It has in the course of millenniums been perfected to a fine art, and recurs like a thread in the weave of succeeding civilisations. The ancient Egyptians resorted to it, and so did the Chaldeans, the Assyrians, the Babylonians and the Jews. There are instances of military espionage recorded in the Holy Scriptures.

Is it a wonder, then, that the idea of espionage, encrusted in the very fibre of our make-up, has at all times gripped the inventive spirit of mankind? The subject is ever topical, and spy stories, true or fictitious, are amongst the most popular with the reading public of both hemispheres.

Our war-ridden world has never been able to do without espionage. History is an almost uninterrupted series of war and armed conflict, which should not, however, be interpreted as meaning that there will always be war. There are, in fact, signs today that some of our more recent means of internecine destruction may prove a healthy deterrent to the activities of our warmongers at home and abroad; which is to be desired in the interest of mankind's continued existence. But even the abolition of war will not put an end to the practice of espionage.

For the range of espionage is not restricted to military purposes alone. There can be a peaceful use of espionage, just as there can be, as we are being occasionally reminded, a peaceful use of atomic power. Essentially, espionage is a method of ferreting out information about the rival's intentions, his potentialities and contemplated course of action, with a view to forestalling him. It is constantly being practised in trade, industry, publicity, even in women's fashions. In the realm of any competitive human activity, there is room for a spy ring. The espionage technique has spread to all walks of life and to a far wider extent than is commonly known. In a sense, the attachés accredited to the various departments of foreign embassies are potential spies.

In this volume, however, the editor has confined himself to present a selection of the most baffling military espionage adventures of modern times, from 1914 to the present nuclear age, via the second world war. It is an anthology of the best-known stories, specially chosen for their veracity and sensational repercussions, which shook the world in the last few decades. They will, it is hoped, fill the bill for the most fastidious addict of the genre, who may now comfortably recline in his armchair and follow the peripatetics of some of the world's most dangerous espionage agents at the safe distance of the fireside.

THE EDITOR.

I

THE LEGENDARY MATA HARI

from

BEHIND THE SCENES OF ESPIONAGE

by WINFRIED LÜDECKE

(Published by George G. Harrap & Co. Ltd., London, 1929)

Nearly four decades have passed since her espionage exploits for the Germans that resulted in her execution by a French firing squad, but Mata Hari is not forgotten. Books have been written and films made about her; in the course of years she has assumed a quasi-legendary stature.

Although a native of Holland, where she was born in 1876, Mata Hari was a truly cosmopolitan figure, who had widely travelled all over the world as a variety performer before succumbing to the lure of adventure and offering her services as a spy to the Germans during the first world war. Beautiful, elegant, clever and reckless, she was able to supply much useful military information to the German High Command, which paid her handsomely for her activities.

Her background of variety artist, combined with the fact that she was a citizen of a neutral country, enabled her to travel freely in war-ridden Europe and to collect valuable information for her employers in France, Belgium and England. She was eventually caught by the French in 1917, tried and condemned to death.

★

MATA HARI, "the Eye of the Morning," was the poetic Javanese pseudonym adopted by a famous variety artist, who, according to her papers, was a divorced woman named MacLeod, née Margareta Gertruda Zelle. She was born in 1876 in Lèeuwarden, in Holland, and became one of the subtlest and cleverest secret agents thrown up by the first world war. This international courtesan, the mistress of ministers, officers and artists of all nations; this woman, whose insatiable thirst for luxury and money brought many a man of substance to beggary, was at the same time a dancer, who, with the play of her supple naked body in Indian temple dances, roused to thunderous applause the music-hall public in London, Paris, Berlin and Rome. This adventuress, who was as much at home in Sydney, New York and Cairo as in her elegant mansion, No. 11 rue Windsor, Neuilly, Paris, paid for by a millionaire marquis; this *demi-mondaine* with the airs of a great lady, who, in Germany, raved over her disappointed love for the Crown Prince, and, in France, indicated the Russian Captain Marov as the one man whom, in all her life, she had truly loved; this bewitching sorceress of love and art also entered the dangerous province of espionage, for which, by her beauty, her great intellectual gifts and her daring, she certainly seemed remarkably well qualified. Was it the titillating stimulus of danger that she sought, or was it the lust for gold that this career promised so quickly to satisfy, that made her enter upon the path that led her in the end to Vincennes?

In the trial that took place in the year 1917 behind closed doors in Paris the story of her life that was unfolded was like some sensational film drama. Some interesting details have been made public by Major Count Massard.

On the day of the declaration of war Mata Hari was in Berlin, where she was appearing in the Wintergarten as an Indian dancing girl. By the German secret service, who registered her as H.21, she was commissioned to go to Paris, which did not entail any great difficulty for her, seeing that she was a Dutch subject and therefore neutral. She received the handsome sum of thirty thousand marks, and went via Belgium, Holland and England to Paris, on the pretext that she was going to break up her house in Neuilly. From Paris she went, after a time, to the French front, staying in Vittel for many months disguised as a nurse. It was here that she devoted herself to the severely wounded and blinded Russian officer Marov, whom she appears to have tended with really touching care, asserting that she loved him passionately. All through this period she was in uninterrupted correspondence with the chief of the German intelligence service in Amsterdam. Her letters were forwarded by the Dutch Embassy in Paris, who were under the delusion that she was corresponding with her daughter in Holland. It was a simple matter for the beautiful hospital nurse to gain the confidence of the French officers, and especially of the flying-officers, from whom, no doubt, in moments of amorous delight, she obtained valuable military information. She was able to give the German Army command most useful details as to the disposition of French spies on the German front, and betrayed the preparations that were being made for a French counter-offensive in 1916.

The British secret service was the first to warn the French authorities against her, and at last they too had their suspicions aroused. When she became aware that she was being observed she quitted the front and returned to Paris. But even here she did not feel safe. What was she to do? She did what most spies are wont to do in such circumstances: she offered her services to the other side. She went to the second bureau of the French General Staff and made a statement purporting to give the points on the Moroccan coast where German submarines were

THE LEGENDARY MATA HARI 3

sheltering: the statement was, of course, an invention. At the same time she proposed that she should be sent to the occupied zone in Belgium, to convey instructions to the French agents posted there. The French secret service pretended to accept the offer, and handed her a list of all the names of their people employed at the time in Belgium. But this list was really a trap; for, of the names included in the list, only one was genuine; and this exception was that of an agent who, they had good reason to believe, was a double spy. Three weeks later this man was shot by the Germans in Brussels. Only Mata Hari could have given him away, by communicating that list, somehow or other, to the enemy.

She had not yet left Paris; but as she belonged to the neutrals and there was no absolutely clear proof that suspicion was well founded, they did not care to proceed at once to arrest her. She was allowed to leave France.

Here the account of her movements is somewhat obscure. It is certain that she managed to find her way to Germany, for a personal friend of the Crown Prince ran across her in the street in Cologne, and had a long talk with her. She gave him to understand that she intended to go back, sooner or later, to France and would not be dissuaded, alleging that she had professional engagements to keep. On leaving him she used these curious and telltale words, "Remember me as a woman who has done and suffered much for Germany."

It is also certain that the British authorities were aware of her movements. They managed to secure her person, probably arresting her on board ship, and conveyed her to London, where she was subjected to a very thorough cross-examination by Sir Basil Thomson, the chief of Scotland Yard. With consummate skill she strove to avoid all the traps he laid for her, and the interview ended most unexpectedly on her admission that she was indeed a spy, but for France, not for Germany. She was sent off to Spain; with what commission is not stated.

Her arrival there was, of course, known to both sides, and from the moment she set foot on shore in the port of Gijon, a French secret agent attached himself to her, following her wherever she went and taking care never to let her out of his sight. He was, from the start, so successful in his job that, on the very day of her landing, he had a photograph taken and sent to his employers, which showed himself and the all-unsuspecting dancer on the one plate. In Madrid she took up her abode in a well-appointed suite of rooms in a fashionable hotel, and was soon on very intimate terms with a particularly fascinating German attaché there. Her relations with him developed quickly into a regular liaison. There was no opportunity of bringing her charms to bear directly upon the King, who would certainly have known much of what mattered most at the moment concerning Entente policy, so they endeavoured to bring about an association between her and the French military attaché, who lived in the same hotel. But of him she could make nothing. Having been warned beforehand, he successfully repelled all the advances she made to him, on every conceivable pretext.

The German attaché gave the lady one or two dainty trinkets, but Mata Hari needed money, always money. So, as they could make no further use of her as an agent in Spain, it was decided to send her back to Paris, where in any case, as she had told her friend in Cologne, she wished to go. And it was then that the thing was done which sealed her fate.

The attaché sent an urgent wireless message to the chief of the intelligence service in Amsterdam requesting him to have fifteen thousand pesetas paid to H.21, by the intermediary of the Dutch Embassy, on her return to Paris. This wireless message was intercepted by the Eiffel Tower; and as the French were by this time informed of Mata Hari's letter and number, it was resolved to arrest her. She was allowed to return to Paris, in order to receive payment due at the Dutch Embassy, and almost immediately after she had paid this call the police conveyed her to the St. Lazare prison.

The proceedings before the court martial were not without dramatic episodes. Mata Hari made ingenious efforts to defend herself. She admitted quite frankly the various remittances from Amsterdam and her correspondence with the chief spy in Holland, whose mistress she said she was. But, she protested, it was not a question of espionage at all, but simply of a love affair. She had certainly been a courtesan, but never a spy. Her advocate, an old gentleman of seventy-five, who appeared to be in love with her, and chivalrously lavished flowers and sweetmeats upon her, cited as a witness for the defence a French diplomatist who occupied a very exalted post in the Foreign Office. He had been her first lover after her divorce, and with him she had spent three evenings on her return from Madrid. He testified that the subject of their conversations had been Indian art. A very intimate document from a French Minister of War was read aloud and provoked in the court a significant smile. Apparently Mata Hari had used these connections to give herself the necessary importance in the eyes of her employers.

She was unanimously condemned to death, and heard the sentence with a convulsive sort of smile and a shrug of the shoulders. On the day before her execution she was dancing in her cell and took a bath. She had asked to be allowed to bathe in milk, but had to be satisfied with water. The execution took place at six o'clock on the morning of

October 15th, 1917. The Dutch Government had vainly tried to intervene at the last moment; and, as vainly, her counsel had tried to obtain a reprieve by appealing to a certain article of the criminal code, affirming that she was pregnant by his agency. Mata Hari would not have anything to do with this line of strategy, and refused to undergo the medical examination. She wrote a few letters of farewell, and then entered the motor-car that conveyed her, accompanied by a military escort, to Vincennes. As proud as a princess she walked past the file of soldiers, who were standing at the present. She bade farewell to her advocate, who embraced her, and to the Sister of Mercy who had watched over her and tended her in her cell, and then received the last words of consolation from the priest. A gendarme led her to the stake to pinion her, but she objected. She likewise refused to be blindfolded. The officer in charge of the firing party raised his sword. The drums rolled. The clergyman stepped aside. Mata Hari smiled and threw kisses to the lawyer and the priest. Then, short and sharp, came the order, "Fire!" A sergeant-major gave her the *coup de grâce* by firing his revolver into her ear. The doctor certified her death. The body of the beautiful dancer and spy, once so ardently loved and admired, was thrown into a plain whitewood coffin. *Finita la commedia!*

II

THE HUMAN CHAMELEON

from

BEHIND THE SCENES OF ESPIONAGE

by WINFRIED LÜDECKE

(Published by George G. Harrap & Co. Ltd., London, 1929)

*Ignatius Timothy Trebitsch-Lincoln's life was one long, uninterrupted chain o,
adventures, and his actions can only be accounted for by the fact that he was a born
adventurer. And he was a chameleon as well; in the history of espionage and
double-dealings, there is no instance of a man who changed professions, nation-
alities and religions as frequently and nonchalantly as the erstwhile Hungarian
Trebitsch-Lincoln.*

*Frankly, he did not do so well as a spy, for both the British and the Germans
suspected him of double-crossing them, which, given the chance, he would, of
course, have had no compunction to do. His greatest achievement, in our
opinion, was to become a British M.P. in 1910, as the Member for Darlington.*

*Although his nefarious activities date nearly half a century back, his rôle as a
traitor and double agent has not been surpassed since.*

★

IGNATIUS TIMOTHY TREBITSCH-LINCOLN, the international adventurer
and spy, may justly lay claim to the doubtful glory of being acknow-
ledged as the greatest political charlatan and humbug of his time, for he
managed to take a hand in an extraordinary number of notorious
scandals and disturbances in public life. His versatility in the province of
political crime and the chameleon-like gift he displayed in changing
his coat bordered on the marvellous. He was an actor, or, to speak
more accurately, a quick-change artist, with the talent of a professional
in the performance of all the parts demanded by his dangerous game,
while the scenes of the amazing dramas in which he appeared embraced
the continents. We find him not only in Europe, but also in America
and Asia, as a journalist, political agent, priest, Member of Parliament,
forger, double spy, Buddhist monk, and mandarin. What led him to
adopt this many-coloured kaleidoscopic sort of existence? Was he
merely cool and calculating, with an irresistible thirst for wealth
acquired anyhow and at any cost? Was he impelled by morbid ambition to attain political power, and skilful enough, for a time, to choose

the easy path opened to him by unexpected but favourable opportunity? Was he possessed by the love of adventure, the desire for
exciting experience, the exhilarating enjoyment of danger? We cannot
tell what it was that brought this remarkable Hungarian, for a brief
period, into such a prominent position upon the political stage. This
only we know, that his meteoric career was run on bluff; that it was as
full of sensation as an American film; that it came to a sudden end, after
all its brilliance, falling to earth like an exploded rocket.

Lincoln, or, to give him his real name, Trebitsch, was born in the
Hungarian town of Paks, situated on the Danube. It was not a big
place, but its trade was prosperous. There his father, who was a Jew in
comfortable circumstances, had a thriving boat-building yard. Ignatius
was a younger son, and as he was destined for the profession of rabbi, he
received a very careful and thorough education. His chief intellectual
interest was the study of foreign tongues.

When he reached the age of twenty years he set off on his travels,
and presently arrived in London. Here he took a rather unusual step for
a budding rabbi: he joined the Anglican Church. After a certain lapse
of time he returned home and found his father very naturally indignant
at the conduct of his renegade son. Ignatius, therefore, found it advisable not to postpone too long his second departure. In fact he left the
house of his parents with all possible speed, and betook himself to
Hamburg, where, in 1899, he changed his religious denomination for
the second time, on this occasion going over to the Lutheran Church.
By his brethren of this persuasion he was sent to Canada, as a missionary
to the Jews. But, strangely enough, he had not long exercised his new
functions when the mission was transferred to the Anglican Church,
with the result that Trebitsch promptly changed his faith again. For
some years he remained in that position of Anglican missionary,
earning a reputation as a sound and able preacher. Then we find him on
furlough in Germany. At his own request he was appointed by the
authorities of the Church in England to the living of Appledore in
Kent. However, the worthy villagers in this parish appear not to have
taken very kindly to this ex-Hungarian Jew as a pastor, and the latter,
after remaining with them for some fourteen months, decided that his
best policy was to leave his flock to their own devices. He went to
London, where he discovered a talent for journalism, and contributed
for a year or two to several newspapers.

The year 1906 brought with it a decided turn in the affairs of
this man. He went in for politics. He made the acquaintance of Mr.
Seebohm Rowntree, the well-known Quaker, who was also a distinguished member of the Liberal Party. The young Hungarian was

undoubtedly capable and gifted, and Mr. Rowntree was so much attracted to him that he made him his private secretary. It must be admitted that Trebitsch had a strange way of showing his gratitude, for he rewarded the trust of his patron and friend by relieving him of the handsome sum of seven hundred pounds: he forged his signature to a bill. His crime was not discovered till years after, but it was paid for.

His efforts to win political laurels were crowned with success, for, in 1910, he made his entry into the House of Commons, as Member for Darlington. The House did not take him very seriously, however; he was a stranger, and his foreign pronunciation often excited noisy mirth. He was sent at various times by his party on tours of investigation, for the purpose of studying economic conditions on the continent of Europe, and was thus brought into touch with eminent politicians and diplomatists. But these continual journeys began to excite a certain degree of suspicion. When he lost his seat in Parliament at the last election before the 1914-18 war, he found himself in a financial situation that was anything but favourable.

Then came the war. His civil status, as an alien and really a subject of one of the hostile belligerent Powers, made his position decidedly more difficult. However, there were influential people to supply him with credentials, and he applied to the War Office for employment as censor of Hungarian and Roumanian correspondence. And he actually received such an appointment! He was not maintained in it very long, for his colleagues naturally looked askance at him, considering him as an enemy within the gates and suspecting him of double-dealing, although, possibly, he had not yet been guilty of any conduct that would have justified their attitude. In any case, he was obliged to give up his post in the censorship. Once more, then, he found himself in difficulties. In the club which he frequented people began to turn the cold shoulder to him, and it seemed evident that his expulsion was merely a matter of time.

It was then, so far as we can judge, that the thought entered his head of avenging the insults he had suffered at the hands of Englishmen, by betraying them; and he did not delay long in taking the steps necessary to achieve this purpose. Trebitsch became a German spy. He immediately got into communication with the British intelligence service, and, again with the aid of influential persons who could not believe the late M.P. capable of any evil design, he succeeded in obtaining an interview with responsible officials of the secret service, to whom he intimated his desire to assist in the work of counter-espionage. But Trebitsch did not present himself empty-handed. He was in the unexpected position of being able to submit to the British naval staff a plan, a really ingenious plan already fully worked out, which, in his opinion, would prove of the utmost value and importance to Britain. This fantastic scheme was, in a few words, as follows: Britain was to send out into the North Sea a small squadron, and he would then inform the German Admiralty of the fact. The Germans would send out a more powerful fleet and annihilate the British ships. But that would have enabled him to gain the confidence of the Germans. After this manœuvre had been repeated two or three times the great affair was to follow. The British would have a mighty fleet of dreadnoughts in waiting, and thus the whole German navy would be wiped out. That was Trebitsch-Lincoln's plan—far-fetched and stupid at one and the same time.

But somehow the British did not show any great appreciation of the naval strategy evolved by this zealous ex-M.P., for they saw through the sly proposals of the crafty Hungarian. They understood what he was after. Had such a project been realised, he would have acquired very reliable information concerning the station and distribution of the British naval forces, and would then have passed it on to the Germans. After ten days of futile expectation, he was told very dryly that his suggestions could not be accepted, as the authorities had no intention of letting him know anything of the whereabouts of British ships.

Trebitsch was never at a loss, however, and he had another proposal to lay before them. He offered to go to Rotterdam. He would pretend to place himself at the disposal of the German espionage service, and so be in the best possible position to serve the interests of Britain, by procuring information at first hand. The British authorities affected to approve of this scheme. He was given his passport, and in December he went to Rotterdam, where he at once made advances to the German consul-general. What he did not know was that his every step was being most carefully observed by agents of the British counter-espionage, who, before long, were quite convinced that it could not be Britain that he was working for. The information that he brought back from Holland was examined by Sir Reginald Hall, the chief of the naval intelligence staff, and proved to be utterly worthless. He was kept hanging about for a week or two, and was then summoned to appear before the chief, bringing his passport with him. Sir Reginald Hall had no doubt whatever of the fact that he had been playing the dangerous part of double spy, and gave him clearly to understand that the sooner he turned his back upon England, the better it would be for him. He realised that the game was up so far as his stay in England was concerned; and, very much relieved at not finding himself under arrest,

Trebitsch did not wait to be told twice. The very next day he sailed for New York on board the steamer *Philadelphia*.

He arrived at New York on February 9th. The first thing he did on landing was to present himself to the German secret service, but they refused to have any dealings with him. Apparently they, too, distrusted him. So Trebitsch resumed his journalistic activities and contributed articles to the pro-German American Press.

In the meantime his act of forgery had been discovered in England, and the British Government made an application to the American authorities for his extradition. This was granted only after protracted negotiations. On August 4th, 1915, Trebitsch was arrested and at once conveyed to England, where he was tried and sentenced to a long term of imprisonment. His time expired during the summer of 1919, and on coming out of prison he was to be deported to Hungary. But it happened that Bela Kun's reign of terror was just then raging in Budapest so Trebitsch-Lincoln's expulsion was delayed for some weeks. In September of that year he was sent out of England, and found himself once more in the capital of his native land, where, however, the atmosphere proved, after a short stay, rather uncongenial. He therefore quitted Hungary and went to Germany, where there were then brighter prospects of fishing in troubled waters.

He made some attempt to approach the ex-Kaiser Wilhelm, in the palace of Amerongen in Holland, but had no success in that venture. That did not stand in the way of his being taken up by the reactionary and monarchist circles of Berlin, who had grouped themselves round Kapp. He managed to win the confidence of men like Colonel Bauer and Captain Pabst; and, his journalistic ability once more standing him in good stead, he became the director of the Press campaign that was being carried on in preparation for Kapp's abortive insurrection, in the execution of which he also played a considerable part. After the failure of this rising a warrant was issued for his arrest, but he fled with the other bravoes to Munich, where their new headquarters were established.

Here Trebitsch succeeded in doing what Major Stephani had failed to do, that was, to induce Pöhner, the chief of police, and Kahr, the Bavarian Prime Minister, to join the new project of the conspirators, who were planning to bring about the simultaneous action of Bavaria against Saxony and of Mecklenburg against Berlin. But as money—a great deal of money—was absolutely necessary for this purpose, Trebitsch received from the chief of police in Munich a false passport and went twice to Berlin, to interview Ludendorff or some other member of the initiated, who had control of the funds required. The Berlin detectives were on the look-out for him, and were occasionally close at his heels, although the Bavarian police had expressly warned him to be on his guard against them. On the occasion of his second visit to Berlin, he happened to come across Captain Pabst, who was still in possession of a large sum of money remaining from the treasury of the original conspiracy in Berlin, and who also knew Ludendorff's secret place of abode—a lonely house in the forest, in the neighbourhood of Rosenhain. The two of them went to call on Ludendorff, where Major Stephani also put in an appearance. It was resolved, for reasons of personal security, to transfer the headquarters to Budapest. The idea was, that the Hungarian and even the Russian monarchists should be persuaded to interest themselves in the movement, and that the revolution should be organised and directed from Budapest and Vienna. On May 8th a monarchist congress was to be held in Berlin. Trebitsch, therefore, betook himself once more to the German capital, but, for some reason or another, he was not very warmly received by the other partisans, who advised him that the police were after him and that he should make himself scarce. He followed their advice and disappeared, at least for the night, finding shelter in Trebbin, a little town near Potsdam, in the house of a governess who had once been employed by him. Next day he was standing on the platform, waiting to get into the train for Berlin, when he was recognised and stopped by an official of the criminal police. Trebitsch got the latter to allow him to go back, under escort, to his own quarters, in order to pack his things. The attention of his warder being distracted for a moment, the prisoner took advantage of the fact to jump through an open window, and so he made his escape.

But the police did have something to show for their trouble. One valuable piece of booty fell into their hands: a trunk containing the secret correspondence of the conspirators.

Trebitsch remained concealed for a short time in Potsdam, being sheltered by a political sympathiser. Then he made his way by Frankfort to his friends in Munich. Pöhner, the chief of police, gave him a note of introduction to the Hungarian consul-general in Munich, who was so well satisfied with his initiation into the immediate plans of his fellow countryman that he supplied him with a guardian angel as far as Vienna, in the shape of a consular official. In Vienna his difficulties threatened to become serious, for he noticed that he was being followed by detectives.

However, he found Gratz, the Hungarian Ambassador in Vienna, quite willing to have a new passport made out for him, and he arrived without further molestation in Budapest, hoping to obtain congenial employment. Without any loss of time he made the acquaintance of the deputies Gömbös and Eckhardt, and of Colonel von Pronay, the chief Press agent of the Hungarian Government. To them he unfolded a plan that was comparable in value to the one he had proposed to the British Admiralty during the war. A large number of German soldiers, dressed as civilians, were to be smuggled into Hungary, and there to receive their military equipment, after which they were to be sent against Vienna and Czechoslovakia. Colonel Bauer, who had accompanied Trebitsch, had actually received from Ludendorff plenary powers to conclude a preliminary treaty with Hungary. But Colonel Pronay did not look with approval upon this mad project, which struck him as being risky in the extreme. The whole scheme ended in smoke.

Trebitsch now understood that there was no further opportunity of using his talents in Germany and Austria, so he moved to Italy, trusting that, among the Fascists, there would surely be scope for his activities. And he was not disappointed. There is still a dark veil of mystery surrounding the intrigues in which he became involved as a Fascist, and perhaps this is not incomprehensible, if it be true, as has been alleged, that he had some connection with the murder of Matteotti.

Then, for a fairly long time, nothing more was heard of him, until people concluded that he was dead. But it was not so. He had certainly shaken off from his feet the dust of an ungrateful Europe. The astonished world heard through the reports from an American correspondent in China, that were being published in the New York *World*, of a certain Chilan, said to be the political adviser of Wu Pei Fu, and to have organised the anti-British propaganda in China. At the same time we learned that this Chilan was no other than the notorious Trebitsch-Lincoln, who had found a new outlet for his energies in the turmoil of the Far East. With cynical frankness he had related to the American newspaper-man the vicissitudes of his adventurous life, making no effort whatever to conceal his employment as a double spy during the first world war. It will hardly astonish anyone who knows his previous history to hear that in China he had once more changed his religion and gone over to Buddhism.

The last news of this incorrigible adventurer, that had interest for the world, was the announcement that he was returning from China to England. His son was under sentence of death for murder, and Trebitsch wished to see him once more before his execution. The British Government was magnanimously willing to put no obstacle in his way. But as a matter of fact the father was too late. During the course of his chequered career he had many a time had vast sums of money placed at his disposal for various purposes of conspiracy and underhand work. To mention only one case, Lieutenant-General Krauss had once opened for him a credit of 230,000 dollars. On this occasion, however, by the time he reached France, his financial resources were so completely exhausted that he was not able to pay the fare that would have brought him over the last short stage of his journey to London. He never saw his son again in life.

Since that last melancholy appearance, Trebitsch-Lincoln has faded completely from public notice.

III

CAPTAIN VON RINTELEN SURRENDERS

from

THE DARK INVADER

by CAPTAIN VON RINTELEN

(Published by Lovat Dickson Ltd., London, 1933)

Captain von Rintelen (Franz Rintelen Von Kleist), one of the most famous secret agents of German naval intelligence during the first world war, is reputed to have perfected sabotage to a fine art. This claim seems amply substantiated by his own account of thrilling exploits in neutral Europe and America.

As a young naval officer of remarkable intelligence and organising talent, Von Rintelen went abroad in 1915 and successfully accomplished a series of secret missions. His most outstanding successes were achieved in the United States, technically still neutral at the time, where he managed to establish an organisation of German seamen for the purpose of sabotaging the Allied war effort. He was ruthless and efficient, and the split-second timing of his action resulted in the sinking of a great number of ships carrying munitions and war materials to the Allied ports.

Von Rintelen was held in high esteem by friend and foe alike, and Admiral Sir William Reginald Hall, to whom he finally surrendered when arrested by British naval intelligence officers at Ramsgate, expressed his admiration "for the manner in which you have retained your balance of mind and your courage." The chief of the British Naval Intelligence Division was lavish in his praise of his German opponent, who, whatever methods he employed, always acted in the sacred service of his country.

★

I AGAIN became E. V. Gaché from Solothurn, and booked a passage on the *Noordam*, of the Holland-American Line. Accompanying me was a man whom I had engaged to help me during the crossing. He was a genuine American citizen and appeared in public as my friend.

I went on board full of despair at the thought of the work I had left unfinished; and as we left New York Harbour in the evening twilight I tortured myself with the mystery of the telegram which had ordered me to return. My companion pulled me out of the depression into which I had fallen, by announcing that he was hungry and it was time for dinner. He was powerfully built and had crossed the ocean more than once to give advice to the German Government. He had hit upon a splendid idea which gave him time to think when anyone addressed him unawares. He pretended to be stone deaf and always carried a gigantic ear-trumpet about with him. Every question had to be thundered into the trumpet, and this enabled him to prepare his answers. We descended to the dining-room and I ordered a bottle of wine to disperse my unenviable thoughts. As I looked round I received a dreadful shock. Sitting at a table opposite was a man whom I had known well in Berlin and had often met at dances, Count Limburg-Stirum, of the Dutch branch of the family. I must have grown pale, for my companion whispered:

"What's the matter?"

Limburg-Stirum had already crossed over to greet me, and asked: "Do you think you are going to get across safely?"

I registered astonishment and replied:

"Why not?"

"Well, after all, you are a German!"

"I? A German? Good heavens, I am a Swiss. In those days I was attached to the Swiss Legation in Berlin."

Limburg-Stirum looked at me in amazement. He hung round me during the whole crossing. He had of course seen my name "E. V. Gaché" on the door of my cabin and at my place at table, but he was certain that that had not been my name when he knew me in Berlin. Every time I saw him I had an odd feeling that he was going to remember just at that moment who I was, so I kept out of his way.

The good ship *Noordam* continued her voyage, and at last the chalk cliffs of England lay to port. I gazed at them with mixed feelings. It took a whole day to pass them, and I found it necessary to visit the bar at intervals to fortify myself. The chalk cliffs still lay on our left, when early in the morning, at seven o'clock on Friday, August 13th, as I was lying in my bath, a steward knocked at the door, and said:

"Some British officers wish to have a word with you."

This was the darkest moment of my life!

Nobody who had done what I considered it my duty to do in America, and was in possession of a forged passport, would have been anxious to converse with British officers opposite the white cliffs of England. Certainly not before breakfast. But I had no alternative. These gentlemen desired to speak with me, and there was no possibility of avoiding their welcome. I put my head outside and listened. The officers were not inspecting the other passengers, but had inquired exclusively for me, and I can truthfully say that it made an impression on me. I had an immediate intuition that I was discovered, and the only thing that could help me now was "bluff."

I went on deck in my bath-robe and found two officers and ten sailors with fixed bayonets waiting for me.

"You are Mr. Gaché?"

"Yes. What can I do for you?"

"We have orders to take you with us."

"I have no intention of disembarking here. I am going to Rotterdam."

"I am sorry. If you refuse, we have orders to take you by force."

"If you threaten me with force I have no alternative, as a Swiss citizen, but to follow you. Before I leave the boat, however, I demand the right to telegraph to the Minister of my country in London. In any case, I must dress and, above all, have breakfast. I am sure you will agree."

"How much time do you need?"

" About two hours."

"All right. We shall return at nine-thirty."

Punctually at nine-thirty the British escort came on board again and politely requested the Swiss gentleman to enter a steam pinnace. I was then taken on board a British auxiliary cruiser, where I was kept for three days. Morning, afternoon and evening there was a bottle of champagne available in the captain's cabin, presented by the British officers to keep the Swiss citizen, whom they all pitied so, in a good humour. One evening one of the officers poured his heart out to me. He told me that he had been consul in Karlsbad for seven years, knew all the German dialects, and could tell whether a man was justified or not in claiming to be a "neutral." He was tired of being the scapegoat every time a neutral traveller had to be put through the mill on his way up the Channel. He was completely fed up. "But," he said, "there is a fellow sitting in London who never gives up, and when we capture a neutral, we have to carry out our job as best we can. Just imagine! There's an old bear with a sore head in charge of the department and he's got a fixed idea that every neutral is suspect."

"Who is he?"

"Admiral Hall."

. . . . . .

On the last day of my stay on board the cruiser I was subjected to a surprise. I was confronted with my deaf American friend, who had also been taken off the *Noordam* as a suspicious character. He was being questioned on deck by an officer, who pointed at me.

"Wait a minute," cried my friend. With slow and deliberate movements he began to extract his great ear-trumpet from his case. The electric battery failed to function at once, so he turned a few screws and said to the officer: "Excuse me just a moment." He then applied the trumpet to his ear and roared:

"What did you say?"

The officer saw his great confrontation scene ruined, and turned crustily away without deigning to reply. My friend shouted at me:

"What are these people saying?" and then proceeded to run about the deck, as he fiddled with his ear-trumpet, and to call out continually to the officers on the bridge: "What do you want of me? What's that you say?"

It was easy for him, since he had a genuine passport and nothing much to fear. My position was more serious.

We were taken ashore at Ramsgate. We were examined, our papers were inspected, we were re-examined, and our papers once more inspected, and in the interval we were taken with great courtesy by car to an hotel and invited to tea. In the lounge I saw a man, a waiter, whom I had seen before somewhere, and I suddenly remembered. He had been at the Hotel Bristol in Berlin, where I used to be a frequent visitor. As we drank our tea I informed my deaf friend in a whisper of my disturbing discovery.

"That makes another old friend we've met," he complained. "Can't we go anywhere in the world without meeting somebody you know?"

We returned to headquarters.

"Please show your passports again for inspection."

"Yes, of course. Passport inspection."

We entered the room, and stationed in the corner I saw the waiter from the Bristol. I told myself to keep cool. The officer in charge, the Rt. Hon. Dudley Ward, M.P., a very eminent man, put to me the same questions that I had had to answer in the morning. Suddenly a shrill voice, full of hate and fury, broke in from the corner:

"Don't talk such rubbish! You are Captain Rintelen from Berlin."

I did not move an eyelash, for I had caught sight of the man in time, but calmly replied to the officer's question. A man talking nonsense in the corner had nothing to do with me! It was a pity there were such ill-bred people about.

The man roared again:

"You stop that! You are the German Captain Rintelen. I've known you for a long time."

It would have been suspicious if I had continued to take no notice, so I turned round towards him and said in astonishment:

"What's that?"

My deaf friend joined in and shouted, as he fixed his ear-trumpet:

"What's the man saying? What does he want of me? Or is he talking to you?"

His trumpet being by now adjusted, I thundered down it:

"There's somebody saying that I am . . ." I turned to the waiter. "What was the name? Will you spell it, please?"

An alphabetic pandemonium broke loose, and there was grotesque confusion between the English *a* and the German *e*. The name I shouted into the American's trumpet was one that had never existed. The sounds were all distorted, and we got thoroughly mixed up, until at last the American packed his trumpet into its case and said angrily: "I've had enough."

To which I replied: "There are always ill-bred people in this world who insist on interfering with bona fide travellers."

The officer motioned the waiter, who was a Belgian, out of the room with an impatient gesture, then went to the telephone and reported that a mistake seemed to have been made. To our astonishment and my boundless joy we were allowed to return to the *Noordam*. Our luggage was already on board, and the Fatherland beckoned.

As the pinnace approached the ship, the British officer stationed on it called through his megaphone:

"Turn back!"

When we were on shore again, I was separated from my companion and taken by train, under the escort of a detective and a naval officer, to London, where, to my amazement, I was driven to Scotland Yard. The storm was about to burst.

We entered a building like a castle, and crossed a courtyard to a mighty curved staircase. Through broad corridors instilling an atmosphere of peaceful dignity we came to a door which opened suddenly and admitted us to a room occupied by a group of naval officers in gold-encrusted uniforms. It was not long before I learned that two of them, who wore the aiguillettes of royal aides-de-camp, were Admiral Sir Reginald Hall, the Chief of the British Naval Intelligence Service, and his right-hand man, Lord Herschell. To the left of the fireplace stood a heavy table, behind which sat the Chief of the C.I.D., Sir Basil Thomson, wearing horn-rimmed spectacles.

This pleasant gathering in my honour offered exciting prospects. They all sat there and bored me through with malevolent eyes. Admiral Hall stood up.

"Do you know a Captain Rintelen?"

"I am not obliged to answer you."

Sir Basil Thomson:

"You apparently do not know where you are!"

"Wherever I am, I have been brought by force. I have no business here and I shall not reply to any questions until I have spoken with the Minister of my country. Or am I, perhaps, to be charged with a crime?"

Sir Basil Thomson:

"You are a German and have to explain why you are on English soil."

"I did not land on English soil of my own free will. I was brought here by force in violation of all justice."

My reply caused a great uproar. Hall and Thompson grew irritated, while I pretended to get angry and, keeping faithfully to my rôle, began to shout that I protested against the whole proceedings and demanded to be taken to the Swiss Minister. I insisted on this right, until they actually became uncertain of their case.

But my faithful "A.D.C.," the naval officer who had accompanied me from Ramsgate, promptly bet me a sovereign that I shouldn't even be admitted. By the way, he paid up like a gentleman—after the war!

The meeting broke up, and I was informed that I should be escorted at once to the Swiss Legation. The Minister, M. Gaston Carlin, was a dignified old gentleman, tall and with white hair, and he spoke to me in German.

"Now, tell me," he said, "what this is all about. I was unable to do anything when your telegram arrived, since I was away for the weekend. What do the English want with you? I have heard from my office that your passports and military papers are in order, but the English maintain obstinately that you are the German Captain Rintelen. Can you explain how they conceived the idea?"

I decided to risk a great bluff.

"I can disclose it to you, Your Excellency," I said. "Captain Rintelen really was on the boat, but the British have got hold of the wrong man. The *Noordam*, as I have read in *The Times*, has already reached Rotterdam, and the German officer, whom I did not want to betray to the English, is far away by now. You see, Your Excellency, my sympathies are with Germany. I spent my boyhood there, and you will remember that my father was Swiss consul at Leipzig."

" Oh yes! I remember your father. Your attitude has been quite correct."

He came from behind his desk and stretched out his hand.

"Accept my thanks for your truly neutral conduct."

He telephoned in my presence to the Admiralty and communicated the disconcerting solution of the mystery, after which my escort took me back to Admiral Hall. Everybody was foaming with rage at having let the German captain slip through their hands, but the Admiral, who alone remained perfectly calm, came up to me and said:

"So you are not Rintelen?"

"I gave all explanations to my Minister."

Nevertheless I was not immediately set at liberty. I was to be kept in custody until the evening of the following day, and should then be allowed to resume my journey. Two "adjutants" were attached to me, a naval commander and a detective, and I took up my quarters at the Hotel Cecil. I felt that the battle was won, and ordered a drink. Nothing could happen to me, and I only had to wait for the settling of a few formalities. I began to wonder how soon I could be in Berlin.

My two companions sat in the adjoining room, with the communicating door ajar, so that they might keep an eye on me and see that I did not escape. I walked to and fro and heard them conversing. Suddenly a remark was dropped which made me prick up my ears and listen intently:

". . . a special inquiry in Berne by the British Legation?"

"Yes. It isn't merely a consular matter. Admiral Hall has specially asked the Legation to find out whether it is possible that Emile Gaché is now in London."

I had heard enough to know that my position was serious, that I had lost the fight, when a minute before I had been convinced that I had won. I raged round the room. The Legation in Berne was bound to discover that the real Emile Gaché was living in Switzerland and could not now be in London. When the English knew that, I should be in a hole.

I reasoned as follows: as I had been the only passenger, with the exception of the American, to be examined and taken off the boat, they must be aware that I had embarked on the *Noordam* in New York, and if they knew that they must possess information concerning what I had been doing in America. That meant that a blow had been struck against us in the United States, which I had only escaped by my departure. When the answer arrived from Berne, I should be regarded as a civilian and sent back to America in custody, where a disagreeable welcome would await me. Whatever happened, they would not let me go, so it was better to be a prisoner of war than to be sent to an American jail. After I had rapidly reviewed the situation, I knocked at the door and said to one of my "warders":

"Excuse me. Is it possible to have a word with Admiral Hall at once?"

"I don't think so. What do you want? Is it so urgent?"

3

"Yes, it is. Admiral Hall will be highly interested in what I have to say to him."

"Well, tell me, then."

"No. I cannot do that. I must speak to the Admiral himself."

He went to the telephone. It was already eight in the evening, but the Admiral was still in his office and prepared to receive me at once. Rain was streaming down as we crossed the courtyard of the Admiralty. Hall was standing in his room, and asked:

"What brings you here at so late an hour?"

I stood to attention:

"I surrender."

"What do you mean? We have just wired to Berne on your account . . ."

"That is why I have come. It is no longer necessary."

"What does all this mean?"

"Captain Rintelen begs to report to you, sir, as a prisoner of war."

IV

A GIRL DEFIES THE GERMAN STEAM-ROLLER

from

THE STORY OF LOUISE DE BETTIGNIES

by ANTOINE REDIER

Translated by Olive Hall

(Published by Hutchinson & Co. Ltd., London)

Louise de Bettignies, heroine of the first world war, was a young girl of noble birth when the Germans invaded her home town, Lille, in October 1914. She fled to England. The British intelligence officer who interviewed her at Folkestone was struck by her vivacity and charm and had a long talk with her. It appeared that, apart from her high intelligence, she spoke both English and German fluently, in addition to her mother language.

It was not difficult to persuade her to return to France and to supply the British authorities with information on German military movements. Operating from Lille, where she was known under the name of Alice, she organised her own espionage service which soon had its ramifications all over northern France. Extremely valuable and accurate information reached the British intelligence service in messages she managed to smuggle out of the country through German territory and Holland.

When she was finally arrested by a suspicious German guard, she succeeded in swallowing the secret message she was carrying.

Louise de Bettignies was not to survive the war. Tried by a German military court, she was sentenced to death, but the sentence was later changed to imprisonment for life. She died at Cologne on September 27th, 1918. When the British troops occupied the Rhenish city a couple of months later they found the freshly made grave of the girl who had served them so well.

★

MONSIEUR LAMOTTE had had great difficulties in procuring a passport for Alice, and a traveller to accompany them to Tournai, where she had asked to be driven that morning. She had impressed on him the necessity of finding a stranger willing to make the journey with them. Alice, who, it seems, was losing some of her self-confidence, thought she would feel more at ease passing the German guard-house in the company of someone who knew nothing about her.

Having heard that Mademoiselle Seynaeve of Herzeaux had obtained a *sauf conduit* (printed permission) to attend a first communion of a niece at Tournai, Lamotte requested the girl to let him have the use of it for the Wednesday morning, saying it was for his daughter, and promising to return the paper at midday. The passport was lent, so Alice was provided for.

The next problem was the finding of a traveller for Tournai. He thought of Mademoiselle Marguerite le François, who, he knew, was anxious to do some shopping there. She was quite agreeable to go, but had no passport.

Determined to secure her presence at any price, he said rashly: "That doesn't matter; you can have Mademoiselle Seynaeve's."

On the Wednesday morning, while harnessing his mare, Ernest Lamotte fell to wondering what Mademoiselle Alice would say when she knew he had only one passport for two travellers. He felt worried himself, but reckoned she had been in tighter corners, and her resourcefulness would be equal to tricking the authorities on this occasion.

So the imprudence which was to cost Louise de Bettignies her life was not committed by her, but by one who had caught the audacious courage which made her one of the finest agents in the secret service.

"She will manage somehow," he thought, starting off towards Herzeaux, where the parents of Marguerite le François lived in a beautiful house, the typical house occupied by wealthy bourgeois in the smaller towns. Alice had given orders that a girl who knew nothing of the real object of the journey was to accompany them, and Mademoiselle François was certainly far from suspecting Lamotte of being engaged on work of the highest importance. She was a slight girl of about twenty, lively and charming. Eager to be off, she lost no time in seating herself in Lamotte's high cabriolet. This antiquated carriage, lightly constructed of polished oak, and well sprung, was a great favourite with Alice, who gratefully made use of the big box under the seat, where an attaché case, an umbrella, a fur and many other things could be concealed—and perhaps the old vehicle, reminding one of an old engraving, appealed to her artistic sense. But this is a digression. Mademoiselle le François was unaware of Lamotte's real plans; she did not know that underneath her seat Alice's attaché case was hidden, or that its owner, giving a false name and behaving to Lamotte like a perfect stranger, would presently join them, or that a secret message for the Allied Armies was lying in the lining of his cap.

It was seven o'clock; they had just left Herzeaux and passed the house of La Grenouille, a woman detested in the locality and employed by the Germans to search persons arrested on suspicion. Mademoiselle le François and her companion seemed to find amusement in exchanging comments on the atrocious stories told of this female.

Suddenly, on turning a corner, they saw a young woman walking quickly in the same direction as the vehicle; when they had caught her up she signed to Ernest Lamotte to stop. He did so, grumbling a little to himself.

"Are you going far?" she asked.

"To Tournai."

"Would you give me a lift? I am going there too."

They moved up to make room for her; the man on the right, Mademoiselle François in the middle, and Louise de Bettignies—the new arrival—on the left. She engaged them in conversation, saying she was a dressmaker going to town to get work, and discussing fashion with the authority of one in the trade. How her accomplice Lamotte must have smiled to himself. But he was in no smiling mood, thinking continually of the passport difficulty.

"Ah!" said the newcomer suddenly. "I have forgotten my identity card. What shall I do?"

She waited, expecting Lamotte to say he had an extra one on him, as had been agreed. This not being the case, he was obliged to remain silent.

At this period of the war, the identity cards bore no photographs and so, with a little risk, the same card could be used by different people.

Marguerite le François said kindly:

"Take mine, and I will go back."

But Louise, for reasons of her own, desired the company of this girl.

"No, mademoiselle, I could not think of depriving you of your treat. We will both pass with the same card. I will manage it all right."

But she was not feeling as confident as she sounded, for she had already been nearly caught at this particular guard-house of Froyennes at the gateway of Tournai. She had hoped, at any rate, to have things in order this morning.

It had begun to rain. They stopped to put up the hood, as a darkening sky threatened its continuation. The road was cobbled and the vehicle rattled along, turning sharply to right and left as do these narrow Flemish roads. Between Mouscron and Tournai are fifty-four of these sharp turnings; it would be tiring for the eyes if the outlook were not always the same. In the fields soldiers and civilians were busy gathering in beetroot and preparing the ground for the sowing of corn. The church steeples of different villages could be seen in the distance.

The cabriolet reached the town and passed the well-known school of the Frères de Passy at Froyennes, which was then a hospital. On the left is a vast German cemetery. The travellers were silent as they passed over the railway, beyond which there are no side streets which can afford shelter in case of danger. There is now nothing for it but to drive straight on towards the spot they know to be dangerous.

With a nonchalant gesture Ernest Lamotte now takes from his cap the tiny piece of paper which he has charge of until this moment. He passes it to Louise de Bettignies, who slips it between her ring and finger. They arrive at the group of houses in the middle of which is the German barrier.

The wide road edged with trees has suddenly narrowed into a short passage bordered with sombre masonry. A hundred yards farther off, beyond the German barrier, the road widens again, and its venerable elm trees, apparently so near and yet such a distance off to the girl who must pass without the necessary paper, afford a welcome shade, which she longs so to enjoy. Approaching the first of the houses, they no doubt try to picture themselves on the other side of the barrier. But will they pass. . . .

This gateway to Tournai is an important point in the army zone, and those who would pass through safely had better attempt no tricks. Beyond this place the sternness of Germans on duty is slightly relaxed; one feels one can breathe.

The conveyance has stopped on the right near the inn Palais Royal. The three travellers jump down, and while Lamotte unyokes and stables his horse, Louise de Bettignies mingles with the crowd of soldiers, civilians and urchins. Spotting one of these, she whispers something to him, and then, with a firm step, arm-in-arm with her companion, walks towards the German barrier, which is on the left, at the sign of Le Canon d'Or, just before the pastry-cook's "Mamour." About twenty yards from the sentinel she leaves Mademoiselle le François, who walks straight on, passport in hand. Louise sidles off into a small triangular yard from which point of vantage she can easily follow the manœuvres of Lamotte, still busy with his mare. The little urchin is beside her again. She smiles at him, and he, gazing intently at the passers-by, smuggles into her hand the identity card which he has fetched from Mademoiselle le François, now safely on the other side of the barrier.

These kiddies, trained in peace-time to help in the smuggling of tobacco, were invaluable to our secret service. This particular one now closes his hand over a few coppers and runs off to earn his living elsewhere, and Marguerite le François, under the trees on the other side of the guard-house, waits for her new friend, the dressmaker, to pass the sentinel with the same identity card that has proved a talisman to her. To their surprise, all goes well; the German soldier finds this passport as valid as the first time, and our two friends, smiling and triumphant, behave like birds escaped from a trap. The gullibility of these bogys, so easily duped by a little self-assurance, seems to amuse them. Well, it is a great relief to be on the right side of the barrier, all the same.

While they laugh and prattle two men, two civilians coming from Tournai, look at them, wonder at their high spirits, and approach.

"Your papers?"

"But we showed them over there," said Louise de Bettignies.

"Show them again."

Then she lost her head.

"Who are you?" she asked.

One of them pulled out a medal and said in a hard voice: "German authority. If you have your passports I want to see them."

Louise held out hers. He turned to the other girl.

"And yours?"

Marguerite le François, trembling like a leaf, pretended to look for it in her bag.

"That will do. Off to the guard-house, both of you."

From this moment, as though they sensed the value of their prey, of which, of course, they could know nothing, the Germans behaved like brutes to Louise de Bettignies. The two girls were taken back to the guard-house and pushed into the narrow corridor. On the right was the little room of the general officer. The man who made the arrest proved that the girls had only one passport between them.

"Right. I will inform Tournai. Keep them."

He took down the telephone and the two girls were conducted back through the narrow corridor to the principal room. The inn, Le Canon d'Or, which the Germans commandeered for a guard-house during the war, is today in possession of its rightful owner, and in the room in which used to be a table littered with letters and entangled telephone wires a little boy in a black pinafore now learns his lessons with a commendable application. He scarcely raises his head while his parent explains to me how they abandoned their house in the early days of the invasion, fleeing in terror for the safety of this little child, who, so the rumour went, the Germans would not hesitate to maltreat.

With these good folks we go into the principal room that served as a guard-house during the war, and where the two girls were conducted. Poor Lamotte, who had no idea of the unfortunate turn of events, was fetched from Le Palais Royal, and it is he who reconstitutes today, in all its details, the tragic scene which was to follow. This room looks out on the street. With one's back to the window, along which are benches, one faces a large counter; on the left is a glass door, leading to another room, small but well lighted.

They seated Lamotte near a window, and Mademoiselle le François was placed between the counter and the wall of the little room where Louise had been put. Some soldiers were engaged in dressing themselves. One of them, naked to the waist, was washing himself in a bucket less than a yard from Marguerite le François. Suddenly he straightened himself up and, pointing with his finger to Louise de Bettignies on the other side of the glass door, he shouted in a hoarse voice:
"She is a criminal. Look at her."

The girl was swallowing the secret message.

The detective Rotselaer then arrived, followed by La Grenouille. This degraded woman, frequently called off to Tournai, happened to be on duty that day. She ran straight to Marguerite le François and ordered her to undress.

"Here?" asked the poor child, looking round at the soldiers dressing.

After taking off her blouse and undoing her skirt she fainted. A tooth-glass belonging to one of the men was filled from a jug of dirty water and put to the girl's lips. She remained unconscious for about ten minutes, during which time La Grenouille took off all her clothes and, having searched her thoroughly, left her, and passed into the next room—where her task proved a more difficult one. For Louise de Bettignies, who spoke this woman's language, did not mince her words in defending herself. But it was an unequal match. She did not give up the five or six identity cards that she carried about her person, but they were discovered and snatched from her. Every inch of her clothes was examined.

Meanwhile Rotselaer, chief of the detectives of Tournai, and another important personage were cross-examining Lamotte. This detective was a small, wiry man with a short moustache and piercing eyes. He was said to be a Jew from Frankfort, and to have lived many years in Antwerp. Usually correct in his demeanour and dressed in good taste, he only resembled the Germans in his coarseness when under the influence of anger. He gathered from the very first that one of the women was innocent. He never suspected for a moment that Lamotte was an accomplice, and accepted without question the story of the dressmaker encountered on the road; he did not even have the cabriolet searched. At last he ordered the three of them to be driven to the offices of the secret service at Tournai. Louise de Bettignies was seated next to a military policeman, and opposite her Lamotte and Mademoiselle le François: in the front sat Rotselaer and the chauffeur. Before starting he turned to the three prisoners and said, in his best French:

"Not a word, you three. You are watched."

La Grenouille and the detectives followed in a second car. In a few minutes they arrived at their destination, a beautiful house the Germans had commandeered, and which today is inhabited by peaceful citizens. In the front is a huge dining-room ornamented with a richly carved wooden mantelpiece. In this room, around an enormous table, worked young and elderly German typists. The prisoners were questioned separately, beginning with the one already called "the spy." The other two were sent out. Louise was seated near the fireplace, looking so pale, her hands on her knees, waiting; while her captors conversed in low tones, and the typists, curious to see what a real spy looked like, stole many glances at her. Suddenly her eyes met those of Lamotte, who had been put in a little room separated from the large one by a corridor. The doors, thank God, had been left open, so this man, before whom La Grenouille had just heated some milk into which she had mixed a yellowish powder, was able, by a gesture of the fingers to the mouth, to make Louise understand she must presently refuse to drink.

"You must be exhausted," said a voice at her elbow, "drink this." And the simpering German woman presented a bowl of milk.

"No, thank you, madam. I am not thirsty."

The woman insisted; Louise de Bettignies refused again politely, then definitely and finally.

The detective Rotselaer then interposed.

"Come along, no nonsense. Swallow it, or say why you won't."

She was careful not to reply to this man who was watching for her mouth to open. Louise made a brusque movement knocking the cup over and spilling its contents on the parquet floor.

The message was well hidden and safe, and the Germans seemed to understand that, unless they killed her and opened the stomach, they would never get it.

So, being now sure the girl was a spy, they decided not to waste time in further questioning, but to imprison her straight away.

Disarmed by the obvious innocence of Marguerite le François, whose emotion and terror were really pitiable, they sent her back in Lamotte's cabriolet, and in his charge to her parents at Mouscron.

V

THE FRENCH LADY PREFERS NAVAL ATTACHÉS

from

I SPIED FOR FRANCE

by Marthe Richer

Translated by Gerald Griffin

(Published by John Long Ltd., London, 1935)

Captain Georges Ladoux, head of the "Fifth Bureau," or French counter-espionage service, in 1915, who enlisted Marthe Richer, nicknamed the "Skylark," for the dangerous rôle of double agent, wrote that she was the first woman spy whose name was recorded in the history of France.

Marthe Richer, a war widow and pre-war airwoman, was attracted to espionage by the danger and hazards of the secret service that somehow seemed to respond to her adventurous nature. She gladly accepted Ladoux's offer and went on her first missions at her own expense, for the "Fifth Bureau" was rather short of funds in the early days of the war. As a matter of fact, she not only worked without getting paid for it but actually contributed funds to the empty coffers of her organisation from the money the Germans paid her for pretending to spy for them.

For over two years she was stringing along Johann von Krohn, the elderly German naval attaché in Spain, who had hopelessly fallen in love with the attractive young Frenchwoman. She was sent by the Germans on various missions, including one to the Argentine; on the latter assignment she was supposed to carry two thermos flasks of vermin to a German agent in Buenos Aires, the bugs to be used to infect the Allied grain stores in South America. Marthe simply drowned the insects and handed them over dead.

The chapter of her book selected for our collection deals with the final settling of her account with Herr von Krohn.

★

WHEN the Baron turned up he knew instinctively that there was trouble ahead. The moment his eyes met mine his face fell.

"What's wrong, Marthe?" he said, as he sat down.

I was in no hurry to reply to him. I was thinking very hard. My silence was the calm that heralded the storm. I looked pensive, but my mind was in a regular tumult.

"Marthe, please tell me why you are so terribly preoccupied," purred the Baron. "Feeling ill—or what?"

"I'm fed up with Spain," I thundered. "I'm sick of living in exile. I want to go back to France."

Von Krohn stared at me in amazement. "You are overwrought, Marthe. You want a change. Have a little patience; I'm sending you to Morocco in a fortnight's time."

So he in his turn now was prescribing "patience" as a remedy for my troubles!

"I want to go back to France," I repeated doggedly, bringing down my gloved hand on the table with such force that all the cups rattled.

"You can't do that, Marthe. It would mean death for you, and well you know it."

"And whose fault is that?" I asked bitterly.

"Wait until the end of the war, Marthe. That can't be far off. And the minute the war is over you can depend upon me that I shall take steps so that you can return to France."

With my face set hard and my shoulders hunched and my hands clenched, I glared straight into Von Krohn's eyes, and, yielding to an irresistible impulse, I shouted:

"I am a Frenchwoman! A Frenchwoman! Do you hear that? Do you know what that means? Well, now I'm going to tell you what it means. It means that ever since the first day I met you I have been working for my own country. I have been spying on you. I have kept an eye on all your movements, and duly reported them to Paris. Now do you understand what it means to be a Frenchwoman?"

I jumped to my feet, staring rigidly at him all the time. Von Krohn went red, pale, livid and tallowy green in turn. A diabolical smile played along his thin lips. He found it hard to realise that I was telling the truth. Such was his profound self-sufficiency, such was his confidence in his infallible knowledge of mankind, that he refused to accept the fact that he had been fooled by a young Frenchwoman. He tried to delude himself into the belief that my outburst had just been prompted by bad temper and female whimsicalness. I read all this in his face, and was goaded to greater frenzy by the man's abysmal fatuity. Well, now I was going to give him the *coup de grâce*.

"Ich bin Französin!" I shouted in German.

He gasped like a stranded fish, and his face became all puckered with sheer horror, as he heard me speaking for the first time in a language which I had pretended I did not know.

"Ha, you seem to think that I am just playing a stupid joke on you, do you?" I went on. "Just half a minute. Here's something that will convince you."

Opening my handbag I produced the return half of my ticket from

Paris to Hendaye—the ticket I had used on the journey during which I had met the Greek consul.

"Look at it!" I said, holding it right under his nose. "Look at the date on it! I did not wait until the war was over to return to France, you fool! You see for yourself clear proof that I have been in Paris quite recently!"

"Impossible, impossible, Marthe!" gasped Von Krohn, still incredulous through sheer fatuity. "Say it isn't true. I know what happened, somebody gave you that ticket."

"No! I bought it. I've fooled you all along the line."

He put his hand to his throat. His face went purple. I thought that he was going to have a fit.

"You!" he gasped, hoarse with rage.

"Yes, I! I! I!" I repeated. "I fooled you completely for nearly two years. Just look at the date on the ticket. In fact, you can ask the Greek consul, and he will tell you the name of the station at which I boarded the train. Get this into your thick head, Baron Von Krohn, naval attaché in Spain to the All Highest, William II, Emperor of Germany. I came to Spain to serve my country!"

Von Krohn stared at me aghast. His fury had for the moment merged into numb despair.

"I don't believe you. I don't believe you. Even a woman couldn't possibly be guilty of such treachery and such falsehood, Marthe."

There was an expression of intense agony in his living eye, while the artificial one stared spectrally at me. Beads of perspiration stood out on his brow. His artificial eye glared glassily while his other eye had the expression of a wild beast at bay.

"I told you that my husband had been killed in Switzerland," I went on. "You believed me. Well, now, read this. Now do you believe me?"

I extracted from my handbag the official proof that I was a war widow. He stared at it for a long time, as if he were mesmerised. Then all of a sudden he realised how he had been imposed upon, and, overcome by a fit of uncontrollable frenzy, he struck me across the mouth with such fury that he broke one of my teeth. I believe firmly that, had we not been in a public place, he would have killed me.

I was too dazed for a bit to speak, but as soon as I regained possession of myself I addressed him in a defiant, challenging tone.

"You have signed your own death-warrant. I'm going to let Prince Ratibov know all about you tomorrow. He will be able to judge for himself how easy it has been for a young Frenchwoman to tweak the nose of the German naval attaché."

A satanic sneer overspread the features of the hideous Cyclops. "You won't get the chance to do anything of the kind."

He jumped from his seat and fled out of the restaurant with the precipitancy of a scalded cat. I wondered what his next move would be. I really did not care what he intended to do, as I felt that I had him well on the run now. I was out for his ruin, and I felt confident that I would succeed.

.   .   .   .   .

When I reached the hotel, the porter told me that a man had just called to see me. To judge by the porter's description of him it was nobody whom I knew even by sight. I was pondering about the mysterious caller as I proceeded to my room. I was barely outside my door when there was a ring at the telephone. Obviously my mysterious visitor returning.

Immediately afterwards my door was thrown open, and a Spaniard dashed in unceremoniously.

"Police!" he announced curtly.

"Police? Why, pray?"

"You've got to come along with me, madam."

"What for?"

"You tried to blackmail the German naval attaché."

Instead of answering him directly, I picked up the receiver and asked the girl at the switchboard to put me on to the German Embassy. As soon as I got in touch with the Embassy, I insisted on His Excellency, Prince Ratibov, granting me an interview at the earliest possible moment. After a lot of negotiation I was told to call next day. Thereupon the official who had come to arrest me retired with profuse apologies, looking extremely silly.

A junior officer in the Embassy met me next day, but I insisted that I should immediately be brought face to face with Prince Ratibov. After a considerable amount of further tedious negotiation, I was brought before Prince Ratibov. The Prince, who was just then preparing to go out, was a dapper, trim little man of about sixty, very well dressed, who was obviously doing his utmost to look twenty years younger than he was.

"You are surprised at my visit, I presume, your Excellency?" I said.

"Yes, madam. You are, if my information is correct, one of Baron von Krohn's agents."

"I was nominally one of his agents, Your Excellency, and I have just come to inform you that Baron von Krohn has been consistently fooled by me ever since I entered his service. I took advantage of the fact that he was infatuated with me to make him spend money on me which he got for secret service work."

Prince Ratibov stared at me for some minutes in dumb amazement. He seemed somewhat appalled at hearing such disclosures about the naval attaché from the lips of a Frenchwoman.

"But—but—I don't quite understand," he said, with a bewildered expression. "Is it not a fact that the Baron arranged your journey to France by the secret passage?"

"Yes. I played upon the idiotic infatuation which the old fool had for me. I told him that I was ill, and that I wanted to consult a French woman doctor."

Prince Ratibov seemed dumbfounded. "Tell me, madam," he went on, "is it not a fact that Baron von Krohn sent you on a mission to the Argentine?"

"Oh yes, Your Excellency. I rather enjoyed the trip. I was curious to see that country; that was why I went there."

An expression of extreme uneasiness darkened his face.

"Answer me candidly, madam, one question. While you were in the service of the naval attaché, did you come into possession of any vital information concerning us?"

"No, Your Excellency. I was only out for having a good time at his expense. But I had the key to his safe in my possession several times. Oh, by the way, here's the combination for it. You can have it as well as the love letters which the silly ass wrote me. Keep the lot. Goodbye."

The look which Prince Ratibov gave me at this point made it clear to me that if I did not beat a hasty retreat he would have me thrown into the street. I knew, however, from the impression my revelation made on him that I had effectively finished Von Krohn's political career.

I bowed frigidly to the Ambassador. He responded with an even more frigid bow.

As I was leaving the Embassy I saw Von Krohn approaching the building. When he saw me he shot me a murderous glance. I really believe that, given the opportunity, he would have assassinated me there and then.

I fled down the street shivering with sheer terror.

VI

HE DIDN'T WANT TO BE A SPY

from

RUSSIAN HAZARD

by DORIAN BLAIR AND C. H. DAND

(Published by Robert Hale, London, 1937)

Dorian Blair wanted to be a soldier, not a spy. His father was a Scot, his mother a Slav, and he himself, though born in St. Petersburg, British to the core. His story began in August 1914, when the Russian consul at Hull, where Dorian lived at the time, convinced him that it was his duty to serve the cause of the Allies by doing a spot of spying for the Russians. Dorian demurred but finally accepted a mission to go to St. Petersburg, where he was to contact certain people, including an important person at the Imperial Court.

Soon he found himself in the centre of Russian court intrigue. He became an officer in the Czar's Flying Corps, but his real objective was to ascertain whether Rasputin was using his influence with the Czarina to assist the Germans. The figure of Gregory Rasputin, the mysterious monk who wielded such an incredible power over Russia's bigoted Empress, comes to life in this fantastic narrative. Blair found out that Rasputin was collaborating with the Germans, who had conceived the devilish idea of destroying the entire population of St. Petersburg by means of bacteriological warfare. The plot was averted by the anti-Rasputin faction and Rasputin was killed.

Blair later witnessed the first months of the Bolshevik revolution and came in touch with the early leaders of the new régime, such as Lenin, Trotsky, Kamenev, Radek, Lunacharsky, Krylenko, et al. At one time, he actually arrested Trotsky, Zinoviev, Tchicherin and other Bloshevik leaders in a house in Viborgskaya, but they were released the same day by order of Kerensky.

Dorian Blair's career as the Scarlet Pimpernel of St. Petersburg came to an end on Christmas Eve, 1917, when he was arrested by the newly formed Cheka. He spent several months in prison, had his fair share of the Red terror, and was actually condemned to death. He managed to escape and was helped out of the country by the American Relief Administration.

★

FOR the first few days after the massacre the prisoners remaining in the Cross Prison were bewildered, stunned, horror-stricken, resentful. Grief, where it applied, can be taken for granted. The warders and even the soldiers went about the place subdued and shamefaced. A new relationship required to be established. On both sides was the feeling

4

that any bonds which had existed before had been finally broken. Before, they had been prisoners and guards, the same human clay with differences of class, creed or political opinion. Now they were two opposite and different worlds which were suddenly seeing one another clearly for the first time and realising the impassable gulf which must divide them. The real class war had begun.

My lucky plea to have the origins of Moroshkin's revolver investigated began its repercussions on the third day after the massacre. I was summoned to be interrogated by Madame Krilenko, wife of the generalissimo of the Bolshevik army and a member of the Petrograd Tribunal. She was a plain-looking woman of middle age, a schoolmistress in appearance and evidently determined to stand no nonsense.

When I finished my story of the revolver episode Madame Krilenko looked quizzically at me.

"Don't think I am misled, citizen. I don't expect you to tell me the truth about that revolver—yet. Is it not the case that when we do know the truth of where it came from we shall find it closely connected with a plot for the capture of Petrograd and the overthrow of the Workers' Government?"

"I'm sorry," I replied timidly, "but I don't know anything of any plots to capture Petrograd."

Her eyes became gimlets.

"I think you do. Do you deny knowing Commander Crombie of the British Embassy?"

"I have never known any Commander Crombie," I answered.

She drew back slightly to observe me.

"It does not interest you to know that Commander Crombie is dead?"

"No, not in the least, since I never knew Commander Crombie."

Madame sank back in her chair, glared at me and shuffled her papers. Cromwell's revolution was the sensible one. He kept women out of it.

"I'm not taken in by your pretences," she suddenly began again in a high screech. "You can't fool me with your gentlemanly manners and your clumsily acted bourgeois obtuseness. We know your plots against the workers and your schemes to betray them to the capitalist governments. We got the evidence of them when we took possession of your British Embassy. Commander Crombie was shot while trying to resist the right of the workers to make an entry. He was a fool, but we have all his papers and codes. We have made prisoners of the Embassy staff and we know all his spies and agents. Commander Crombie's plot against the Workers' Government is broken. And so is Lockhart's. Lockhart is our prisoner in Moscow. His plot to murder

our commissars and bribe our Lettish soldier-comrades to turn against
the workers has been revealed and all the necessary steps have been
taken. Now will you tell us what you know? Now will you tell us
who helped you to smuggle that revolver into the prison and what you
were going to do with it?"

While she was screeching at me I was drinking in every word and
trying at the same time to keep my face set in stolid indifference. All
she was saying was news and exciting for me. But it was all something
I had played no part in—if it was true—and when the woman wound
up her tirade by dragging in that wretched revolver as though it had
been a factor in a plot to overthrow the Bolshevik Government, the
whole interview became so childish and absurd that I laughed right out
at her.

The effect of my laugh was electrical. With another piercing shriek
she shot back from me, opened the door, pushed aside the astonished
guard outside it, and ran along the corridor calling: "Comrade
Pavlov! Comrade Pavlov!" The guard glanced into the room to see
what had happened and saw me sitting there every bit as astounded as
he was. In a few minutes she was back with Pavlov, the prison com-
mandant.

"Comrade Pavlov, this man has grossly insulted the representative
of the Workers' Justice. I shall not interrogate him further. From his
whole behaviour it is obvious he is an enemy of the working class and
will do all in his power to overthrow the Workers' Government. I
shall report what I have learned of him to the Tribunal and it will
be for them to decide what shall be done with him. Take him back to
his cell and keep him under close observation night and day. You will
hear in due course regarding him."

The female of the species is more deadly than the male. Madame
Krilenko's reply to my insult came next day in the form of a deputation of leather-jackets, one of whom read me in theatrical tones a
wordy recital of the reasons why the Russian workers and their soldier
and peasant friends could no longer tolerate having me on Russian
soil and ending with the intimation that it was proposed to remove me
from it by means of execution to be carried out at the Cheka headquarters in Gorokhovaya Street the following morning at six o'clock.

The paper was handed to me and I was asked to sign.

"Sign what?"

"Sign the order to certify that you are aware of what it contains."

"What is it you want from me, comrade—a reply to the invitation,
a promise that I'll be there? Take it away. I won't sign it. I don't
admit a word of what it says."

"It makes no difference whether you sign or not. The execution will be carried out just the same. It is only that you won't complain when we come for you and say you didn't have notice of it."

"I refuse to sign until I have seen Commissar Pavlov."

"Very well."

The deputation shuffled outside.

I had a brief but useless interview with Pavlov. The Tribunal had decided my case on the report of Madame Krilenko. There was no appeal. I persisted that I had had no proper trial and that there seemed small point in saving me from Bokia's squad to let me fall victim to the petty malice of a woman. He replied that the Workers' Government was fighting for its life and could not waste ceremony on an enemy whose guilt was plain. This was a new Pavlov with a new function and a new faith.

I was roused about three o'clock in the morning to be conducted to Gorokhovaya Street. The journey was made in an open automobile. I was sandwiched in the back seat between two guards with fat revolvers in their hands. The fit was tight and I was afraid to ease a muscle in case the guards would think I was about to make a bolt for it and slug me one. Rain was falling, wetting my eyelids and my mouth. A goodbye kiss, I thought.

It was eight months since my last visit to No. 2 Gorokhovaya Street. Everything was considerably dirtier. There seemed to be eight months' litter of cigarette ends. Evidently the Extraordinary Commission was too busy sweeping the undesirable elements out of Russia to find time to sweep its own rooms and corridors out. The white marble had the marks of greasy fingers on it. What draperies remained were torn and soiled. Justice embellished for the Tsar's generals and colonels was wearing badly in the hands of the proletariat. Everywhere, too, there was a heavy proletarian smell, the pungent smell of old sweat-laden clothes, of unwashed, undernourished bodies, the smells of toil and grime, of brutish souls and stunted minds, the doss-house smell in which the workers of the world unpleasantly unite.

Petrograd was asleep, perhaps uneasily, but not the Cheka. The traditions of the Tsarist police that raids and arrests have an added terror in the night-time had been taken over with the building. Guards marched out and in; officials hurried out and into rooms with files of papers. Prisoners of all classes crouched on benches. I was stopped for a few minutes beside an old woman in a black shawl whose twitching fingers clutched a cloth-wrapped parcel out of which a knuckle of dirty white bread stuck like a knee through a hole in a stocking. She was presumably a "speculator" who was learning the new lesson badly. Every official carried arms and an air of busy purpose. In that respect that atmosphere was different from my last visit when everyone, even Dzerjinsky in his funeral chamber and the armed guards, had been slack in manner, amateurish and ineffective. Here everybody seemed to be going at tension, winding himself up. Something, the shooting of the five hundred or the approach of the Allies, had released a spring in them. Thought of the five hundred sent a shudder through me. I looked around, half expecting to see blood somewhere. Among these officials bustling around me must be some of the executioners. They could not have carried out so wild a slaughter and left no traces, at least figuratively, upon their persons. I was leaving Russia at an interesting moment, it seemed, and under strange new auspices. I hoped they would be short-lived, anyhow.

"The English spy, is it? Bring him here, then."

A brisk-looking clerk with a leather portfolio interrupted my musing. We marched behind him down a corridor. Walking slowly in front of us was a tall, thin figure which was vaguely familiar. When it turned to glance at us as we passed, I saw it was Dzerjinsky. I had not expected to find him in Gorokhovaya Street, as he had accompanied the Bolshevik Government last February to Moscow. I had an impulse to appeal to him and might have done so but he spoke first, addressing the clerk with the important-looking portfolio.

"One moment. Where are you taking him?"

"This is a British spy sentenced to be shot by order of the Military Tribunal, Commissar. I am taking him to sign his acquaintance with the order for the execution which he refused to sign when it was first presented to him."

There was a pause while Dzerjinsky turned his unblinking eyes on me and looked me over.

"For what hour is the execution ordered?"

"Six o'clock, Commissar."

"He will sign later. Bring him to my room."

We followed him along the corridor and this time into a bare room furnished with no more than a table and a couple of chairs—Chippendale.

"Wait outside," he told the guards, and to the clerk, "I'll send for you."

"Sit down, citizen."

He motioned me to a chair and himself remained standing. He had exchanged the Norfolk jacket in which I had last seen him for a plain dark coat. There was no sign of the cartridges appearing although I waited for them. But he couldn't mask the queer theatrical fascination of his eyes, which seemed to be looking with their unblinking stare, not at my eyes, but into them as if he could see through my eyeballs and watch my brain working. The feeling was the same when one removed one's eyes from his. He could see through the top of my head and pierce my temples. I had fully five minutes in which to experience the sensation, for he had not given up his habit of silent probing of his victims. At last he smiled, sweetly. It was strange to see how his smile lifted the eerie look from his eyes without the eyes themselves changing.

"This is a fortunate meeting, citizen. I am not often in Petrograd, and I am afraid if we had not met things might have gone with you rather sadly."

I brightened up perceptibly at this remark and tried to meet his friendly smile with one of answering sweetness. It was probably not very convincing. My difficulty was to think quickly of a suitable reply.

"So you think I may not—have to die?" I stumbled.

"But of course not," he replied in his softest voice. "It is curious I should have forgotten someone who could have been of so much help to us."

I knew what he meant, but my mind ran out to meet his. I was scared, really scared. I didn't want to die. Sitting in that room, I was horribly conscious of all that was going on in the rooms around it, of the clerk waiting with his paper for me to sign, the inexorable approach of six o'clock which would produce the courtyard and the short walk to the wall and the end of everything. I found something to like in this man and wanted to make him like me. If a man takes a liking to you, he doesn't send you out to be shot, does he? But what to say? I could only try to convince him that I wasn't holding anything back, that there was nothing in my head which, if given to him, would enable Bolshevik Russia to fight its enemies with one more hope of success or one less danger of defeat.

Dzerjinsky was speaking.

"Our Workers' Government is in very serious danger. Why should I conceal anything from you? Internally, we are young and inexperienced. There are too few who understand what is needed of us. We are handicapped by lack of technicians of all kinds. We have few doctors. We have fewer motor mechanics. We lack also foremen, captains, men who can be the sub-leaders of our enterprises. Over all Russia we lack simple means of conveying simple ideas to the people, particularly the peasants, among whom the need of a new education is most urgent. There is a great new world to be built, all over the world, but first in Russia. I am convinced that we shall build it if we are given time. We must have time to cut our teeth. We have started on the most stupendous task men have ever consciously set themselves. The bigger the job, the more the enemies. We have many enemies outside and many enemies inside. Our Red Army must deal with the enemies attacking our front. It is my commission to combat all enemies attacking from the rear.

"Citizen Blair, I am determined that this new world shall be allowed to grow. If it takes twenty-five years, even fifty years, of struggle and sorrow, it will not be too big a price to pay. Whatever time is needed, I shall see that we secure it. I shall protect this new world of ours against its enemies, whatever the cost.

"The purchase of time has already begun. In the last week we have killed more than a thousand of our enemies in cold blood. Threats of terror will be met with greater terror. For every life a hundred lives. We shall be relentless in the suppression of counter-revolution, all forms of resistance and sabotage. The more ruthless we are, the shorter will be the period of our ruthlessness. What other way is open to us?"

As his eyes looked into the balls of mine he seemed to be addressing not me but the world behind and beyond me.

"What else can we do with the world outside against us? We have England, America, France, Japan, with armies on our territory. Counter-revolutionary armies are marching from Siberia, from the Don, from Archangel. The peasants may turn against us any day. The bourgeoisie within is impatient for our collapse and thousands are working for it. The governments of England, France and America are using secret agents to foment revolt and sabotage against us. We must defend ourselves. Hesitation would be suicide. If we fail now it will all have to come again. History has given us this opportunity. It would be treason to abandon it. I am not a cruel man, not even a hard man. But if the success of the revolution demands that I be a hammer, I am a hammer. If it needs a sickle, I am a sickle."

It was queerly impressive to hear Bolshevism's chief executioner thus justifying himself and his terrorism.

"So you see, citizen, why I should like to have your assistance. Within Moscow and Petrograd there are British agents at work, organising a counter-revolution of the bourgeoisie, and they must be run to earth and dealt with. We have just unmasked one of their plots to bribe the Lettish contingents of our army to turn against us. Lockhart, the envoy of the British Government, was implicated and has been arrested. Commander Crombie, the British naval attaché, would also have been arrested, but he resisted our guards who came to search the Embassy and was shot after he had murdered one of our men. I have come to Petrograd to examine the papers we have discovered and to follow up certain clues. But we know that the real organiser of this plot and other dangerous plots is a certain Captain Reilly, who is still at large. Now, Citizen Blair, I want you to help me. How can I find Captain Reilly—Captain Sidney Reilly?"

The name Reilly struck no chords and rang no bells in my mind. Nothing rushed up to my lips to be blurted out to buy my freedom with. The name Reilly meant just nothing to me at all.

I shook my head.

"Reilly? I don't know any Reilly."

"Come, citizen, I have been telling you of the situation in which we find ourselves that you may understand how important it is for me to track down Captain Reilly and all his associates. I thought we were past beating about the bush with one another."

Dzerjinsky's voice was still soft but, as the Russian peasants say, he showed his teeth in his eyes.

"But I assure you I know nothing about any Reilly. I've never heard of him."

"Perhaps you do not know him by that name. Our information is that he is tall, lean, dark and military-looking when he is Captain Sidney Reilly. But he really is a Russian by birth, and a master of disguises. At least, that is what they tell me. They say he is never the same person for two consecutive days, that he appears in a place like a weed in a cornfield and disappears again like water. But I don't believe these stories. They are merely the romantic apologies of those who are too stupid to catch him. But I shall get him yet. There is no spy so clever that he does not fall into a trap some time. Is there, Citizen Blair? Surely you have heard something of this master spy of the British Government?"

I was crying inside me for sheer desperation. I wanted to convince him that I really could not help him.

"You see, Mr. Dzerjinsky, you say this Reilly has been operating with Mr. Lockhart from Moscow. I don't know Mr. Lockhart. He was only a name to me when he was consul in Moscow. I didn't even know he had been made an envoy to your Government until I read it in your newspapers when I was a prisoner in the Peter and Paul Fortress. Perhaps Reilly came to Russia with Lockhart in January. You see, I've been in prison for the last eight months. For eight months I've been dead so far as any secret service work is concerned. There's nothing so dead as a spy who falls into the hands of the enemy. You must know that. I don't know anything about anything unless——"

But the words I was about to say died on my lips.

I stared down at the floor.

When I raised my head I met Dzerjinsky's eyes.

"Your hesitation does you credit, Mr. Blair. I think I understand something of what you are experiencing. But you seemed about to tell me something. Perhaps you were going to name someone when you interrupted yourself. Would you like to go on now?"

I shook my head. All I wanted was the squad to come quickly and get on with it.

He tapped the table impatiently.

"But, Mr. Blair, I thought you had decided——"

I shook my head again.

"I've got nothing to say. I'm sorry if I misled you."

It was a miserable, disgraceful mumble.

"You know the alternative. There is a sentence of death already passed on you. It will be carried out within an hour now."

I made no reply. I stared at my boots and felt sick with misery.

"Very well. I'm sorry, but if you refuse to help me you are my enemy and I have my duty to perform with the enemies of my Government."

He walked to the door and asked the guard to summon the clerk who had taken charge of me. I followed the clerk to another room and signed acknowledgment of my own death sentence. I was left in the room with the two guards who had accompanied me from the Cross Prison.

I passed the next hour like a small boy recovering from a whipping.

At last they came for me and I was led through more musty, grime-smelling corridors into a courtyard. I tried to walk firmly, uprightly, but my head would jerk awkwardly on my neck and my feet felt loose and oddly detached from me. It was broad daylight, but there was no sunshine in the yard and everything had a raw, night-chilled, early morning feeling. A file of five soldiers waited by the opposite wall under charge of some sort of an officer. The walls of the building were grey with years of soot. Several motor-lorries with dull grey hoods stood around. The scene was cheerless and dispiriting. The guards marched me to the wall and left me without ceremony. The commander gave an order and the soldiers shouldered their rifles and lined up opposite me. A leather-jacketed mechanic swung the starting-handle of one of the lorries, a big Packard. The commander and the soldiers had their eyes on him. Apparently they were waiting for him to get it started. Vaguely I remembered hearing something of a practice that had been employed at some executions for disobedience or desertion among the troops behind the front line. They started up a noisy motor-lorry engine, but whether it was to drown the volley or annoy the victim or dull the perceptions of the firing squad I was uncertain. The fellow swung and swung again without result, dashed round to adjust the throttle, dashed back, swung and got a kick and a back-fire. He scratched his head as if the behaviour of the engine puzzled him. Incompetent Russia. . . . The morning air after the stuffy rooms and this fellow's incompetence brought back to me a slight feeling of superiority.

The commander approached me and produced a cloth.

"Your eyes," he explained. "Turn round and let me bandage them."

"No, no," I pleaded.

"The prisoner's eyes must be bandaged according to the regulations," he announced gruffly and seized hold of my arm to turn me. I resisted and he slapped my face. But as he did so he glanced up to a window on his left as if afraid of a reproof for his action. I followed his glance. The window was open and beside it stood Dzerjinsky and another man. Dzerjinsky must have made some sign which I did not see because the commander desisted.

"I shall tie your hands, then."

"No, no. Please!"

The Packard engine suddenly roared. There was no exhaust pipe on the lorry and the din was terrible. It made me frown and the commander of the soldiers grinned at my annoyance. I could not hear what he said, but he took several paces to the right of me and waited. I had made up my mind what I should like to do. I would give myself one last fling by waiting until the instant before the officer gave the word to fire, when I would hurl myself bodily at him and bring him to the ground. It would be a poor little abortive fling, for I should be shot or clubbed to death the next moment, but at least I would go down fighting. I wasn't afraid of dying now. I was solacing myself with the thought of my feeble gesture.

The Packard was roaring on. The officer raised his hand. I could see him clearly. He was slightly in front of me. The soldiers had their rifles levelled.

"One!"

I could barely hear his voice above the roar of the engine. The soldiers certainly could not hear it, but they were watching his hand drop.

He raised his hand again.

"Two!"

The hand fell. Up again. I held my breath. I had every muscle tense for that side-spring. The hand went a shade higher than before in preparation for the final signal and I willed myself to leap sideways and forward.

"Stop!"

As my body moved a voice called faintly through the engine roar from the window above me. It was Dzerjinsky. I was in the air, hurtling towards him, when I saw the surprised commander turn and look up, his hand still uplifted. Then commander, courtyard, everything went reeling high over me and my head banged against the flagstones.

VII

HERR HAUPTMANN HAPPENS TO BE BRITISH

from

MY MASTER SPY

by MARTHE McKENNA

(Published by Jarrolds, London)

In My Master Spy, *Marthe McKenna, herself a British secret agent in the first world war, tells the story of Captain Clive Granville, one of the most audacious English spies who enlisted as an officer in the German Army a few days after the Germans had overrun Belgium and occupied Brussels. It was a dangerous bluff but the Germans were fooled by the Englishman's amazing physical resemblance to a Prussian junker, Alberic von Schultz, rich landowner with vast possessions in Belgium. The latter happened to be in Belgium on the day the war broke out and was abducted by a Belgian patriot. Captain Granville, better known as Special Duty Agent "Three-three," simply took his place.*

The physical resemblance alone would not have helped him much had his German not been absolutely flawless. It so happened that Captain Granville had spent several years in Germany and had, moreover, been educated at a German university; impersonating a German officer was child's play to him. His messages to London were transmitted by Belgian patriots.

Needless to say that Agent "Three-three" nevertheless had to take great personal risks, especially after he aroused the suspicions of the German counter-espionage service. The following excerpt thrillingly conveys the sort of danger spies cannot always avoid.

★

CLIVE's heart missed a beat as he glanced with a fleeting startled look at the threatening German. As though straddled on the deck of a rolling battleship, the Admiral stood square in the centre of the room, his revolver held menacingly.

Fortunately whilst attempting to read Clive had sat with his back to the light, leaving his face in deep shadow.

The Englishman did not stir his body, but fumbled for his monocle, found it, stuck it hastily into his eye, and glared fully at the bristling Von Kramann.

In those priceless seconds it flashed through Clive that the cool and collected pose would be useless. Only by the superb acting of Alberic von Schultz's character would he momentarily escape. As Alberic, he had been living the life of an indolent, partially brainless officer, and one who would most certainly be unnerved by such a sudden attack. That character he must live up to, and unless you have something definitely opposite to say, Clive knew, it is better to remain silent . . . but silence here would mean consent to the Admiral's accusation. His talk must be opposite and definitely hostile.

"*Gott in Himmel!* Who are you? Who are you to come here threatening a Prussian gentleman?" Clive demanded, his voice rising to indignant protest. He stood up and placed his book on the table with trembling hand.

"A Prussian gentleman, eh?" sneered Von Kramann, "we will soon sweat the gentleman out of you, and then we will see what's left of the Prussian, Herr Captain Granville."

"He's escaped from a madhouse," ejaculated Clive. "*Lieb Gott*, who are you, madman!" and vociferously Clive called: "Hi, Fritz! Fritz! *Kommen sie hier*, at once, I am attacked," and as they heard the heavy footsteps of the batman, Clive went on: "Put that weapon away, you fool madman, it might blow off." And he displayed all the nervousness of a man used to firearms himself, but distrustful of them in the hands of others.

With a grim gesture Von Kramann lowered his revolver as Fritz, with startled face, showed in the doorway.

"Send your man away," Von Kramann demanded harshly.

Purposely Clive hesitated, pretending to be still nervous of this strange formidable visitor. Then he waved Fritz dismissal.

Granville, for a moment, looked vacantly at Von Kramann, and then, affecting a nervous cough, he asked, "Now, Herr, perhaps you will explain this mad-dog play?"

"I have come to arrest you, Herr Captain Granville," gritted Von Kramann.

"Arrest me? Who the devil in hell are you?" demanded Clive, playing for precious time, and still keeping his blank, scared look. Was the confident Admiral bluffing? Clive thought so. In arriving alone the Admiral demonstrated he had as yet no definite proof. In any case his instinct led Clive to believe that his best riposte to the Admiral's attack was to persist with Alberic's rôle to the bitter end. There, and there alone, lay safety for the moment. Afterwards . . . ?

The German looked at the clock. "In five minutes two of my men will arrive. Meanwhile I will have a serious talk with you, Herr Captain, a talk in which if you do not speak willingly of everything you know, then—" the lips parted in a crude snarl, and his long white teeth protruded as a row of fangs, "we have means of squeezing it from you . . . you dirty English swinehound."

Ignoring the deadly insult, thrown purposely, Clive demanded in a well-adopted, mystified voice—"Will you please tell me who you are, and who I am supposed to be?"

"Sit down," commanded Von Kramann, "but remember one little move towards your revolver holster and you are a dead man. I have you covered."

"I give you my word," returned Clive in a feigned weak voice. "I do not intend to quarrel with an armed madman."

Clive sank slowly into the settee. The Admiral sat himself on the edge of a chair, watching Clive closely as he explained with a meaning leer:

"As you well know, I am Admiral von Kramann, and unfortunately for your clever little schemes, Herr Captain, we had a meeting once on a train, when I gave sound advice to the Herr Captain. We meet again, but under very different circumstances!" He bent menacingly forward again, pointing his revolver at Granville. "Since our last talk in that train we have found out all about the clever Herr Captain. The day you left London . . . the day our secret service clods lost you. We know of the mission which that fox the Herr Colonel Templeman has sent you on."

Clive's heart sank at the mention of the name of Templeman. Yet he took what comfort he could from the fact that a man of Von Kramann's calling would certainly know his opposite number in the British Intelligence.

"We know also the day the interesting exchange was made with the Herr Alberic von Schultz." His voice sank into a harsh whisper. "My only reason for questioning you now is . . . shall we name it vanity? It is my wish to capture the whole of your damn spy-nest, capture it alone, with my own two hands. And perhaps to make a suggestion to you. A little suggestion which might be the means of allowing you to leave this country in safety." He paused.

Clive somehow had a feeling, a warning, that the real object of the German's visit had not yet come to light. His face in the shadows, Clive watched narrowly, whilst in an attempt to force the Admiral to declare himself he held his tongue, knowing that silence would be disconcerting to Von Kramann. He was not quite certain, but it seemed to him the German hesitated, seeking for a diversion to help.

"Denial, Herr Captain, is useless!" and again came the hesitation. "I have a confession, a full confession from that old decayed Notaris, your fellow conspirator."

With a nervous laugh, but now with absolute conviction in his voice, Granville answered: "Herr Admiral, with the exception that you undoubtedly appear to be mistaking me for some other person, your talk is fathomless riddles to me! Chinese puzzles."

And Clive's heart began to lighten. The conviction came to him that the Admiral was playing a strong gigantic bluff, for he had passed too far with Verhagen. Brut Verhagen, even under all the tortures of hell, the Englishman was convinced, would never confess. And then the warning of the jungle came again. *Be not elated, in that elation there lies deadly danger.* The German was on the right track, dangerously right. As yet he may not be in possession of tangible proof, but the tiny accident might supply it, and it was for that accident the Admiral was fencing, seeking an opening to force the Englishman into a mistake. He was definitely convinced that the lounging form before him was the Englishman Captain Clive Granville.

Then in the next words Clive learned the reason of Von Kramann's visit and the deadly fear at the German's heart.

"Last night you dined with the Baroness Galie Fhel. She, too, is convinced of your correct identity, but it is not of that I would speak. In the Pannier d'Or last night a code was handed to you. Under her very nose you smuggled this secret code away. A code, Herr Captain," he declared solemnly, "that no other hands but German hands may touch and live. You saw what happened to that meddling traitor last night? Those fools of gendarmes did not communicate with me until this afternoon, but immediately I knew . . . and in those few short hours you have been able to secrete that book of death. Now, Engländer, there is one minute to go. Hand to me the code, and I swear you go free from this country. Refuse, and I take the law into my own hands and shoot you like a dog," he threatened in a tense voice.

Clive's mind now worked with bell-like clearness. That Galie Fhel had expressed such an opinion he doubted. As for Brut Verhagen, he was convinced the German's statement was sheer bluff. Admiral von Kramann had made the common mistake of overstating his case. But would the Admiral go so far as to arrest the man whom he thought to be an English spy? Apart from his convinced suspicions, what evidence had he? He was overplaying his bluff in a desperate endeavour to regain the code before it changed hands.

Clive decided the moment had arrived to attempt to call the German's bluff.

And simultaneously a cold clutch of fear gripped his heart. Any moment now, and Henri would arrive, and the curtains were at the "all clear." Would that supply the persistent Von Kramann with the accidental clue? At all costs he must give the danger signal and warn off the unsuspecting Henri, carrying the book of death.

Clive stood up, coolly stretched himself, and sneered. "It is well, Herr Admiral. I shall accompany you to the Commissar. But," he muttered fiercely, his eyes glinting, and shaking a trembling finger at Von Kramann, "I warn you, Herr Admiral, I make of you the laughing-stock of Berlin. I will publish your damn-foolishness in the comic papers . . . I, who have the ears of the Press, will make you the joke of the German Army—yes, and the whole of our Fatherland."

A German, Clive was well aware, can stand almost any shame, but not ridicule. In the vocabulary of the official Prussian the word "joke" is buried as deep as the Sargasso Sea.

The Admiral's face turned fiery red with passion, but his eyes followed Clive's movements with hatred and doubt. The glance turned to blazing suspicion as he saw the Englishman move towards the window and commence tinkering with the curtains, apparently arranging them for the light.

The bent form of Henri was in Clive's mind, and as he looked out of the window he thought he was suffering from hallucinations, for across the street his startled face saw Henri shuffling away from the house. Away, back towards the Boulevard Botanic. Clive had been too late with the signal. But what had warned Henri?

Quickly noticing Clive's tense attitude, Von Kramann followed the eyes of the Englishman, and then as the two pair of eyes stared at the bent form of Henri he turned and glanced up at the window.

"Ah!" grunted Von Kramann, "one of Verhagen's vultures."

With a hurried hiss of excitement he wrenched open the door and raced down the street, and turned into the boulevard following the unsuspecting Henri.

The German's movements had been so rapid Clive was left dumb-founded, but as he crossed the room and rapidly felt for his revolver holster and belt he called for Fritz. There was no answer. Then he remembered this was the hour Fritz would attend at the nearby military depot to draw rations.

His reasons for following in the wake of Henri and Von Kramann were purely mechanical. To sit in his rooms waiting, waiting for he knew not what, would have been impossible, was repugnant to his battling spirit.

Darkness had fallen as Clive, hugging the shadows of the tall buildings of the Louvain Gate, came into view of No. 5. He halted suddenly, for he saw the house was already guarded. On either side of the door stood a tall secret service man. Clive recognised he could do nothing for the moment, less than nothing.

He turned into a quiet café almost opposite, and asked the waiter for pen, ink and paper. He sat at a table near the window and pretended to write a letter, whilst his eyes, through a crack in the blind, closely watched the door of No. 5.

Only the ingenuity of the devoted, gentle Henri could save the situation. Could he secrete the fateful code? Apart from the code book Clive knew that nothing of an incriminating character would be found in No. 5. Brut Verhagen, without exception, destroyed all messages immediately, and he carried all the particulars of his vast organisation in his encyclopædic brain.

Clive suppressed a glow of thankfulness that the Admiral was bluffing. The shrewd German was too close, too terribly near the truth, to encourage any feelings of equanimity. Would he find the accidental damaging clue behind those dark walls opposite?

At long last he saw the door of No. 5 open and three men come quietly out. Eagerly he scrutinised the three figures, but not one was the bent-shouldered Henri. He recognised Von Kramann, as the Admiral brusquely commanded one man to remain on guard, whilst the others moved quickly away.

Clive immediately understood. The front door had been forced, so Von Kramann had left a man on guard. He reasoned further that no other policemen would be in the house itself as one had been left outside on duty.

He felt for his small electric torch, and under the table he drew out his automatic and released the safety catch. He replaced the weapon carefully in his holster, called the *garçon*, paid and left.

A short detour brought him to the rear of No. 5.

Whether Verhagen would approve of his actions or not Clive did not pause to consider. He had decided it was his duty to risk the investigation of No. 5, and if possible to help the faithful Henri. If, indeed, Henri had not already been arrested and taken for interrogation.

Clive unlocked the back door and passed along a covered corridor which ran along one side of a spacious garden. He was well acquainted with this part of Verhagen's property, for this was where he had lodged, and hidden, for ten weary days. At the end of the corridor he tried the latch of the kitchen door. It opened to his gentle pressure. Noiselessly Clive entered and attempted to cross the kitchen, but when near a door which led into the hall he stumbled over an upturned chair. His heart beating furiously, he breathlessly waited. There was no stir of alarm in the house, then carefully he moved forward and reached the hall. Again with great caution he moved along the lofty hall. No sound or light came from any of the rooms. For the first time he turned on the electric torch, and carefully slid open the door of the drawing-room. The place was a shambles. The upholstery on the furniture was ripped and torn off, pictures were wrenched from the walls and lay smashed in the middle of the floor. Even large tracts of wall-paper had been torn off in an attempt to find a secret hiding-place. Priceless *objets d'art* had been senselessly thrown about and smashed in this ruthless search.

Clive turned away from the scene of destruction with tightened lips, and a sickening fear of being too late gripped him.

Slowly he opened the door of Verhagen's study.

The place was even in worse case than the drawing-room. Documents and legal papers lay ankle-deep, and then Clive's eyes fell on the rigid form of Henri, and slowly under his breath terrible invectives hissed through his teeth.

But the pitiful battered face of Henri showed not the agonies he endured in his last moments, for the eyes were closed, and a gentle curve, almost a smile, lay on the lips. The upper part of the body was naked, with just a coat flung roughly over the body to hide the desecration, and where the dead flesh showed Clive saw huge gaping scars, evidence of a ferocious flogging. The trouser legs were torn off to the knees and the bare legs bore similar furious marks . . . the signs of infuriated maniacs.

Clive had once before seen such a sight. A native soldier in German East Africa had been left thus under the blazing sun, and abandoned still breathing. They had been more merciful to gentle Henri, for Clive found, under the coat, a bullet wound which had passed through the heart. As on that day in the African bush a berserker rage swept his soul, and as he heard now the chugging of a motor-car halted at the front door, he snapped off his electric torch, and gripped his automatic.

The murderers had returned to spirit the dead body of Henri away. Blindly he stood at the ready in the hall. He would shoot them down like rats—destroy them as beasts of prey. . . .

But the mesmeric eyes of Brut Verhagen glowed through the darkness, and the high cracked voice beat insistently on Clive's distraught senses. . . . "By no pity or sentiment must we endanger our position . . . the greater good must always outweigh the lesser . . . even our personal feelings . . . our honour. . . ."

His mind was pandemonium, chaotic, but with almost a sob of rebellion in his throat he obeyed the instinct and slowly backed out down the hall and through the kitchen as he heard the guttural voices enter the front door. They would spirit the body of Henri away, and that would be the last heard of the dastardly murder.

As in a nightmare Clive walked back to the Rue Rumbeak, and it was with almost a lack of surprise he noticed that his rooms, too, had been ransacked. Omitting to call for his batman Fritz, he sat down and attempted to think. But he felt a nausea, a revolt against the whole of degrading mankind, against his terrible position.

Here he was alone, by nature an open honest fighter, a battler who asked nothing further than to ride openly out with his fellows, and die fighting joyously in clean strife. The herd instinct, and the feeling that the herd is nigh, no matter how brutal the issues, has the saving grace of sustaining one in a crisis. And here he was alone, condemned to sneak into devious ways . . . to disobey an honourable instinct . . . to forget honour, and sink his identity in another's.

Presently Clive heard a low knock on the door. For a few seconds he could only watch without speaking a word as Fritz quietly entered. Then:

"Well?" asked Clive, as he saw the soldier lay a small white parcel on the table.

"Two lousy policemen were here, mein Herr Hauptmann," explained Fritz, "and they only left a few minutes ago."

"Yes, I see it," replied Clive, trying to keep up his usual front before the searching eyes of his batman, as he looked ruefully round the room.

"That Prussian sailor, the Admiral," volunteered Fritz, as he moved his eyes from his master to the parcel, "has been here again asking questions about you, mein Herr Hauptmann, and he then searched this room. He said he was searching for a small book. He found it not."

Clive nodded absently as Fritz continued imperturbably, but this time on a different strain. "This evening going to draw the rations I saw that old penwiper of yours Notaris. I said to him, 'Hi, Belgian, do not go near the Herr Hauptmann, there's a mad-dog Prussian sailor there waving revolvers.' 'Ah' he said to me, 'it is not for much I want to see the Hauptmann, Herr Soldat,'—yes, Herr Hauptmann, he named me Herr Soldat," and Fritz nodded his head at the appreciation, "'it is only to hand this small parcel to your master. Perhaps, Herr Soldat, you would hand it to him when the mad Prussian sailor has departed?' Of course I agreed, and as he handed the parcel he warned, 'But beware, Herr Soldat, the parcel is valuable . . . as valuable as the Herr Hauptmann's life. He and he alone must have it,' and this, Herr Hauptmann, is the parcel."

Fritz took the small white object from the table and handed it to Clive, who, with eyes aflame, ripped off the string and paper and disclosed the fatal code book.

Eagerly Clive searched, and under the flap of the cover was a neatly written warning penned by the hand of Henri, now stilled in death.

Beware! death will follow this book as your own shadow. It is the latest of the Imperial Naval Codes.

In the hands of the British Admiralty this fateful little book would throw grit into the machine of the German sea forces from which they could never escape.

"Fritz Berger," warned Clive, "I have heard your words, watched your lips, but of this," and he held the book before the soldier, "I have seen or heard nothing. You, too, have now forgotten. Is that not so?"

"Herr Hauptmann," Fritz replied, "my eyes have seen, my ears have heard nothing. I have already forgotten."

VIII

SIDNEY REILLY EXPLORES SOVIET RUSSIA

from

THE ADVENTURES OF SIDNEY REILLY, BRITAIN'S MASTER SPY

Written by himself, edited and completed by his wife
(Published by Elkin Mathews & Marrot, London, 1931)

Sidney Reilly had an Irish merchant sea captain for a father and a Russian for a mother. Speaking fluently German and Russian, he was an ideal choice for the job assigned to him by the British secret service towards the end of the first world war to work against the Germans in Russia.

A man of immense courage and great resourcefulness, Reilly's previous exploits in Germany had already become legendary. Penetrating into the Kaiser's wartime Germany on various occasions, usually crossing the front line by plane, he had been successful in supplying Britain with valuable military information.

He was less lucky in Russia, where his mission finally proved disastrous. There was a price on his head, his life was constantly in danger. Moreover, it was quite impossible for him to pick up the threads of his activities in Petrograd following the events of the Bolshevik revolution. All he could do was to escape from Russia with his bare life.

A few years later, in 1925, he was, however, lured back to Russia by the Soviet counter-espionage network, and nothing has been heard from him since. Rumours have it that he was executed on his arrival in Russia, but it is just as possible that he is still alive in some forced labour camp in Siberia.

The following excerpt from his own narrative describes his hazardous flight from the Soviet Union after the first world war.

★

I was well satisfied with the change in my appearance. Looking in the mirror I was sure that nobody would recognise me. My beard was a really formidable affair, and gave me a most ruffianly appearance. I had allowed my hair to grow and entirely neglected the civilised practice of washing. This, in conjunction with a very shabby coat and a pair of shabbier trousers, presented a spectacle which any tramp might envy, and which the most suspicious comrade would pass unchallenged.

My intention now was to leave Russia as soon as I could. The mission on which I had been sent by the British Government had failed disastrously. There was little or no chance of picking up again the threads of my organisation in Petrograd. I had been formally condemned to death by the Bolshevik Government, the sentence to be executed whenever and wherever I was found. In short, there was little point and much danger in my remaining in Russia.

There were two ways of getting out of the country.

(1) I might take the train from the Finland station at Petrograd and cross the frontier near Viborg. This was the favourite route of *émigrés*. The Finns were always ready to assist, but the Red patrols were correspondingly alert. However, escapes by this route were frequent. It entailed securing another passport and running the usual barrage at the railway station.

(2) There was the way over the frontier bridge at Bielo Ostrov. This necessitated a handsome bribe to the station commissar and to the sentry on duty at the bridge.

Fortunately I was well supplied with money. The notes at the Cheremetev Pereulok had remained undiscovered, and, although the evacuation of my agents from Moscow had proved a costly business, I still had a considerable sum left.

Not caring about facing the inquisition at the station, I determined to follow the latter route. The panic which had followed the shooting of Uritzky had now died down. Five hundred prisoners had been executed by way of a reprisal, and the Bolsheviks had proclaimed their intention of revenging in the same fashion any further attack upon their authority. It seemed to be known that I had travelled from Moscow to Petrograd. But the Cheka raids had ceased in the latter city and the place had resumed its normal state of stagnation.

I resolved accordingly to show myself in public and test the efficacy of my disguise. In Petrograd I had stayed with friends, moving from place to place as I had done at Moscow. This was necessary owing to the vigilance of the house committees, particularly in the days following the discovery of the plot, in watching for unregistered lodgers. The slightest carelessness would not only lead to my discovery, but would bring the wrath of the Cheka on to the heads of my hosts.

I was obsessed with the impression that Petrograd possessed eyes and all the eyes were focused on me. Everybody was watching me. The man I passed just now—did he not turn round and look after me? The woman opposite, staring at me across the pavement? I was certain to be recognised and arrested. Well, I had a Colt in my pocket, and there would be a few fresh faces in Hell before I put the last bullet into my own head, rather than fall into the hands of that scum.

Gradually I grew more confident in the extent of the change in my appearance. I did not venture out in broad daylight to start with, but remained under cover until dusk. But as time went on and I still remained unrecognised, I made excursions into the more frequented streets at all hours of the day.

I passed people whom I knew. I did not force myself upon their notice, however, but shuffled hurriedly by in the gait which I had assumed to suit my general appearance.

It was in the Nevsky Prospekt that I met the man who recognised me. I passed someone whose appearance was vaguely familiar to me. He seemed to know me, too, for he shot a keen and suspicious glance in my direction as he passed. Then he turned round, overtook me by about ten paces, then came back and looked at me again. I pushed ahead quickly, but before long I heard his steps tap-tapping after me again.

Then my heart missed a beat. A voice hissed over my shoulder in a hoarse whisper.

"Sidney Georgevitch!" Then as I neither turned round nor said anything he went on: "Do not be afraid. It is a friend." Thereupon he gave me an address and a number in the Kamenostrovsky Prospekt, and added—"In half an hour."

I shuffled on. Should I go? Was it a trap? No, surely if he had been an enemy he would have given the alarm there and then. Well, trap or not, I was discovered now. Might as well face it. So I went down the long Kamenostrovsky Prospekt and knocked at the door of the house indicated.

I was admitted cautiously by the man who had recognised me, and ushered into a room bare and almost denuded of furniture. My unknown acquaintance then swung round and peered at me narrowly.

"That beard changes you, Sidney Georgevitch," he said. "Your closest friend might not have known you."

"Perhaps that is why I have grown it," I suggested. "But may I ask who you are and how you came to know me?"

"I am the man who used to prevent that beard from growing, Sidney Georgevitch," he replied, "Don't you know me yet?"

Then memory came to me. "You are the barber," I said. "You are Alexander, who used to be in Maullé's saloon, and shaved me in the old days."

Alexander seemed as pleased at the meeting as I was, and prepared the samovar in high spirits.

"Why you should have come to Russia again I do not know," he said, "when you were safely out of the place. Do you think I would return if I had a living elsewhere?"

So I told him that I had come back in the service of my country, and added that at the moment the dearest wish of my heart was to get out of it.

"It is easy neither to get in nor out, Sidney Georgevitch," said Alexander sadly. "Which way did you think of going?"

"I am trying to find someone who will bribe the station commissar at Bielo Ostrof to turn his back while I cross the bridge," I told him.

"It is no good," he said, shaking his head gravely. "Anybody else, perhaps—at a price. But you—no. Nobody in Russia dare let you go, however much you paid him. I recognised you. So will others. Perhaps you are not aware that at every station people are posted who know you. The rascals have traced you to Petrograd, and I may tell you that the Redskin who let you through the barrier was summarily shot. They are pretty certain that you have not left the city, and when they say that you seem to have escaped from Russia it is only to tempt you out of hiding. There are too many eyes watching, Sidney Georgevitch. No, we must think of some other way."

I could not but agree with him, especially since it had been proved so conclusively that my disguise was less effective than I had hoped it would be.

"Meantime," said the barber, "you are quite safe here. So far I have given no cause for suspicion. I have a clerical post in a Soviet institution. If you will stay here I have an extra bed, and I shall be honoured by your company."

I stayed for about a fortnight with Alexander, and, having learned caution, did not venture out of the apartment. Nor did the house committee ever suspect my presence. As Alexander said, with a rueful glance round his bare room, they had taken all there was to be taken and so were not likely to trouble him again.

And during that two weeks Alexander was searching every channel for a means to smuggle me out of Russia.

Then one day he came in bringing with him a portly, heavy-faced man, who might have been a prosperous merchant or stockbroker—if such phenomena were to be found in Russia.

"Mr. Van den Bosch," said Alexander by way of introduction. The heavy-faced man bowed perfunctorily. "Mr. Van den Bosch is a Netherlander, who has come to Petrograd to do a little business with the Soviet Government. His boat—it is quite a small boat, a motor boat—lies in the river now." Alexander paused to add emphasis. "I have explained to Mr. Van den Bosch your predicament and your requirements. Mr. Van den Bosch is of opinion that he might be able to help you."

I thanked the stranger in German.

"I understand," said Van den Bosch, "that you are in some trouble with the government—such government as it is in this country. What sort of trouble it is not my business to inquire. Of course you will understand, Mr.——"

"Bergmann," said I.

"You are a German?" (I bowed). "Of course you will understand, Mr. Bergmann, that my assisting you might very seriously prejudice my position. Not only would the very delicate trade mission on which I am engaged be ruined, but I would render myself liable to imprisonment for assisting in the escape of a man who is wanted by the authorities."

"Of course, I will make it worth your while," I assured him. "How much do you want?"

"Sixty thousand roubles," said Van den Bosch.

"You shall have them."

"And when may I expect payment?" asked this hard-headed business man.

"Half now and half when you land me," said I, and counted out to him thirty thousand roubles on the spot.

"I shall be sailing at midnight tomorrow," said Van den Bosch, pocketing the money. "Be early. I cannot wait for you. Your friend here knows where my boat is lying and will guide you to it. A dinghy will be waiting by the quay. There will be no moon. But if you are followed don't try to come aboard."

Van den Bosch then left us. The following day I sent Alexander round to my old quarters, whence he succeeded in retrieving a suit and some linen in not too bad a state of disrepair. The faithful barber clipped my beard and moustache, and dressed my hair with a pair of rather blunt scissors. As a result I looked rather like a naval officer who had run a little to seed.

The good fellow then left me. We were to meet at eleven o'clock by the Kazan Cathedral. I was to board the boat at the last minute. A visit from the Bolshevik agents before she put to sea was almost inevitable.

The day seemed interminable. I amused myself by reading the copies of the Communist papers which Alexander had brought. I was not a little edified to find several references to myself and to the abortive conspiracy in which I had played a part. But there was little news. Most of the matter consisted of propaganda and the approaching war against the Imperialist powers of the West.

The night fell stormy and overcast. Great clouds were chasing one another across the sky and there were several downpours of rain. The streets were deserted when I set out for the ruined Kazan Cathedral.

Alexander was waiting for me. When he saw me he signalled a

warning and slipped behind the hoarding which covered one face of the edifice. I joined him there.

"All is clear, Sidney Georgevitch," he whispered. "I have been down to the quay. The boat is waiting, as Van den Bosch promised. A commissar has been on board with a soldier, but left at about eight o'clock. Since then the quay has been deserted. I will go ahead. If I see anyone suspicious I will pretend to stumble. That will be a signal to you to get under cover. If anything goes wrong make your way back to the Kamenostrovsky Prospekt. But go circuitously. You might be followed."

I let Alexander get some fifty yards ahead and then followed him. It had begun to rain hard, much to my satisfaction. But I was drenched to the skin before we reached the quay. Nothing untoward had happened. Alexander stopped in the shadow of a large building and signalled me.

"Wait here," he whispered when I joined him. "All is not well. There is a light showing in the boat. Mr. Van den Bosch promised to show a light if you could not go aboard. Stay, while I go and investigate."

The faithful barber disappeared into the rain in the direction of the quay. By and by he returned looking anxious.

"The boat is showing a light, Sidney Georgevitch, and the dinghy is not at the quay as Van den Bosch promised. Something is wrong. We must return at once to the Kamenostrovsky Prospekt."

"Too late, Alexander. You have been followed." Out of the downpour in the wake of the barber a man had appeared, a giant of a fellow who towered above myself and my companion in the uncertain light. My hand closed on the butt of my revolver. My adventures seemed to have come to an end at last. But a pleasant surprise awaited me.

"Herr Bergmann?" The newcomer addressed me in German. "I am Mr. Van den Bosch's mechanic. I recognise your friend. I have seen him with my master. Herr Bergmann, there is a commissar on board the boat. You cannot come on board until he leaves"

"And when does the commissar intend to leave?" I asked him.

"Not until the boat sails," said the mechanic. "The Communists are suspicious about something. A man came aboard yesterday night, when Mr. Van den Bosch was away, and asked many questions. He was very anxious to know where Mr. Van den Bosch had gone. And when Mr. Van den Bosch returned he was followed. Tonight the commissar came aboard again, and insisted on examining each one of the crew. Mr. Van den Bosch does not wish to offend the Bolsheviks. He expects to do business with them. Therefore he is entertaining the commissar in his cabin until we are due to sail. The commissar has expressed the polite intention of seeing us off and waving goodbye from the quay."

"And when do we go aboard?"

"When the commissar comes off."

"And if he sees us?"

"Herr Bergmann, the commissar will not be in a condition to see anyone."

Sure enough, shortly after one o'clock the commissar was brought ashore dead drunk. Hastily gripping Alexander's hand, I hastened across the quay with the mechanic and dropped into the dinghy.

Van den Bosch provided me with a change of clothing and some hot toddy. As I heard the screw thresh the water, a flood of exhilaration surged through me. I felt as a man feels who, after being almost suffocated, gets a breath of air. Slowly the rare lights of Petrograd dropped astern. Chug, chug, chug! In front of us was the open sea, Helsingfors, Copenhagen, England. At that moment running the gauntlet of the German naval base at Reval seemed but a minor risk. Chug, chug, chug! The drifting clouds were being chased out of the sky by the quickening breeze of morning. Here and there a watery star looked dimly down. Already the long grey fingers of dawn reached from the eastern horizon. Chug, chug, chug! England, home, safety.

"Where are you bound for?" I asked Van den Bosch.

"The German naval base at Reval," was the answer.

IX

AN INCURSION ON THE KU KLUX KLAN
from
I RODE WITH THE KU KLUX KLAN
by STETSON KENNEDY
(Published by Arco, London)

One of the most hateful of secret societies ever to be formed is the Ku Klux Klan, which has most of its adherents in what is known as the "Deep South" of the U.S.A. The headquarters of this organisation is at Atlanta, Georgia, the "Imperial City of the K.K.K.'s Invisible Empire," as its members refer to it.

The Ku Klux Klan never make any bones about their aim, which simply is to eradicate from the face of the earth all Negroes, Jews, Catholics, Communists, trade unionists and all others who incur their hatred on racial, religious or political grounds. Negroes especially are singled out for destruction ("Dead niggers make good fertiliser") and lynching has always been one of the Ku Klux Klan's favourite methods.

Stetson Kennedy became a member of the Ku Klux Klan for the express purpose of spying on them with a view to obtaining dissolution of the society. In his first book, Palmetto Country, published shortly before the outbreak of the last war, he debunked the lie that the original K.K.K. was founded in 1865, to "save the South from rascally Negroes, scaliwags and carpetbaggers." In order to gain a footing with the K.K.K., he had to change not only his place of residence but also his name. From Miami, Florida, he went to Atlanta, Georgia, where he managed to worm his way into the confidence of the society's leaders, under the name of John S. Perkins.

★

I AWOKE with a start, my hand already instinctively reaching for the ·32 automatic I kept under my pillow. No sooner did I have the comforting cool steel in hand than I became aware that the ringing of a bell had awakened me. It was dark, and my first thought was that the alarm clock must have gone off ahead of schedule. Cursing under my breath, I flicked on the bed light. It was 2 a.m. Then I realised that the bell had stopped ringing, and I knew it was the telephone.

Trouble, I thought. But I knew that failure to answer it might mean worse trouble, so I stumbled out into the hall and picked up the receiver.

"Who is this?" asked the caller. I recognised the voice—rather like a cement-mixer running at half speed—as that of Cliff Carter, "Chief

Ass-Tearer" of the hooded Ku Klux Klan's Klavalier Klub murder squad.

"John Perkins," I replied, giving him the alias under which I had lived ever since I joined the Klan as a secret undercover agent to gather evidence against it.

"What's your number, Perkins?" asked the voice bluntly.

"Seventy-three," I replied, this being the number on my Klavalier Klub membership "Kard."

"White—" he said, giving me the first half of the Klan's current secret password.

"—man," I replied, returning the countersign.

"Native—" he continued.

"—born," I concluded.

Satisfied that I was indeed his "Brother Klansman" and Klavalier, Carter dropped the recognition ritual we Klavaliers always used for telephonic conversations.

"This is Clearwater," he said solemnly, giving the code name by which he as Chieftain was known to us. "And this is a Fiery Summons! Remember your oath to be ready when called! The call is imperative! Bring your robe and *come prepared*—to Black Rock!"

Wide awake now, I was thinking hard. When Carter said "come prepared," I knew he meant for me to bring whatever deadly weapon I had available. "Black Rock" was our secret code name for the Atlanta suburb known as Buckhead—one of the key mobilisation points which the Klavaliers had designated throughout the city. Someone—Negro, Jew, Catholic or labour unionist—had been tagged for a K.K.K. flogging or worse that night. Or perhaps I was literally being invited to my own funeral—which was always a possibility when I attended a Klan function.

I wondered whether I could rouse Dan Duke—the state's Assistant Attorney-General under whom I worked as an anti-Klan agent—in time to nip the Klavaliers' projected flogging or lynching party in the bud.

"Clearwater," I said weakly, "you know I've been very sick with the flu lately. I don't think I would be much good to you tonight."

"Klansman!" Carter roared. "You know the oath as well as I do! And I happen to know you are not bedridden! No other excuse is tolerated! *You must go!*" There was a click as he hung up.

I knew there was no way out—that I myself would be subject to "banishment" as a "citizen" of the Klan's "Invisible Empire" if I failed to respond to the summons. "Herein fail ye not! By mandate of His Lordship, the Imperial Wizard" is the way the little printed cards read in red ink, when a Fiery Summons is sent by mail. All action undertaken by the Klavalier Klub, which serves as the "Military Department" of the K.K.K., has the approval of the Wizard or Grand Dragon. All Klansmen are sworn not only to obey the edicts of the hierarchy but to enforce obedience upon any Brothers who fail to live up to this oath. I had seen one Klansman, who chose punishment to banishment, forced to run nude through a gauntlet of Klan belts. I had no desire to let myself in for the same thing.

I put in a rush call for Dan Duke, using the direct private telephone he had installed in his home to keep our Klan probe out of the hostile ears of telephone company switchboard operators. Duke had been out of the city on official business, and I had an anxious moment until I heard his sleepy voice on the phone. Briefly, I relayed to him the details of the Fiery Summons I had received.

"Got any idea who they're after this time?" Duke asked.

"Not the least," I had to admit.

"Well, I'll do my best to get my men out to Buckhead in time," Duke said. "If you get a chance to call me back without making anybody suspicious, phone me when you get more details."

"Right," I said. "I'd better get moving—it isn't healthy to be late for one of these affairs."

A few minutes later I was speeding in my car through the city's deserted streets—my automatic in my pocket and my black Klavalier's robe tucked under the seat.

As I approached Buckhead I could see, scattered over an area of several blocks as we had been trained to do to avoid suspicion, the cars of other Klavaliers who had arrived ahead of me.

Cars were still converging on the intersection, so I knew I would not be the last arrival. I wondered about Duke's men—whether they were somewhere on hand. Our whole "Operation Anti-Klan" was so ticklish that Duke had kept my identity from his other hand-picked undercover agents of the Georgia Department of Law, and I in turn had no idea who they were. So deep was the K.K.K. infiltration inside the state's law enforcement agencies that my cheque was even drawn from a special account, as a precaution against real Klansmen on the state payroll discovering my identity.

Parking my car in the shadows of a side street, I went around to the parking lot behind an abandoned theatre which was our meeting place. I estimated that there were nearly forty Klavaliers assembled there, each one carrying his robe in small briefcase-like bags (which the Dragon sold at a neat profit for $10 each) or in paper bags or simply wrapped in newspapers. They were just standing there, smoking and

6

talking in low tones, waiting for Carter to give them their riding orders for the night. Carter was checking those present by a list of numbers he carried. Finally he was satisfied that all those who had been summoned—thirty-seven, hand picked for reasons known only to himself—were present. Raising a hand as a signal for us to gather around him, Carter said:

"So far so good. You are all to be commended for getting here in good time. Keep your robes off for the time being, disperse, and proceed to Wingo's Café. Take your robes in with you. And keep a sharp lookout to see whether you are being followed!"

Wingo's Café was a joint in the East End of Atlanta, specialising in steaks, and open all night. We Klavaliers met there for steak dinners and corn liquor one night each month, but I couldn't imagine why we should be ordered there at two-thirty in the morning. I wondered if Carter were mean enough to do a job on the Negro chef, who on our last visit had refused to cook when he detected that we were Klansmen.

I decided to try to give Duke a ring on the way to Wingo's. Starting off slowly, I waited until I had turned the corner before cutting on my lights. Adjusting my rear-view mirror, I looked back to see if I were being followed. Just as I was about to relax, I saw that I was being tailed by a car without lights. Was it Duke's men—or Brother Klavaliers keeping an eye on me? The car kept too far behind for me to recognise it.

I tried speeding and I tried slowing down. Neither worked. Finally, putting all the distance I could between us, I careened around a corner, cut my lights and motor, and coasted far up into the dark driveway of the first house I came to. Immediately, a dog inside the house began to bark. I had visions of what might happen if lights began to go on inside. It seemed a long time before the following car turned the corner, and I held my breath in anticipation that it might spot me and slam on the brakes. It roared on down the street, hesitated at the corner, and then disappeared in a cloud of red Georgia clay dust.

The dog inside the house was barking louder than ever, and I wondered whether I had escaped my pursuers only to be accosted by an irate householder. I stamped on the starter and accelerator simultaneously. As the motor roared, the lights in the house flashed on, but in a matter of seconds I had backed out and was off down the street—on my way to an all-night drug store where I could telephone.

The tailing episode bothered me chiefly because, had my pursuers turned out to be Klavaliers, it would have meant I was under suspicion as the much-sought-after "spy" in the Klan. It would also have prevented me tipping off Duke to the new mobilisation point at Wingo's Café, in case his men failed to get there on their own.

I circled the drug store twice before deciding it was safe to make the call. Inside, I made certain that no one was in the adjoining phone booths. Duke said he had just had a call from his men, who had lost the trail after trying to tail a Klavalier car from Buckhead. They had been shaken, he said, without getting close enough to the car to describe it.

"It's a good thing you called," Duke said. "They're going to phone me back in five minutes, and I'll send them on to Wingo's!"

All this had taken time, and I raced to Wingo's without seeing any further signs of being followed. Most of the Klavaliers were already assembled in the private dining-room where we always convened. Carter was at the door.

"Enrobe, but do not put on your mask," he ordered.

The Brothers were all seated around a long table which had been formed by placing a number of tables together. Most of them had ordered hamburgers, and Carter had provided half a dozen bottles of cheap "drinking whisky" as a reward for their "faithfulness." Even with their masks off, they were an awesome sight. I was the last to arrive, and Carter, taking his place at the head of the table, lost no time in asking:

"Were any of you followed?"

"I was," I said promptly. "A carload of Duke's men got in behind me without any lights, and I had one hellova time shaking them. That's why I was late getting here. There's no doubt about it—the damned spy is still on the job."

Carter looked at me and blinked.

"Are you positive you shook them?" he asked finally.

"Absolutely," I replied.

"Anybody else followed?" Carter asked, looking around the room.

"Yeah, they tried to tail me too," said a Klavalier named Nathan Jones, "but I finally got rid of them. Somebody ought to pay me back for all the gas I had to burn."

This got a laugh from the brethren, but Carter cut it short.

"This is no laughing matter!" he roared. "The Judas we've been trying to catch so long is sitting right here at this table tonight! At last I know who he is! That's why you men were summoned here—to close the trap and mete out fitting punishment!"

It was a cold January night, but I began to sweat under my robe.

"Name the s.o.b.!" several Klavaliers shouted—and I joined in the chorus with what little enthusiasm I could muster.

"Take it easy," said Carter with a grim smile. He was playing cat-and-mouse, studying each man's face carefully. For a brief moment I thought of making a break for the door. It was closed, and while no guard had been posted outside of it to my knowledge, it occurred to me that Carter might have locked it. I wondered, too, about the odds of backing out of such a room even if I could succeed in getting the drop on them all with my automatic. The odds, I decided, were not too good—and when I noticed that Carter was keeping one hand under the table I decided to sit tight and sweat it out.

"I told you all to come prepared!" Carter said. "Let's see what you've got to work with!"

From under his own robe he pulled a ·45 Police Special revolver, and laid it on the table in front of him. Amidst a tumult of curses to "let us at him," the Klavaliers followed suit. Soon the table was covered with an assortment of pistols, switch-blade "nigger-killer" knives, blackjacks, brassknucks, and a flogging whip made by sewing a piece of sawmill belt to a sawed-off baseball bat handle. Adding my automatic to the collection, I decided that the chances for a getaway were now non-existent.

"We're prepared, all right!" shouted one Brother. "Just name him!"

Carter only smiled, and the clamour arose like the frenzied "treed" baying of a pack of hounds gathered for the kill—gnashing their teeth in anticipation of rending their prey asunder. Carter kept smiling and watching.

"What are we gonna do with the rat?" one man shouted.

"You know the penalty," Carter spoke up. "Death, death at the hands of a Brother!" He was quoting the oath we all took upon joining the Klan, wherein we swore to accept the death penalty if we ever betrayed the Klan's secrets.

"Let's take him out in the woods, fasten him to a log with a staple over his testicles, set fire to the log, give him a knife and tell him to 'Cut or burn!'" shouted one enthusiast.

Other proposals came thick and fast, each more blood-curdling than the other. I tried without much conviction to make some suggestions of my own.

Every now and then Carter would toss them some more bait.

"We've waited a long time to corner the rat," he said, "and every one of you who is paid up in his dues can have a free hand in working him over. I'm going to start things off by standing him in front of a Klan altar and wearing off both my arms up to the elbows!"

"Don't you think we ought to banish him from citizenship in the Invisible Empire first?" one stickler for protocol asked. Banishment proceedings are a long-drawn-out ceremony, including a mock trial and concluded by a symbolic "burial" of the banished Brother.

"When we get through with him he won't need banishing!" Carter said solemnly, still watching.

But he had stopped smiling.

Suddenly, I almost smiled with the realisation that Carter was bluffing—that he had no idea whom to put his finger on. Fortunately, I didn't smile, for Carter was clever enough to have interpreted a smile at that moment. But I kicked myself mentally for not having considered the possibility that Carter had merely set a trap and hoped that someone would make a break and dash into it. I took a long pull at the "drinking whisky" and rejoined the debate with far more enthusiasm than before.

At last, when he could stall the men no longer, Carter stood up.

"Brother Klansmen and Dirty Rat," he began sardonically, "I'm sorry to have to disappoint you, but we're going to have to put off the killing a little while longer. I don't know who the rat is, but I hoped that by giving him a little rope here tonight he would hang himself by trying to make a break for it. I wish he had. Knowing the penalty, I can't understand how any man would dare rat on the Klan! Anyway, we've narrowed the prospects down to thirty-seven men—the men right here in this room. We're hot on his trail, and it's getting hotter all the time. We know he's here tonight, or we would never have been followed. Our Klokann investigating committee is made up of the best detectives on the Atlanta police force, and we'll catch the rat yet!

"I want to congratulate you all for your quick mobilisation tonight. There is plenty of good work that needs to be done, and we will attend to it just as soon as we get rid of the rat. As long as he is in our midst, our hands are tied. Catch him, and I promise you we'll light up the skies with fiery crosses! There'll be something doing every night!

"Disrobe now, and go back to your homes. And if any of you are stopped by Duke's men, remember the marks of a Klavalier—not only to be ready when called, but to have guts and a tight lip! Sew up your mouths, and they can't hold you! Disperse!"

There was a scrambling for what was left of the whisky, and a great deal of profanity, but nothing new was proposed by way of punishing the "rat."

I was never so happy to disperse in my life.

X

IRGUN OUTWITS BRITISH INTELLIGENCE

from

THE REVOLT

by Menachem Begim

(Published by W. H. Allen, London, 1951)

Menachem Begim, erstwhile leader of the Israeli underground movement during the postwar insurrection in Palestine that led to the abrogation of the Mandate, was the master mind who brought about the emergence of the sovereign Jewish State of Israel. He played a decisive rôle in the Jewish struggle for national independence and his cunning and resourcefulness as head of the Irgun Zvai Leumi was dreaded by the British authorities, who were trying to maintain the status quo.

The British did their utmost to capture the man who at the time was described as "Terrorist Number One" but they never succeeded in laying their hands on him. He was as slippery as an eel and used more aliases even than the legendary Count of Saint-Germain. British Intelligence in Palestine was no match for Menachem Begim, who lived to instil the old fighting spirit into the Jewish race.

To use the words of Sir Edward Grigg (now Lord Altrincham), former British Minister to the Middle East: "The primary cause of our failure in Palestine was the failure of our intelligence service."

★

AFTER some time I forsook McMichael's sheets and moved, this time with my wife and son, to a little house in the Hasidoff Quarter. There I became Israel Halperin.

The Hasidoff Quarter consists of a row of low houses on the road to Kfar Sirkin, near Lydda. It is a workers' suburb, within the municipal boundaries of Petah Tikva, built opposite the well-known Arab village of Fejja. In that period, 1944-5, its houses were frequently without water and had no electricity at all. But it was a verdant neighbourhood, with cultivated fields, blooming gardens, woods and orange groves. An outside observer would no doubt assume that it was because of the abundance of trees that we chose the place as headquarters. This was not so. We found it almost by chance. It was quiet and cheap, and in accordance with our "open underground" tactics we went there to expose ourselves as a means of hiding more effectively. We assumed that it would not occur to the authorities that the "chief terrorist" lived in a place where everybody knew his neighbours. We were not mistaken.

For nearly a year I lived in this small suburb among silent friends of the underground and its vigorous, vociferous opponents. One of the inhabitants knew. He recognised me the first time I went out on to the sandy walk that ran along the length of the row of houses. But he said nothing. My hosts, too, were mercifully silent. The rest of our neighbours had not the least suspicion. They found it all natural and understandable. They were told that the Halperin family was a family of refugees from Poland who had been unable to find accommodation in the town. True, the head of the family did not go out to work every day, but for this too a plausible explanation was found. We voluntarily told the neighbours that we lived off an allocation from the refugee aid organisation and that I was preparing for the Palestinian law examinations—hence my working at home. It is characteristic that the landlord, the good Mr. Malkieli, who knew what "business" I was in, assumed that it was connected with law. Malkieli had been a member of the Irgun and knew Meridor, who had been his commanding officer, as well as Eitan and Daniel and Benjamin. He saw all these officers coming on frequent visits to his tenant. But on trying to deduce the object of these visits he came to the conclusion that it was to get legal advice in connection with the trials of undergound fighters. It seems that his tenant made the impression of being a bookish lawyer rather than a "commander." Later on he learnt the truth. But, in spite of the danger to himself, he unhesitatingly allowed me to stay on in his house. Malkieli gave me a good deal of help, but I do not believe that he ever changed his opinion about the external appearance of his tenant.

We were soon on friendly terms not only with the landlord, who knew, but with all our neighbours, who did not know. My son used to play or fight with the children. We exchanged visits with the neighbours. Our house was filled with law volumes which were as open as the house itself. It is not surprising, therefore, that it was in the Hasidoff Quarter, at the midst of the undergound fight, that I came near to receiving my first fee as a "legal adviser." One of the residents got into a dispute with the Petah Tikva Municipality over a small structure he had put up without a licence from the Health Department. He asked me to draft a polite but firm letter to overcome the opposition of the Municipality. I could hardly refuse. I slaved at that letter— not at the contents, but at the handwriting. My handwriting is not very legible. And a Petah Tikva official is, after all, not Ruhama, our all-knowing secretary who knew not only how to keep secrets but even how to decipher my handwriting. Moreover I realised that officials upon whose good humour the fate of the request depended should not have hieroglyphics inflicted upon them. I therefore tried to write in large round letters. I had to work even harder to explain to the applicant, a milkman, who saw how much effort I was putting into his letter, that I was doing it purely out of neighbourliness and expected no payment.

I have many other happy memories of the pleasant Hasidoff Quarter. In the tiny kitchen, by the light of a small oil lamp or a candle, we held meetings of the High Command, took important decisions and planned operations. The "friends" who visited the "Halperin" family aroused no suspicions. Occasionally they helped the Quarter out: they would make up a "minyan"—the quorum of ten required for Jewish prayers—in the little synagogue. At times, on Sabbath afternoons or of an evening, we would go out for a refreshing stroll in the fields and groves and while walking hold a "session" and take decisions on policy. An Arab shepherd would go by with his flock and greet us, Jewish youngsters played games around us. Nobody could have imagined that these innocent chatting strollers were being hunted by the British secret service and police throughout the length and breadth of the country.

I remember also the little synagogue which stands on a rise opposite the houses. In that synagogue where we all used to attend prayers on Sabbaths and Holydays, I was given a new underground name: Israel. On the first Sabbath after our arrival I was honoured, as befits a newcomer, by being "called up" to the reading of the Law. The good warden asked what my name was. I was afraid to mention my first name lest, in combination with my father's name, it might recall something to somebody. I said hesitantly "Israel the son of Ze'ev Dov." I picked Israel, I suppose, because of the deep affection which bound me to my very close friend Israel Epstein. Thenceforward, until I left the underground, I was always "called up" by that name. I must ask forgiveness from the Almighty for dissembling my real name even in Divine Services, but He will understand that in the circumstances I had no choice.

It was in the Hasidoff Quarter that we experienced the first great search conducted by the Palestine police with the aid of whole regiments of the Occupation Army. On September 5th, 1944, Petah Tikva was surrounded by large forces of soldiers and police. The town had a special attraction for the Mandatory authorities. They used to say inelegantly: "Bloody Petah Tikva is full of terrorists."

They were not altogether wrong. Petah Tikva, with its free people, attached to the soil, rendered great service to the underground. Our fighters freely used its orange groves without mishap. The soldiers did not even dare look into these orchards. Its fields and woods and trees could tell many a tale of concealed armouries, secret training forces, of rendezvous and exercises. The trees kept their secret as did the youth of Petah Tikva, bouyant and free and fearless who, as often as they suffered blows, recovered and rose again to fight and resist. Twice the military authorities almost succeeded, with the help of Jewish information organised from high up, in liquidating the local detachment of the Irgun Zvai Leumi. But each time our ranks were replenished with young blood and emerged more energetic, more numerous and stronger than before the "liquidation." Petah Tikva was blessedly "full of terrorists."

The authorities, then, began their search at dawn that day. The town was surrounded on all sides. A curfew was imposed. Soldiers toured the streets on tenders, calling through loudspeakers:

"Curfew, curfew! Stay in your houses! Anybody who leaves risks his life!"

Every house was searched. Every resident was examined. This was indeed the first great search. The soldiers and police wished each other "Good hunting."

At sunrise the neighbour who "knew" woke me up and told me what was happening. He was, naturally, somewhat worried. His tale was not cheerful.

"I have tried to get to Petah Tikva itself," he said, "but the patrols sent me back. They are everywhere. Nobody is going in or out. They will certainly come here too. I think you ought to try to get away through the orange groves."

I rejected his advice. Daniel, who had spent the night in the house, agreed that there was no sense in rushing to the groves. Such a flight would not only "finish" us with the neighbours, but was likely to deliver us to the enemy. It was better to wait for troubles than to meet them half-way. The situation was of course serious. But we relied to some extent on the contrariness of the military and police and, having no choice, on our own good fortune. So we stayed where we were, Daniel in his room, I in ours. But we wanted the neighbours to see that we were not concerned by the propinquity of the police. Accordingly, we left our rooms and went out and sat in front of the house. We witnessed an interesting spectacle. On the main road about two hundred yards away, British tanks and armoured cars, filled with soldiers, were on the move. A Jewish policeman, who had previously lived in the Quarter, ran up and down and consoled us by assuring that we would

not have to wait long for the searchers and would then be done with
them for a long time. His promise did nothing to cheer us up. Nobody
looked pleased.

Our neighbour, Mrs. Seigel, mother of Rahel and Micky, my
favourites in the Quarter (my three-year-old son was a dangerous
rival for the affections of two-year-old Micky), showed considerable
distress. My wife tried to calm her but in vain. Finally, out of confidence
in "Mrs. Halperin," with whom she had become very friendly, she
confessed: "Of course, it's all right for you, Mrs. Halperin, you have
nothing to worry about. But I have got a *military blanket* in the house.
What am I to do? What am I to do?"

There was no need for her to do anything. We waited in vain for
the police and soldiers. They searched Petah Tikva thoroughly, but
for some reason slipped the outlying Hasidoff Quarter. The morning
passed. At noon, the curfew was lifted. Daniel, without saying goodbye
to Mr. Halperin, whom he "hardly knew," went off to his work. We
breathed freely again. The danger had retreated from our threshold.

The search brought a crop of rumours in its train. Our comrades,
thoroughly alarmed, racked their brains for a way of saving us, but
Petah Tikva was completely sealed off. Afterwards the story went
round among the public, which wanted to believe in the Irgun's
omnipotence, that a strong unit of our soldiers had penetrated the
enemy lines, and borne their besieged comrades to safety. This was one
of many legends about us—recalling the story of how I met General
Barker and the tale about my Russian origin.

The world's Press published a circumstantial story of a meeting
between me and the commanding officer of the British forces in Eretz
Israel. It may be that the origin of the story was the suggestion made by
an officer on Barker's staff that we meet and talk as "enemy to enemy."
A member of the Haganah Intelligence in Jerusalem, who was in
contact with that staff officer's representative, conveyed the invitation
to Moshe Sneh—the Haganah commander—who passed it on to me
at one of our regular conferences during the brief period of our united
struggle in the Resistance Movement. Of course I declined the invitation. I agreed to speak to the commanding officer of the occupation
forces as "enemy to enemy" but I preferred the language of our battle
detachments. Nevertheless I learnt from the foreign Press that I had had
a secret meeting not merely with Barker's representative but with
Barker himself.

The story was highly sympathetic to the underground. It told how
I had made a condition that Barker, like me, should come alone and in
civilian dress to the café rendezvous. Barker, according to this widely

circulated story, accepted the condition, but broke his word and brought a regiment of soldiers who surrounded the café. He went inside but to his chagrin did not find me there. He waited a while, getting more and more restless. Looking round he saw a Catholic priest sitting in the far corner reading a newspaper. Delighted at the opportunity to kill time, he struck up a conversation with him. After some time, seeing that Begim did not appear, he got up, thanked the priest for his company and left the café. The next day he received a letter from me, running roughly as follows:

"You should not break your word of honour. You promised to come alone. Why did you break your promise? You will note that the Irgun always keeps its word. We kept it this time too. I came to the meeting place despite your treachery. The priest with whom you had such a friendly chat was I."

An even more sensational story was published in a Swiss newspaper and from there found its way to every part of the world. Great American newspapers splashed it, and even the Yiddish paper *Bund* treated it seriously. The story was that my real name was not Begim but Freiman, that I had had a special training in the Kremlin, that I had conducted the Communist struggle in Spain and in China and had then been sent by Stalin himself to Eretz Israel in order to make things hot there for the British. . . . An important American journalist was so impressed by this story that on my visit to the United States he telephoned me about it from Chicago to New York.

Another important journalist questioned me about it in a television interview. I replied: "I have read in a Jewish Communist newspaper that I had a secret meeting at the State Department and that I have sold the whole of Palestine to Truman. That paper called me a Fascist."

"What's that to do with our question?"

"Very simple," I said. "I am beginning to find it difficult to decide whether I am Stalin's agent or Truman's agent, or both, whether I'm a Communist Fascist or a Fascist Communist."

These are legends. The truth is that I have never been in Spain or in China, or in the Kremlin or in the State Department. The truth is that I hate all forms of totalitarianism, that I love freedom and free men and believe in their victory everywhere over tyranny and totalitarianism of all kinds. The truth is—to go back to the first story—that I never met nor wanted to meet either Barker or his representative. As for the least important legend of the lot, relating to the search at Petah Tikva, the truth is just as simple: the British authorities searched and did not find.

But there is another, unhappy, truth connected with the search at the Hasidoff Quarter. During the search—and perhaps because of it—I lost my brother-in-law and close friend, Dr. Arnold. It was at his home that I had chanced to meet the seventeen-year-old girl whom I then and there decided to make my wife. I did not err in my choice. I would not like to say as much about hers. The years passed, and we all tasted of the cup of sorrow. Our families were wiped out. Arnold's little son was torn from his mother's arms and murdered in a Nazi gas chamber. The mother killed herself. All his other relatives were shot or gassed by the Germans and his heart took the blows hardly. He was in Tel Aviv when the news reached him that Petah Tikva was surrounded. He knew where I was living, and was deeply distressed. He died that day. And I was underground, unable even to accompany my old friend to his final resting-place. My friends did him that last kindness for me. But they could not prevent the British, who knew of the relationship, from sending several pairs of spying eyes to the cemetery. My wife, therefore, accepting the laws of the underground, did not go to the funeral of her brother, one of the last survivors of her family. We remained at home, bowed down with grief. I said Kaddish (the Prayer for the Dead) in the little synagogue. One had to carry on. There was no choice. But the people outside, what did they know, what could they know?

The period of our stay at the Hasidoff Quarter was not barren. The Irgun rallied solidly round the flag of revolt. Many who had left in the days of internal crisis returned to its ranks. Many volunteered. Our numbers grew. Confidence rose. Most important: belief in our strength was awakened. We were loved or hated—but no longer jeered at. Any underground that passes beyond the stage of inevitable initial ridicule has gone half-way—perhaps the more difficult half of the way—to its goal. During that period I wrote the pamphlet "We Believe" in which I expressed our unshakable belief that "out of our blood will flourish the tree of freedom for our country and the tree of life for our people." And I wrote many other pamphlets, surveys and declarations.

During that period we blew up the British central police headquarters in Jerusalem, forced the police to keep away from the Wailing Wall, stormed the Tegart fortresses, attacked the police stations on the Jaffa–Tel Aviv boundary, and made fun of the Government by confiscating vast quantities of cloth from Government stores under the very noses of the troops. Part of the cloth was distributed among the poor, the rest was sold to buy arms.

But at the end of that period heavy clouds gathered. The storm of internal persecution approached. The "amount of violence" we had given the Mandatory authorities was apparently more than they had expected. The Jewish Agency was subjected to their pressure both in London and Jerusalem. Its leaders were required to extend to the British authorities their "full co-operation in stamping out the terror." Disturbing reports began to reach us. It was rumoured that the Jewish Agency leaders were not refusing to co-operate with the oppressor but indeed were promising that instructions would soon be given to "liquidate the dissidents." The situation became grave. The number of spying eyes increased considerably. Moreover, I learnt that somebody in my neighbourhood was getting suspicious. I could stay no longer in the Hasidoff Quarter. Among the neighbours were members of "Hashomer Hatzair"—extreme left-wing Communist-Socialists who were in favour of co-operation with the British against us. The neighbours were very cordial to "Mr. Halperin." But would they remain so friendly if they discovered who was behind the "lawyer"?

We said goodbye to the Hasidoff Quarter, moved to Tel Aviv, to a little house in Joshua Bin-Nun Street—and I became Israel Sassover.

XI

ADMIRAL CANARIS—HITLER'S MASTER SPY

from

DUEL FOR THE NORTHLAND

by KURT SINGER

(Published by Robert Hale, London, 1945)

Hitler's espionage organisation in the second world war was directed by Admiral Wilhelm Canaris. Responsible only to the Führer himself, Canaris was one of the most powerful personages of the Third Reich, though his name was known to comparatively few.

With the uncanny flair for making the right choice so characteristic of him, the German dictator entrusted this ex-naval officer with the mission of creating the Nazi espionage service, and he could hardly have picked a man more suitable for the job. Cold-blooded, resourceful, afflicted neither with heart nor conscience, Admiral Canaris proved a tireless genius in the service of his master. At the height of his power, his organisation had far-reaching ramifications and he was in control of all foreign departments of Nazi and Fascist parties abroad. It was he who selected, long before they were invested with power, the various puppet-masters who were to rule Hitler's empire, such as Bonnet, Laval, Vidkun Quisling, of Norway, Hacha, of Czechoslovakia, Fritz Kuhn, of the U.S.A., et al.

Oddly enough, Admiral Canaris, who served his master so well when things went well, later found himself in bitter opposition to the régime and participated in the attempt to assassinate Hitler on July 20th, 1944. The attempt failed; Canaris was arrested, tried, sentenced to death and executed.

★

ADMIRAL WILHELM CANARIS began his career like Pflugk-Hartung as a naval cadet, and was picked by Nicolai for espionage work. He was a lieutenant-commander in 1918; it was none other than Hitler who promoted him within a few months to Admiral.

Hitler knew perfectly well why he was advancing this man over the heads of so many others, and why he gave him blanket powers such as no other Nazi leader possessed. For the story of Wilhelm Canaris is inextricably bound up with the history of Germany's preparations for a war of revenge, and with the history of the German secret service from the Versailles Treaty to the second world war.

The peace treaty had been signed. But the Prussian Army insisted it had never been defeated. It was "the stab in the back" that had given Germany over to revolutionaries like Wollweber; Socialists like

Ebert, Scheidemann and the murdered Hilferding had cravenly
abandoned the struggle. The Prussian Army pointed out that Allied
troops have never marched triumphantly through Berlin's Branden-
burger Tor; the Victory Boulevard of the glorious kings of Prussia
had not been trespassed upon even by the revolutionists and republicans
and still bore witness to the fact that the Prussians were a superior
breed of humanity.

The Allies had permitted Germany an army of only one hundred
thousand men and fondly believed that thereby they had destroyed her
for all time as a military power.

It is not Hitler who created the new German Army, nor was he the
founder of the great German espionage apparatus.

The German Army was rebuilt by General Hans von Seeckt, one
of Germany's great strategists. Out of defeat and decay he moulded the
most modern army in Europe, the army that was later to become the
model for the Russian and Italian armies, and still later for the armies
of the United Nations themselves.

Seeckt was a great believer in legality. The peace treaty had pro-
hibited an army large enough to be of the slightest use and so Seeckt
created a peace-time "cadre" army. An intelligence service was pro-
hibited; so Seeckt created a department with quite another name.

The Allies thought Germany could not make war with a hundred
thousand soldiers. It was years before they discovered that these
hundred thousand men were not being trained as common soldiers,
or as lieutenants; every one of the hundred thousand men in the German
Army received a training analogous to that of a junior staff officer. No
army on earth has one hundred thousand general staff officers—and that
is one reason why there are forty-year-old generals in Germany today.
Every one of those hundred thousand men is a commanding officer
in the present German Army. This was General Hans von Seeckt's
gift to Adolf Hitler.

In 1920 General von Seeckt called Lieutenant-Commander Wilhelm
Canaris to the War Ministry and informed him that he needed a
capable intelligence officer of the last war to work in a new bureau that
would have no connection with the Reichswehr. This new bureau required the utmost secrecy; it must be built up carefully and intelli-
gently, and above all its true function must be kept secret from France
and England. The Reichswehr would pay Canaris as a civilian employee, but he would have no official connection with the War
Ministry; he had to disguise all his activities as those of a private person
and must never admit—even should he be brought to court—that he
was working as an agent for General Seeckt.

That September day in 1920 witnessed the birth of the new German secret service. Admiral Canaris became Chief of the Investigation Bureau of the "Black Reichswehr"—the secret army of three hundred thousand soldiers which had been organised in defiance of the Versailles Treaty and camouflaged under the guise of civil service.

The duties of the former intelligence officer were multitudinous. And they were consistent with Germany's flagrant repudiation of her peace treaties. Ostensibly, Canaris checked Communist activities and fought Russia's O.G.P.U. He traced other former officers of the Imperial armies to learn which ones could be enlisted against the republic —and through his investigations found many of them leading the volunteer groups of "Free Corps" which were operating on the Polish border.

A further duty of Canaris was to locate all arms and munitions within Germany. All implements of war were supposed to be turned over to the Allies, but Canaris laid his hands on much armament, which he either gave to the Free Corps or held in readiness for the rapidly growing illegal army. After Canaris had located the chief hiding-places of weapons in Germany and secured them for the Reichswehr and the Black Reichswehr, General von Seeckt, the newly appointed Minister of Defence, set him to new tasks.

Colonel Liese of the Stettin Military District became Canaris's new superior. Liese requested Canaris to organise the *Grenzschutz*, or Border Guard, on all the German frontiers. Outwardly this organisation was a harmless enough civilian defence group somewhat resembling the U.S.A. National Guard. But its membership consisted of such accomplished spies as Pflugk-Hartung and Manfred von Killinger, who commanded hundreds of unemployed army officers, Free Corps leaders, terrorists, putschists and would-be putschists. Colonel Liese, who received financial and moral support from the Third Military District of Reichswehr, became the military leader of this organisation. Freiher von Gablenz, today one of Hitler's generals, was Liese's adjutant; Canaris was the executive organiser.

With the utmost simplicity Canaris had established a new espionage organisation. The civil head was the Commissioner of Public Order, and the agents appeared on the pay-rolls as civil service employees.

The *Grenzschutz* employed men like Heines, who later became Nazi chief of police in Breslau, and the "Hangman," Reinhardt Heydrich, who joined after the suppression of the Halle riots against the republic which he had incited.

Detachments of the *Grenzschutz* were posted on the borders of Poland, Czechoslovakia, France, Belgium, Austria, Switzerland,

7

Holland and Denmark. Canaris visited each detachment in turn to give his espionage agents their instructions and to supply them with false passports so that they could cross the border. They were commanded to locate the most advantageous points for invasion, and above all to find sub-agents who would keep Germany informed of any new border fortifications in the neighbouring country. Thus, Canaris and his spies kept abreast of the construction of the French Maginot Line.

The *Grenzschutz* served its purpose well until it was incorporated into the Investigation Bureau of Ribbentrop's growing espionage organisation.

Canaris was, as ever, restlessly ambitious. He did his duty, but he hated his lowly status, which included not being permitted to hold an official position in the Reichswehr. His great dream was to return to the Army. It was this dream which led him in 1920 to take part in the Kapp putsch; but the putsch failed and he was compelled to put by his ambition for a while.

After this failure he went to see Walter von Nicolai, his former chief, and asked him to help him to obtain an official post in the Reichswehr. Nicolai's influence was great enough to persuade Seeckt, and so Lieutenant-Commander Canaris became liaison officer between the Reichswehr, on the one hand, and the Black Reichswehr and the *Grenzschutz*, his own organisation, on the other.

Since Canaris was originally a Navy man, he was asked to lay the foundation for a new Naval Intelligence Bureau. He set about doing this, but his chief concern remained the organisation of the Black Reichswehr and its espionage service.

In fact, the Black Reichswehr was expanding so rapidly that it became necessary to supply it with funds from new sources. The stratagems the leaders adopted were naïve in the extreme. General Seeckt, the Defence Minister, presented Canaris with funds from the regular army allotment. Canaris invested the money in a large film company (Phoebus) which guaranteed a thirty per cent. return on the investment. A first dividend was paid, but when Germany's inflation policy set in the company was ruined. Canaris had bought for millions of marks stocks of the Phoebus Motion Picture Studios and the money was gone. The people wanted to know from what sources Canaris had received the money. In the ensuing Government investigation the scandal came out. In court, however, Canaris said to the judges: "I am not allowed to reveal my sources. This is on orders from the General Staff."

The investigation indicated that Canaris had worked in a camouflaged outfit called the "Department of Naval Transport" and nobody had suspected his money transactions. Canaris was discharged from the War Department, but he continued to operate from his home and received as his assistant Lieutenant-Commander Steffan, who later became under Hitler military attaché in Sweden, Norway, Finland and Denmark.

Furthermore the investigation indicated that men like Canaris were also personally unscrupulous, for he was shown to be a reckless gambler, overwhelmed with personal debts. Officially, General Seeckt's Reichswehr declared that such men besmirched the tradition and the noble reputation of the Prussian Army.

Nevertheless, Canaris had won the reputation of being uniquely qualified for espionage. As early as 1929 Goering convinced Hitler that Canaris was the right man to build up a first-class spy apparatus for the Nazi Party. Hitler decided to employ him.

Canaris's first job for the Nazi Party was wholly in the realm of personality research. Hitler asked him for a complete study of the political opinions, the private affairs and the economic status of all officers of the Reichswehr. For years before the seizure of power Canaris was thus busy rummaging for potential betrayers of the Weimar Republic in the Prussian Army. He must have done a good job, for the Nazi leaders won over to the party one officer after the other.

Canaris and Papen prepared for the Nazis the fateful documents on General Schleicher. These were presented to Hindenburg and purported to show that Schleicher had undertaken "Bolshevist" experiments in distribution of land. It was Canaris who assembled the documents that sealed the fate of General Schleicher. These documents set forth plans for establishing the unemployed on the vast, unprofitable estates of the Prussian Junkers, and for breaking up these estates, which were subsidised by the State. These Prussian Junkers were Hindenburg's friends. These documents were the sum total of Canaris's "evidence" that General Kurt von Schleicher harboured secret plans to "bolshevise" Germany. Perhaps more than any other factor, these documents precipitated Schleicher's fall from the position of Chancellor of Germany, and helped Hitler's subsequent accession to power.

There is no doubt that Canaris could never have made such headway with his subversive activity within the German Reichswehr without the aid and protection of the Old Masters of German espionage, Colonel Nicolai and Franz von Papen.

Hitler, when he came to power, generously recompensed his faithful spy by entrusting him with the Nazi secret service. From now on the information in Hitler's files was no longer restricted to data on friends and foes within the German Army. Canaris located the friends and foes of Nazism in all the armies and all the police headquarters of the world. The ambitious Admiral went to work with a will, for this was his opportunity to show his ability to organise espionage over the entire world for the coming global war.

For the present, however, Canaris was established as a departmental head in the Foreign Office whose Minister was Joachim von Ribbentrop, the former champagne salesman. Canaris was assigned to re-organising naval espionage.

Ostensibly subordinate to Ribbentrop, Canaris began work on his own initiative, his work taking two forms that interlocked under some circumstances. At the beginning he devoted himself, as it were, to clearing the field for action, employing for this purpose only political and diplomatic agents. During his first years of military espionage, he was extremely cautious in his choice of agents, for during this period he had not yet subscribed to the principle of mass espionage. The few agents he chose were exceptionally competent. They were not the mythical spies with false beards and sham limps, and pebbles bouncing around in their mouths to disguise their voices. They were like the distinguished-looking Pflugk-Hartung, men of culture and good breeding, acceptable anywhere, often men with diplomatic immunity whose friendship was obviously desirable to many. For the present Canaris instructed his agents to listen carefully but not to act. Their duties were pure reconnaissance.

His objective was to place German observers where they could see and hear, and could transmit their information and receive new orders. Partly by sheer genius, partly by plain cunning, Wilhelm Canaris established a harbour espionage system that covered the entire world and yielded incredible results. At heart Canaris was a Navy man. He understood shipping and its vital importance both to the economy and the sinews of war. Other agencies in Germany were building with feverish speed the most effective instruments for ship destruction. It was Canaris's self-imposed task to be informed where and when enemy ships would be available for torpedo, mine or shell. On the face of it, the task was simple; every ship sails from a port and returns to a port, as a plane to its carrier or base. Actually this work was of enormous complexity, but not too great for the malevolent genius of Wilhelm Canaris.

Canaris's broad and diversified plans had one principle never departed from: all persons in this service, whether officials of the Reich or passing as private individuals, must have their places of business and residence as near as practicable to the waterfront.

Naturally, Canaris's first efforts were directed near at home. He set himself to work out plans for the destruction of the British North Sea and Russian Baltic Sea fleets.

His old friend and colleague of World War I days, Pflugk-Hartung, was called to Berlin and given his instructions. Canaris instructed Pflugk-Hartung to assign a German agent to every fifty miles of the immense Scandinavian coastline, so that no fact about the merchant marine of Britain, Russia, Poland and other nations would escape the eye of German espionage. In effect Canaris asked Pflugk-Hartung to transform the Baltic Sea into a German "Mare Nostrum"; he wished to know of the arrival and departure of every ship, the names of all the Baltic captains, the number of seamen in every vessel, the destination, consignor and consignee of every cargo. Such an undertaking was expensive, of course, but Pflugk-Hartung was given a blank cheque.

I investigated the Canaris harbour spy system from Helsinki to Helsingoer, from Esbjerg to the North Cape. Everywhere I found that German consulates or legations "happened" to be located on the seashore. Everywhere I found Scandinavians of German descent living on or near the waterfront.

The most obvious case was that of the German consulate in Malmoe, Sweden. From its windows one could observe with the naked eye, or with weak binoculars, every ship that passed through the narrow sound to enter or leave the Baltic Sea. It was some time before the Swedish authorities unmasked Consul Alexander Bogs as an agent of Canaris; Bogs promptly discovered that the climate of Sweden disagreed with his liver, and left the country.

In the harbour of Malmoe consulate windows gave a view of the traffic of the Baltic just as a house in Bay Ridge, Brooklyn, on the Narrows, may overlook Tompkinsville, or a house on the Staten Island shore may overlook the upper Bay and the Narrows.

Wherever it was feasible Canaris's agents bribed fishermen who were ideally situated to observe passing vessels.

Even after the outbreak of the war, Canaris contrived to keep his agents in every Scandinavian port.

XII

PFLUGK-HARTUNG—MASTER MIND OF INVASION

from

DUEL FOR THE NORTHLAND

by KURT SINGER

(Published by Robert Hale, London, 1945)

Like Admiral Canaris, under whose direction he worked, Horst von Pflugk-Hartung was a young lieutenant-commander in the Imperial German Navy during the first world war. He was always naturally inclined towards political intrigue and secret service work, especially since he had met, in Spain, the now legendary figure of Mata Hari, possibly the most celebrated spy of the century, whose disciple he became.

Immediately after the first world war, in January 1919, he became notorious when, in the midst of the chaos brought about by the German revolution, he occupied with fifty armed men the fashionable Eden Hotel in Berlin, which he used as his headquarters from which he personally directed his terrorist activities. He played a sinister rôle in the torture and killing of Karl Liebknecht and Rosa Luxemburg, who were at the back of the people's revolution. Pflugk-Hartung had to leave the country for a while but his honour was fully restored when Hitler came to power; there was no stigma attached to killing Communists or Jews.

A generation or so after his early exploits in Berlin, we meet him again in Scandinavia; by then he had become the close collaborator of Admiral Canaris, with whom he plotted the conquest of the Northland. The successful invasion of Denmark was due, chiefly, to Pflugk-Hartung's skill and cunning.

★

THE year was 1939. Nothing was done to Pflugk-Hartung, for his agents in the Danish police gave him a clean bill of health, declaring that he had never acted otherwise than as a model newspaper correspondent. But difficulties for him were once more inspired by the Social Democrats.

The Social Democratic Party possessed documents proving that through friends he had bought farms near the German-Danish border. Thus he was able to station German soldiers on Danish soil, soldiers whose farm-hand's costume did not disguise their military bearing. The Social Democrats were planning an interpellation in Parliament. Moreover, they had obtained other documents of even greater importance. On orders from Admiral Canaris, Pflugk-Hartung had undertaken the registration of the four thousand Germans living in Copenhagen, and of all Germans and all Danish Nazis in the provinces. With his usual efficiency, Pflugk-Hartung had prepared a questionnaire to obtain information that would be useful when the invasion came. These were some of the questions:

Do you live near the sea?

Do you live near an airport, railway station, gasworks, electric factory, Government building? If so, where?

Do you own: automobile, motor-boat, sailing-boat, rowing-boat, motor-cycle, bicycle, truck, or other means of transportation?

Are you prepared to place your automobile, motor-boat, sailing-boat, etc., at the disposal of the German Legation?

Do you know any persons in the Government?

Have you any knowledge of Danish industrial plants and communications, or do you know persons who have such knowledge?

The Social Democratic Party turned this evidence over to the Press, creating a national sensation. The case of Pflugk-Hartung was now brought up in Parliament. The German Legation glibly explained that it hoped to borrow automobiles and boats for summer picnics of German tourists, and that the questions on industry and communications were devised with a view to improving German-Danish trade relationships.

This latter explanation won over the semi-Nazi, conservative Peasants' Party, whose members depended largely on exporting to Germany, for England and the other democratic countries had introduced high tariffs on the import of foodstuffs.

Nevertheless, the matter worried Pflugk-Hartung. He wanted to find out how much the Danish Social Democratic Party knew about him and his connections with Pontoppidan and the police. He therefore called a conference with his agent, Carlis Hansen, who had been on the "wanted" list since 1934, for his part in the attempted kidnapping of Wollweber, and had reason to be cautious. Nevertheless, Carlis Hansen promised to obtain friends from the Clausen Nazi Party who would do the job for a hundred kroner per man, and he it was who organised the robbery.

Hans Hedtoft-Hansen, who was looked upon as the successor to Prime Minister Stauning, never dreamed that anyone would dare break into his office. A man without secrets, it did not occur to him to lock his desk or his files.

The Social Democratic Party Headquarters was on the outskirts of Copenhagen, in the Rosenoerns Allé. The Danish Socialists were loyal monarchists who would have felt deeply insulted had they been accused of trying to overthrow the monarchy. They called themselves republicans, but this was a traditional way of speaking rather than a conviction.

Five men, all members of Dr. Clausen's Nazi Party, broke into the headquarters late one night. Carlis Hansen's friend, Inspector Yttesen, was in command of the Copenhagen police that night; this meant that everything was fairly safe. The robbers took their time. They entered the unguarded building with skeleton keys. They found the party chief's office unlocked.

The five Nazis were, like most of their ilk, good thieves; but they did not know which letters among the thousands they found in the files were important. They therefore decided to take along as much as they could and let their employers sort out all this material. Some money in one of Hedtoft-Hansen's desk drawers vanished at once. Books, pictures and placards in the room were torn up. A little incidental vandalism was always a tonic for the Nazi soul.

Pflugk-Hartung was well pleased with the results of the nocturnal visit. The stolen material was fairly interesting, although he found little about himself among the papers and letters. He learned, however, that the Danish Social Democrats were working out plans for the fortification of the Dano-German border, and for laying a large number of land-mines along the frontier.

He also found correspondence with the Social Democrats of Iceland, who warned that the Nazis were erecting secret radio stations on their island. And he found copies of letters to Swedish and Norwegian parliamentary deputies which showed that a widespread pan-Scandinavian anti-Nazi movement was in full swing.

Pflugk-Hartung took his discoveries very seriously. Next day, while the entire Danish Press was raising a hue and cry against the robbery, he flew to Berlin. A murderer returning to the scene of his crime, he went directly to the Eden Hotel. Here Canaris visited him, for he wished to speak with his old friend in private.

Canaris had already received the stolen papers; he was in excellent spirits, laughed heartily at the coup, voiced his admiration for the efficiency of the spies in Denmark, and suggested that the Social Democrats might have some difficulties if their entire correspondence should disappear. But Pflugk-Hartung was in no mood for laughter. His days in Denmark were numbered, he said: he was already suspected by many, and the police would be unable to protect him for ever.

Canaris is said to have laughed jovially, ordered a whisky, and replied, "Horst, you're getting old."

Horst replied that he had no inclination to inspect the inside of a Danish prison.

Canaris tried to cheer him up. From the court records we can infer that he must have said something like this: "You must remain in Denmark until we march in. If you or your men are arrested sooner, it will be so much easier for us to present an ultimatum." Canaris promised him—on the word of a Prussian officer—that he would never desert him, and that "everything is ready; only the exact day has not yet been determined." This was early in 1939.

Canaris instructed him that from now on waterfront espionage was of primary importance, for war in Scandinavia meant sea warfare with England. Before his departure Pflugk-Hartung was awarded the Cross of Merit, First Class, and returned to Denmark with fresh funds and fresh tasks.

Every spy must reckon on detection. Pelving, Pflugk-Hartung's most important agent in the police, had been arrested. The trial of Pontoppidan had resulted in the exposure of his radio company; this in turn had led to the revelation that Kyre and Rambov had tapped the telephone line of the Emigrant Home in Copenhagen as well as of the Russian Trade Delegation. Pelving and Pontoppidan were now behind bars, and Pflugk-Hartung daily awaited his own arrest. It came finally after the outbreak of the war, towards the latter part of 1939, when the British and Russian secret services supplied the Danish Government with the proofs that the Danish police could not or would not find. Great Britain protested vigorously against Pflugk-Hartung's spy network. The protest was so vigorous that it approached an ultimatum. Great Britain threatened Denmark that she would take steps to ensure that the Danish coast no longer harboured spies. The Danish Government was more than disturbed; it was deeply shocked.

Suddenly it found itself in possession of proofs that Pflugk-Hartung had employed two hundred agents in the country and virtually lined the Danish coast with German spies.

Now Pflugk-Hartung's master-stroke recoiled upon him. The story sounds as though it had been plagiarised from some operetta; it appears fantastic and utterly incredible in this era of the second world war. But Pflugk-Hartung was perfectly willing to employ the methods of fiction if they served his ends.

He had known a capable, good-looking young man named Ernst Grueber who had been born on the German-Danish border. The man was unemployed and seemed to Pflugk-Hartung an excellent prospect. The spy master therefore sent him to the espionage school in Berlin. Grueber passed his examinations with flying colours, and Pflugk-Hartung was well pleased with him. In 1936, Pflugk-Hartung assigned him a simple task; he spent the summer, on Pflugk-Hartung's money, at the well-known bathing resort on the Island of Bornholm. All he had to do was to busy himself with learning as much as possible about the island and its inhabitants.

Sunburned, wearing white flannel trousers, an expensive tie and dapper hat, the young vacationeer put in an appearance at Pflugk-Hartung's Strandvejen villa and reported to his employer.

"Do you know where Admiral Tuerck's villa is situated?" Pflugk-Hartung asked him.

"Yes. On the east side of the island. It has a large garden and is close to the sea."

"Can you drive a car?" was Pflugk-Hartung's next question.

"No, Herr Kapitaenleutnant."

"God knows, those fools in Berlin might have taught you that."

This was the end of the conversation. For the next two weeks Grueber did nothing but practice driving for eight hours a day. After he had learned how to drive he again reported to Pflugk-Hartung.

"The Tuercks have a chauffeur," Pflugk-Hartung informed him. "The chauffeur is going to get sick or have an auto accident. Mrs. Tuerck will be looking for a new chauffeur, and you will apply for the job."

Grueber returned to Bornholm. And two weeks later an advertisement appeared in the local newspaper; Mrs. Tuerck was looking for a chauffeur. Her old chauffeur had been run over by a truck.

Mrs. Tuerck was taken with the handsome, sun-browned young fellow who told her he was a fisherman, but would like to change trades; he said that he could also do odd jobs as a handyman.

Mrs. Tuerck asked him how long he had been at sea. Grueber answered, "Three years," which happened to be the truth.

"Well, then, you will feel at home here. My husband is Admiral Tuerck, you see."

With these words Grueber was hired.

For months he worked efficiently for his employers and for Pflugk-Hartung. He bribed and won over to the Nazis dozens of lighthouse guards, fishermen and dock workers. He soon showed that he was destined for higher things than a chauffeur's job, and one day Mrs. Tuerck came to him with the suggestion that he work as her private secretary—he had contrived to let her know that he was an excellent typist.

For a time Grueber was Mrs. Tuerck's private secretary; then he began writing letters for the Admiral. And soon Berlin knew everything of importance that went on in the Danish naval staff. Tuerck was active in promoting Scandinavian co-operation, which gave

Grueber further chances of gathering information about Norway and Sweden.

Bornholm lies close to the German island of Ruegen, and Grueber frequently received visitors from Ruegen. Should the Admiral ask about them, they were old friends of his fishing days; in reality they were German naval intelligence officers, who inspected landing-points, lighthouses and so on. Grueber also regularly secured copies of passenger lists of boats and planes for the Nazi intelligence service. All this material was too important to be sent through Pflugk-Hartung; it was transmitted to Germany via Ruegen.

Pflugk-Hartung now had the police and the Navy under control. But he also needed agents within the Danish Army.

He bribed two young officers, Captain Nils Garde and Captain Winding Christensen. The British, though they knew so much about Pflugk-Hartung's activities and had given the Danish Minister of Defence a great deal of information, knew nothing about these men. But Wollweber had found out about them. His friend, Communist Deputy Aksel Larsen, declared in Parliament that the two traitorous captains had been in Kiel to negotiate with leaders of the German Navy. They were to arrange for the German fleet to make an unopposed landing on the Island of Fuenen. Here the Nazis intended to build a naval and submarine base.

A week later the two officers were dishonourably discharged from the Army; they then entered the German Army. Newspapers, radio and Parliament discussed the case without once mentioning the name of Pflugk-Hartung. Later, when he was at last arrested, he admitted that the two captains had been his tools.

XIII

THE MYSTERIOUS MR. EDDIE CHAPMAN

from

THE EDDIE CHAPMAN STORY

by FRANK OWEN

(Published by Allan Wingate, London, 1953)

The mystery is his exact rôle in the last war. What is known about Eddie Chapman is that he joined the Coldstream Guards shortly after his seventeenth birthday, giving a false age to the recruiting officer. He soon managed to land in the glasshouse with a ninety days' sentence. Discharged from the Army, he wasted no time in embarking on a career of crime. He got himself mixed up with crooks, thieves and prostitutes in the West End of London; was involved in a few robberies and hunted by the police. He fled to the Channel Islands and was arrested and jailed in Jersey at the time the Germans arrived.

Somehow he managed to endear himself to the Germans, who sent him to France and later to Germany, to be trained as a spy. His subsequent successes in the field of espionage pleased the Nazi war lords so much that Eddie was awarded the Iron Cross—probably the only Iron Cross ever given to a British spy.

"This is all of Eddie Chapman's story that anyone is allowed to tell," says Frank Owen in the postscript to his exciting book. "It is only half of it; for telling the other half Eddie was fined fifty pounds and twenty-five pounds costs at Bow Street on March 29th, 1946, under the Official Secrets Act.

"It is perhaps significant, however, that when, through a later indiscretion, he was hauled before a magistrate in 1948 on a currency charge, a senior officer from the War Office who gave evidence described him as 'one of the bravest men who served in the last war'."

★

ONE of the maids brought me a message that Herr Holst had rung me at least four times. She gave me his telephone number, and I got through to him. Johnny answered, and, apologising profusely for last night's fracas, reported that he had a black eye and a split lip, but that Hiller and he were again friends. I made a lunch date with him.

The Ritz was a fashionable restaurant and, like every other place in Oslo, was thronged with German soldiers and officers. It was also the meeting ground of Norwegian Legionaires of the "Viking Regiment," who were the Quisling troops used by Hitler on the Eastern Front. The Legionaires had been admitted to Hitler's élite troops of the S.S., and were highly rated by the Germans.

97

The food we ate was bad; it consisted of *smorbrod*, which is a one-slice sandwich made with different sorts of salt fish. After came the eternal roll-mops, or pickled herring. Happily, to break the monotony, lobster was available too.

From my talk with Johnny Holst, I learned the true state of affairs in Norway—which had always been the most difficult of the occupied countries to control. As time went on I was able to gauge for myself the terrible hatred that eighty (or even ninety) per cent. of the Norwegian population held for Germany.

The Norwegian people and their foreign masters were divided by a vast rift—you were either a Quisling or a Jossing (the latter being the name given to all pro-Allied elements). There was no intervening no-man's-land here. People of all classes and from all walks of life almost openly defied the Germans. They dismissed with contempt every kind of social co-operation, or even civility. They distributed pamphlets, and organised protests and strikes. They committed sabotage, kidnapped, and even killed. Norway, as I can testify, never quit, and never looked like quitting.

It was an uneasy feeling to be a German (or even a *soi-disant* German) in Norway in those days. Everywhere, a wall of hatred rose against you. The Norwegians are a truly brave, patriotic people, and I cannot speak too highly of the struggle which they incessantly waged against their oppressors. Never did they lose hope; never did they waver in their faith that they would eventually be free again.

When the Germans executed their leaders (to say nothing of many innocent hostages), or persecuted them by torture or the concentration camp, they bore their lot stoically. The very horrors they endured served only to weld them more firmly and more solidly together in resistance to their conquerors. The Germans feared the Norse people, and respected them.

In queues for cinemas and theatres, Germans stood patiently along with Norwegians, taking their turn—a thing they seldom did in other occupied countries. They were regarded with contempt. In restaurants, a Norwegian would always obtain a table before a German. In trains and on buses the Norwegians made the Germans feel how much they despised them by giving them too much room. I have seen a German soldier get into an empty bus and sit on a bench capable of holding twenty people. In would come some Norwegians; they would all sit down on the opposite seat, and when that was full, they would stand.

I had been told by Von Grunen that Walter Thomas, who had worked with us both in Paris, would soon be arriving, and on April

THE MYSTERIOUS MR. EDDIE CHAPMAN 99

10th we went to the railway station to meet him. Thomas duly descended from a troop-train, having travelled via Sweden. He was wearing the field green of the Wehrmacht and sported a star on his shoulder, denoting the rank of Oberleutnant. He looked tired and dirty, and complained bitterly at the delays of his journey. He had been three days on the way. It had taken us as many hours in the air to cover the same distance.

Over lunch, he told Von Grunen that Berlin again required the whole of my experiences in England to be typed out and forwarded. The reason for this was, as I had already noted, that if they made me repeat my story often enough I might contradict myself. The German secret service relied on the theory that a man can always remember the truth, but never lies.

Thomas was not altogether pleased at coming to Norway. He had been attending an officers' course for the Eastern Front, and was disappointed at having to give it up to work with me in Norway.

"Not because of you, Fritz," he assured me. "But you realise that I am an idealist; my life belongs to my country, and I think I could serve it better in battle against the Reds than by working in this service. It is a shame, but orders are orders," he added morosely.

Thomas had a hero complex. He was stuffed full of Nazi ideas, and avidly read stories of the German war aces. He would identify himself with any highly decorated hero, especially if he happened to know him.

"Look," he would exclaim, coming across a name in a German newspaper, "Captain Mucklin has been awarded the Iron Cross! And I was at school with that fellow! Now, perhaps if I had been there, I might have got one."

Sometimes, to tease (or irritate) him, I would reply:

"Yes, and by now probably be a nice stiff corpse out in cold, wild Russia."

To which he would retort sulkily:

"Better death for one's ideals than sitting here doing damn all."

April 20th was Hitler's birthday, and a great parade was staged in Oslo to impress the Norwegians with the might of the Wehrmacht. Thomas and I got a splendid view of the procession, which came up the Karl Johannes Gate, past the university, and on towards Drammensveien. A crowd, mainly of Germans, had gathered to watch it from behind the guard of security police who lined the street, three paces apart and facing in.

First came a march past of infantry, next a hundred or so rumbling tanks, then armed motor-cyclists and, finally, a detachment of marines. The band played the Marine marching song "*Wir fahren gegen England*" (We are marching against England). They arrogantly goose-stepped by, to the cheers of their watching comrades.

Farther down the street, opposite the university, Von Terboven, the hated Nazi Gauleiter, was taking the salute. It took an hour for the troops to pass, and they certainly made an impressive show. When the several large mobile guns rolled by I noticed compressed lips on the faces of the few Norwegian spectators. They seemed to say, "You still won't win!"

When the procession was over, I walked with Thomas, whose eyes were still glowing with pride, past the Grand Café. Next to it was a window used by the Nazis to display anti-Allied propaganda. Usually this took the form of a giant cartoon; today it showed Churchill and Roosevelt as two monstrous aeroplanes dropping bombs on German churches and hospitals, while women in Britain were jitter-bugging and drinking cocktails. I thought it did the German cause more harm than good.

The next few days were busy, for Thomas had to complete his report on me. It seemed to meet with his satisfaction. Nevertheless, this recording process, as on previous occasions, left me with an oddly uncomfortable feeling.

When the report was finally completed, Von Grunen took off by plane for the capital. After five days, he returned, and summoned me to meet him at his flat. He was in high spirits.

"Fritz," he said, beaming with pleasure, "they have decided to award you one hundred and fifty thousand marks—that is, a hundred thousand for the sabotage of the aircraft factory and fifty thousand for the ship explosion and the information that you sent over."

I was elated by this news. However, I pretended disappointment.

"It is not enough," I complained. "They promised me two hundred thousand marks; a hundred thousand for the work at De Havillands and another hundred thousand for the ship sabotage and news."

"I am sorry, Fritz," replied Von Grunen, "but unfortunately it was not I who promised you the money for the business in Portugal, but Dr. Braun. He had no right or authority to do so. However, do not forget that one hundred and fifty thousand marks is a lot of money, and in the future you will have opportunities of earning much more. Why, if you play your cards right, there is no reason why you should not end by earning a million marks."

With bad grace, I accepted the money.

It was now formally arranged that Von Grunen should be my banker. I was to draw on him for what amounts I needed, and the money was to be payable in any country I happened to be living in. I signed a note saying that this was satisfactory to me, and Walter Thomas witnessed it. Then came an extraordinary incident. Von Grunen stood up, rather solemnly, behind his desk.

"Now, Fritz," he said, "this is a presentation which I have decided to make to you myself. It was sent to our Dienststelle to be awarded to the member who had shown the most outstanding zeal and success during the year, and after consultation with the chiefs here, you are the choice!"

He then handed me a small case. I opened it—inside was the Iron Cross!

I was astounded—and almost burst out laughing, not at him or at the circumstances, but at myself. Not bad, I told myself—Ober-leutnant Fritz Graumann, with one hundred and fifty thousand Reichsmarks and the Iron Cross!

I thought: If I stay with this mob long enough, I might end up a Reichsmarschall . . .

XIV

THE ORDEAL OF SYBIL KATHIGASU

from

NO DRAM OF MERCY

by Herself

(Published by Neville Spearman Ltd., London, 1954)

Sybil Kathigasu, one of the outstanding heroic figures in the Malayan struggle against Japanese domination in the last war, has been dubbed by Sir Richard Winstead the Odette of Malaya. In point of fact, Mrs. Kathigasu's stature has more resemblance to Florence Nightingale or Edith Cavell than to Odette Churchill.

She was the wife of the local doctor in Ipoh, Malaya, when the Japanese invaded Singapore, and if she did any spying it was only incidental. It would have been easy for her to flee to safer areas but her sense of duty made her stay on. Keeping in touch with the guerrillas, she thought up ways and means of transporting wounded soldiers to her husband's infirmary, where they were treated and hidden until they were ready to resume fighting in the hills.

Eventually both Dr. and Mrs. Kathigasu were arrested by the Japanese, interrogated and tortured by the dreaded Kempetei, the Japanese Gestapo. The amazing thing is that she survived.

After the defeat of the Japanese, Mrs. Kathigasu was flown to England in a state of extreme exhaustion. Despite all medical attention she was given, she died a few years later as a result of her ordeal at the hands of the Japanese, but not until she was awarded the George Medal at an investiture at Buckingham Palace.

★

THE weeks of interrogation which followed dwell in my memory like the confused recollection of a nightmare. I cannot remember the day-to-day details. I would be called for questioning, without warning, at any hour of the day or night. Sometimes I went at least once but sometimes twice a day, every day for perhaps a week; sometimes there was a break of a few days in which I seemed forgotten, after which the proceedings would be resumed as before. There was nothing particularly subtle about the methods used. I would be asked the same question over and over again, and each time I would give the same answer, "I don't know." They seemed desirous of battering the truth out of my body. Each unsatisfactory answer I gave—and they were all unsatisfactory—was followed by a dose of intense physical pain, administered in varying quantities and in many different forms. Usually I was punched and slapped in the face, and beaten with sticks and heavy rattan canes. The places on which the blows were concentrated were those containing no vital nerve or organ so that no permanent injury resulted to the victim; in particular the outside surface of the upper arm, the thigh and the calf were chosen. These parts of my body were soon solid bruises, the pain from which made it impossible to lie down and sleep with any sort of comfort. Sometimes as a change from the beatings other tortures were tried; it might be the water treatment or some other equally diabolical method of inflicting pain. It seemed to me that Kunichika was trying out every weapon in his armoury in an effort to make me talk. Under his supervision policemen, some of whom seemed to hate their task almost as much as I did, would run needles into my finger-tips below the nail, while my hand was held firmly, flat on the table; they heated iron bars in a charcoal brazier and applied them to my legs and back; they ran a stick between the second and third fingers of both my hands, squeezing the fingers together and holding them firmly in the air while two men hung from the ends of the cane, making a see-saw of my hands and tearing the flesh between my fingers; they thrust the rough ragged ends of canes into the hollows of my knees and twisted them until I screamed with pain. I used to find a certain relief by screaming and yelling at the top of my voice, and several times was spared further suffering by falling to the floor in a dead faint. But I held out against Kunichika and his henchmen and told them nothing.

Sometimes he tried to force me to admit that I had treated the guerrillas of my own free will, but more usually the questions were demands for more information. Who was the leader of the Papan guerrillas? What was his name? What did he look like? Where were his headquarters? How many men had he there? Who were they? Where did they get food? Who gave them money? Who brought me their letters? Who were their agents in Papan? Who helped them in Papan? Who was Don Juan? Who was Romeo? Who was the Captain? How were the guerrillas armed? Were there any Australian, Gurkha or British soldiers with them? To all these questions, and countless others, I had but the one answer, "I don't know." The Doctor, too, received his share of the beatings and tortures, but he stuck to the statement which I had made and passed on to him. As the days went by, Kunichika concentrated more on me, and for this I was thankful.

One morning there was a change. The Doctor and I were both taken from our cells and marched under escort to the Roman Catholic Boys' School in the town which the Japanese had taken over as Government offices. We were taken into a room which I recognised as having been Brother Rupert's classroom. A Japanese officer was there. "Good morning, Officer," I said.

My greeting was answered, as I had anticipated, with a couple of hard slaps. "Speak in Malay," shouted the officer, "and address a Japanese as Tuan."

"I speak English," I said, "and I never used 'Tuan' to the British so why should I to you?"

Another torrent of slaps and blows was the only answer.

The Doctor was called first into the adjoining room. I could not hear the questions he was asked, though shouts and the sound of heavy blows were clearly audible. After about half an hour he came out, looking pale and shaken, but determined. I had no time to speak to him as my turn followed at once.

There were several Japanese officers I had not seen before in the room to which I was led. "The Doctor has admitted that he removed bullets from a wounded guerrilla," said one. "What have you to say."

This I knew was a ruse. "It is not true. Your tortures must have forced him to lie. No guerrilla ever came to my house with a bullet wound, and in any case the Doctor never had anything to do with treating the guerrillas. They did not want the Doctor to know what I was doing, and never used to come when he was in the house. I expect he found out what was going on but he never had anything to do with it and we did not even discuss the matter together."

"We have caught the man and he has admitted that the Doctor removed two bullets from his leg."

"Then he is lying. The Doctor never did anything of the sort. I doubt if he could perform such an operation; he hasn't touched a surgical instrument for over twenty years."

"If the Doctor didn't remove the bullets, you must have done."

I said nothing to this, and to my surprise the interview was brought to an end and I was led from the room. For some hours we sat waiting, without being allowed to communicate in any way. There seemed to be great confusion in the building; we later learned that this was the result of the release by the guerrillas of a wealthy and influential Chinese business man they had kidnapped some days earlier. It was after midday before we were led through the streets of Ipoh back to the police lock-up.

We walked barefooted and I was limping badly with a cut leg. We halted at the sight of our own handsome car, now flying the flag of the Japanese Governor of Perak, drawn up outside the house. "What robbery!" I exclaimed, turning to one of the sentries on duty at the entrance. "That is our car, but now we have to walk."

"Please keep quiet, Missy," was the man's anxious reply.

"Am I not speaking the truth?"

The roads were crowded at this hour, and we encountered many friends and acquaintances. Some took no notice of us. They may have been frightened to acknowledge that they knew such dangerous criminals, or they may simply have failed to recognise us. This was not surprising, if so, for we presented a sorry aspect. My face was swollen and misshapen with the blows that had fallen upon it, while the Doctor, who had not been allowed a shave or a haircut, wore a long straggling beard and hair which fell almost to his shoulders framing an unbelievably haggard and pale face. Some, however, recognised us and greeted us with a word or a smile, and we returned their greetings as cheerfully as we could.

Once we were clear of the school building our escort allowed us to talk as we walked along side by side. I told the Doctor what I had said and asked him to stick to my story. He was very upset when I told him I had taken sole responsibility for treating the guerrillas.

"Why did you do that, Bil? They'll certainly kill you."

"They'll kill me anyway; I know that. But I can only die once, and there's no point in your being involved too. That's only common sense."

"I don't like it, Bil."

"You must think of the children, Ziew. Who will look after them if they lose both their parents? Please do as I say, and save yourself. It doesn't matter what you tell the Japs about me. Better admit everything they want you to than try to hold out against them; they might kill you with their tortures and that would defeat our purpose. But you must never admit the truth about guerrilla Panjang or they will certainly cut your head off. Save yourself for the sake of the children, and let me fight my battle alone. They may kill me but I will never give in to them."

My husband said nothing, and our escort would not allow further conversation as we were now near the police station.

That night I wrote a letter to Olga. Now that the Japs had found out about Panjang, the bullets I had so rashly buried in the garden were a threat to the Doctor's life. If the Japs chose to make a really thorough search they would surely find them.

"Dearest Olga (I wrote),

"Please go to Papan and carry out these instructions personally, and at once. Get Dominic to dig up the bottle containing bullets, which we buried in the vegetable garden. Dominic is the only one who knows the place. Smash the bottle, take the bullets and throw them into the river as you cross the bridge before reaching the main road on the way to Ipoh. Do not at all costs be caught by Japs or police with the bullets in your possession. Your father's life may depend on the way in which you carry out these instructions. Do not attempt to reply to this, but send a hard-boiled egg in my food when you have got rid of the bullets successfully.

"Love and kisses to you, Dawn, and Granny;
"Your loving Mummy."

This letter I wrote in tiny letters on a small scrap of paper. When Samy came in to carry out his daily task I gave it to him, and watched him conceal it carefully in a fold of his ragged turban. "Give it to no one but my daughter Olga," I said. "There will be no reply."

"Trust me, Missy."

At times during the night and the next day I regretted having taken the risk of sending such a dangerous note, and thought that I would have been wiser to let the bullets remain where they were. I prayed that Samy should deliver the message safely. My relief was tremendous when I found a hard-boiled egg in my evening meal next day, and I at once got Samy to convey a brief note to the Doctor. "Olga has got rid of the bullets," it read, "and there is now no danger of their being found."

Next morning we were taken once more to the Jap Government H.Q. This time I was the first to be called for questioning and I welcomed this as a sign that the Japs had accepted my statement that the Doctor had had nothing to do with the guerrillas. The interrogation began.

"So it was you who treated the wounded guerrilla?"

"I did nothing of the sort."

"Do you deny that you treated a man with a wound in his leg?"

"I remember treating a man with an ulcer in his leg, if that's what you mean."

"How did he get the ulcer?"

"Lots of people got them. Their diet contained too much tapioca, and I think that was the reason."

"Why did you try to find out the strength of the Nippon Army?"

"I didn't."

"If you won't tell us the truth of your own free will, we shall have to force you to."

They did their best, kicking and beating my body, which was by now permanently bruised and bleeding, and I was led back to the waiting-room feeling more dead than alive.

I could hear the angry shouts of the Japanese, the cracks of rattans and the bangs of sticks. I feared that my husband could not survive such a beating and prayed that he would not try to shield me. At length the ordeal was over; the Doctor was led staggering into the room, his clothes torn and every part of his flesh so exposed showing hideous bruises. His face was grotesquely swollen and a wide gash on his forehead was bleeding profusely. I had no time for a word of sympathy as I was called out at once for further questioning. As we walked along the veranda to the next room the Indian interpreter who had been sent to summon me slackened his pace for a moment. "The Doctor has admitted that you asked him about the Jap forces in Ipoh. Admit it too and save yourself the torture."

This was most welcome information. If I could continue to deny it they might come to regard the Doctor as an unreliable source of information and so lose interest in him. I resolved to hold out against all they could do to me.

"You are a spy for the guerrillas as well as a nurse to them."

"I am nothing of the sort."

"We know that you asked your husband to find out the strength of our forces in Ipoh. He has already confessed it."

"If so he is lying through fear of you and your tortures."

"It is you that is the liar, and you will be punished until you speak the truth."

He was as good as his word. My punishment began in earnest. Every method was used to make me speak. In the end my whole body seemed one great throbbing pain. I screamed and yelled at the top of my voice, but when at intervals my torturers stopped and repeated their questions I stuck doggedly to my denial and my torments were resumed. At length I fell to the ground through sheer weakness and did not move even when they continued to kick me with their heavy boots. I was dragged to my feet and carried out into the waiting-room, where I collapsed in the middle of the floor and lost consciousness.

When I came round the Doctor was supporting my head with one hand and feeling my pulse with the other. He later told me that he thought, from the fearful sounds which had come from the room where I was being questioned, that the Japs had killed me this time. When he saw that I was still alive he asked for water, but the clerks and police constables standing around did not dare brave the wrath of the Japs by succouring their prisoner. One of the Japanese from the Kempetei who had assisted at my interrogation walked in and seemed actually concerned at my condition.

"Officer, please let me have some water," I said.

The Jap gave an order and a glass was brought; he then commanded that we be taken down to his own car. As soon as my husband had given me the water, the sentry, in terror of his Japanese masters, tapped him on the shoulder reminding him that he was a prisoner, and made him stand away from me. I struggled to rise, but was quite unable to do so. A crowd of clerks working in the offices had gathered round in sympathy or curiosity, but such was their fear of the Japs that none dared to assist me. At length one, braver or more compassionate than the rest, stepped forward, lifted me in his arms and carried me down to the waiting car.

We reached the police station after a short drive. My husband was clearly worried by my condition and was almost in tears when they led him away to the Toko cells. My friends at the police station expressed the utmost horror and distress when they saw the condition in which I had been brought back to them. The P.C. on duty at the entrance threw down his rifle and carried me in his arms to my cell. "Missy," he said in a passionate tone, "I'd like to take my rifle and kill every Jap I see."

"Please don't do anything so foolish. This cannot last for ever, and you have a family depending on you."

The corporal on duty came into my cell with some of the constables. "This is terrible, Missy," he said. "When will the British return? Is there anything we can do for you?"

"It is good to be among friends again. I would like some ice to suck, please."

Ice was brought, as well as fresh milk from Harshan Singh's house. I could scarcely swallow the milk, but they fed me patiently, a teaspoonful at a time. When night came they brought a bench into my cell, and covered it with a thick pile of soft blankets from the corporal's house. My clothes were sticking to my body with the dried blood from my wounds; they soaked each place with water and gently drew the cloth away from the raw flesh below. Then, spreading a blanket over me, they changed my clothes and made me comfortable. Trained hospital nurses could not have been gentler or more considerate. They told me that my back looked just like raw meat from my shoulders to my waist.

"Supposing a Jap officer makes a surprise visit? You will all get into trouble."

"Don't worry. If one comes I'll delay him while the sentries lift you on to the sleeping-platform and hide the bench and your blankets. When the coast is clear they'll give you your bed back."

I could not find words to express the gratitude I felt for the ministrations of my kind friends. "Thank you, Corporal," was all I could say.

XV

FILIPINO WOMAN OUTSMARTS THE JAPS

from

JOEY'S QUIET WAR

by THOMAS M. JOHNSON

(Published in the *Reader's Digest*, 1951)

One of the lesser-known but none the less authentic spy adventures of the American war against the Japanese is that of a little Filipino woman who pitted her wits and courage against the brutality of the Japanese invader, shortly after Pearl Harbour.

It is no exaggeration to say that the American final victory in the Philippines was to some extent due to the exploits of Miss Joey Guerrero, who kept ferreting out essential information on Japanese military movements, which she conveyed at the risk of her life to the American guerrillas.

"Joey," as she was affectionately referred to by the advancing American troops, was awarded the highest honours by the United States Government for her bravery and by Cardinal Spellman for her "Christian fortitude and concern for fellow sufferers."

★

ACROSS the battlefields north of Manila trudged a little Filipino woman bearing a knapsack on her bent shoulders. Several of the Japanese soldiers started to question her. Some of them seeing her bloated, scarred brown face, understood and shrank back. To others she bared her chest and showed her sores. When she uttered the one word "Leprosy," no sentry persisted, none examined the knapsack, none found out that—taped on her back—she carried a map of the Japanese defences north of Manila.

The map accurately indicated minefields which the advancing U.S. troops desperately needed to know about. Sick and suffering, Joey Guerrero got the map through and thereby saved hundreds of American lives. It was but one of her great contributions to a U.S. victory in the Philippines.

Among the cleverest and bravest women spies of the war, Joey was decorated by the U.S. Government with the Medal of Freedom with Silver Palm—the highest award for war service by a civilian. Cardinal Spellman presented to her a medallion in recognition of "Christian fortitude and concern for fellow sufferers." The U.S. Government made it possible for her to go to Carville, Louisiana, where astounding progress is being made in treating Hansen's disease (leprosy). Doctors now think that in two years, if all goes well, Joey should be able to go back to her twelve-year-old daughter, from whom she has been separated for years. Even then, Josefina Guerrero, ready for a new life of service, will be only thirty-five years old.

As a little girl, Josefina had wanted to become a nun, but she contracted tuberculosis and the sisters said she was not strong enough for their life. Both her parents died, and a grandmother took the child to the coconut plantation she managed and brought her back to health.

Then Joey went to live with an uncle in Manila. There a young physician, Dr. Renato Maria Guerrero, fell in love with the lively girl who had, to quote Joey herself, a "snub-nosed, funny little mug with unruly features." They were married. The future shone bright. But in the winter of 1941, when her daughter, Cynthia, was two years old, Joey began to lose strength and appetite. Swellings appeared. Her anxious husband called in a specialist. As gently as he could, he told Joey the truth. "It is in an early stage," he said. "You are only twenty-three, and there are promising treatments. But children are susceptible, so you must leave your child." For hours, she sat in the doctor's surgery praying for the surpassing self-control she would need for so many years. She went home. The child was playing in the nursery. It was like dying, but Joey dared not even take the risk of kissing Cynthia goodbye when she sent the child to her grandmother.

Husband and wife then began to plan their fight against the disease and against ostracism. It had not been long since lepers had to ring a bell as they walked in the streets of Manila. Specialists told them that Hansen's disease was now recognised as only feebly contagious among adults, and that Joey was no menace to others. But she did need good medical care and rest.

There was to be neither. Three weeks later came Pearl Harbour. Soon Japanese soldiers swaggered in Manila's streets. One day five Japs stopped Joey and four other young Filipinos and made clear their intent. Joey, five feet and one hundred pounds of outraged womanhood, whacked the largest soldier with her umbrella until he and his companions made off. That night one of the other women telephoned Joey. "Come to our house," she said, and hung up.

Her friend's husband awaited Joey. "A woman of your spirit should join the guerrillas," he said. "You're the kind for our secret service." He told her the Filipino underground was sending information about the Japanese to MacArthur in Australia to help plan the Islands' liberation. Would she join them? "I can't do big things," said Joey, "but every little helps. O.K.!"

Joey was given a trial assignment: "Since you live opposite a Japanese barrack, for the next twenty-four hours count how many Japs go in and out, when, and in what direction. The same for passing vehicles."

Behind drawn blinds, Joey noted everything that passed, and the time. She not only counted a truck-load of Japanese soldiers, but observed that they looked dirty, as if coming from active service. She took a full notebook to the address given her. There she signed an oath of secrecy and loyalty. She had enlisted for what she calls "my quiet war." Her tour of duty was to last for three nerve-racking years.

Joey was assigned to watch the waterfront. There her keen eyes spotted hidden Japanese anti-aircraft guns. She made a sketch and concealed it in a hollowed-out fruit in a basket she carried. A Japanese soldier stopped her, pawed the fruit, greedily chose a large one, and walked on. Luckily she had put the sketch in a small fruit. After that she made only mental notes and did her drawing at home.

Joey was among the group of girls permitted to bring food to the starving Filipino and American prisoners. She radiated courage and faith to hollow-eyed G.I.s, some of whom gave her information they had gleaned from talkative Jap guards. Once a suspicious guard threatened her with a bayonet, finally gestured her on, giving her braided black hair a parting tug. Her hair ribbon concealed a prisoner's report, but it was tied too tightly to come off.

By September 1944 the approaching Americans were bombing Manila, smashing gun emplacements Joey had mapped for them. The Kempetei, the Japanese counter-intelligence police, had stool-pigeons everywhere and many guerrillas were being caught and tortured or shot. Underground operations were now directed by the Allied Intelligence Bureau. After another cryptic telephone call, Joey met Manuel Colayco, formerly a professor at Santo Tomás University, now a captain in the Intelligence. Would Joey join the A.I.B.? It might mean her life, but . . .

"What can I do?" she asked.

He told her to meet a lorry at a rendezvous in the outskirts of the city. She wore wooden shoes, in the hollow soles of which she had hidden thin packets of tissue paper containing guerrilla information about Japanese preparations to defend Manila. The lorry took her fifty miles by rough back roads to Nagcarlán mountain. There a guide led them up a narrow path. A large boulder barred the route, and a voice from nowhere challenged them. Joey gave the password. A light flashed in her eyes from a tree above and then winked out. The guide turned the boulder as if it were on a hinge. Pushing through, they found themselves in a clearing where perhaps a hundred Filipino

guerrillas were living in nipa-palm barracks. Joey watched them set up
a wireless apparatus and send off her message.

She became "just a little errand boy." By various routes to the
guerrilla hideout she brought reports, maps and photographs. And it
was at the camp that she heard the glorious news radioed through:
"The Americans are landing on Luzon!"

The guerrillas made handbills on a smuggled mimeograph machine
—LIBERATION IS NEAR!—and added a ringing appeal for help. Joey
took the bills to Manila. She and other volunteers flitted through the
blackout, slipping them under doors or into the hands of passers-by.

Next she was assigned to spotting Japanese ammunition dumps. One
night she heard a signal at her door. She admitted a man in Japanese
uniform who handed her what seemed to be a bag of vegetables.
"Here's something for Dr. Guerrero," he whispered quickly, and then
slipped from the house. Her husband, who was also in the underground,
took the bag of "vegetables," but said nothing. Many nights thereafter
were thunderous with exploding ammunition dumps. In the daytime
Joey checked to see which dumps needed more "vegetable treatment."

But soon Colayco sent word that she was needed as a messenger
again, so Joey returned to Nagcarlán. She hoped the mountain air
would renew her ebbing strength. With the scarcity of food and
medicine, she was increasingly feverish and exhausted. She suffered
excruciating headaches, her feet were swelling and more sores appeared on her body. Surely, she prayed, God and the returning
Americans would bring help.

Early in 1945, when the Americans were approaching Manila,
Colayco summoned her for the most dangerous mission of all. The
guerrillas had sent the American Army a map of the Japanese defences
which showed a wide section free of mines. The Americans planned to
attack there, but now the Japs had mined the area heavily. The guerrillas
needed someone to take a corrected map to 37th Division Headquarters at Calumpit, forty miles north of Manila. There was fighting
all the way. The Japs guarded every road and footpath, searched all
passers-by. Vehicles could not get through. A woman afoot might,
if she was small, shabby and courageous. Would Joey try it? "Just tell
me where to go," Joey said.

At first she walked under cover of night, but loss of sleep weakened
her still more, and the headaches grew worse. She determined to try
it by daylight. The first day a Japanese officer halted her, approached
as if to search her. The map taped between her shoulder blades seemed
to burn. As the Jap came close, he peered at her face and saw that it
was bloated and spotted with red. He stared at her in fear and then

quickly waved her on. Joey suddenly realised that she had a terrible passport that would get her through.

After two days and nights on the road she reached American headquarters and delivered the map. Weak from sickness and reaction, she could not eat the pancakes and coffee which the Americans offered her, even though she had not tasted them for years.

Her road back took her through heavy fighting. Once, seeking shelter from shell bursts and snipers' bullets, she hid behind an American tank, which exploded and nearly killed her. When she reached Manila, she learned that Manuel Colayco had been terribly wounded during the last days of the fighting. She went to see him in the hospital where he lay dying. He tried to raise his torn body. "Fine job!" he whispered in a last salute.

Joey turned to nursing patients in an evacuation hospital; but her illness, aggravated by overwork, became so serious that the hospital authorities told her she must go to Tala, the Philippine Government leprosarium. She found it a cluster of leaking shacks in a wilderness. There was little food and almost no medical care. Many of the sufferers slept on the same floor which they trod on with feet covered with open sores. This was no hospital, but a charnel house of filth.

In February 1947, Tala was suddenly flooded by six hundred more patients. It was too much for Joey. She had been trying to bring some sort of order and sanitation to the place. Now she appealed to Aurora Quezón, the ex-President's daughter. An exposé in Manila newspapers brought results: new buildings, a laboratory, an operating room; more doctors and nurses; above all, supplies of the new drugs that have brought hope to victims of Hansen's disease.

Through the intercession of friends who knew of Joey's work, Attorney General Clark granted her plea to be allowed treatment at Carville. There patients greeted her with bouquets and a birthday cake. They saw a tiny woman whose brown face was scarred and pale, but whose lively eyes still smiled. Dr. Frederick A. Johansen—kindly, famous "Dr. Jo"—started daily injections and other treatments, and her health began to improve. Now, her sores healed, her face glowing, she is a tribute to Carville's care and skill. She greets her many visitors with a firm hand-clasp and a torrent of eager words. "By heart, I am happy," she says.

When the time comes, Joey Guerrero wants to start out again as God's little errand boy in a new "quiet war." This time her mission will be to bring mercy and good cheer to those who suffer what she has suffered from Hansen's disease.

XVI

IN THE ANKARA SPY JUNGLE

from

OPERATION CICERO

by L. C. Moyzisch

(Published by Allan Wingate, London, 1950)

L. C. Moyzisch was an attaché at the German Embassy at Ankara when he was approached by "Cicero," who offered to sell him important secret documents from the British Embassy. Cicero was the code name given by the Germans to the soi-disant valet of the British Ambassador. Nobody knew his real name or his nationality. He himself claimed to be an Albanian who "hated the British."

How Cicero managed to gain access to the papers he sold to the German Embassy is still shrouded in mystery. Moyzisch's version of the affair naturally reflects the German attitude, and while it seems probable that the facts are accurate, the story still has to be confirmed by release of Allied documents.

The "Cicero Affair" took place during the comparatively short period between October 1943 and April 1944. The filched documents, or rather the photographs thereof, must have been highly valuable to the Germans, for they paid Cicero the fantastic sum of three hundred thousand pounds. This generosity, however, did not cost the Germans very much, for it later turned out that most of the lovely, crisp pound notes were "made in Germany."

★

DECEMBER was Cicero's great period. Never before and never again did he deliver so much or such important material. There could no longer be the slightest doubt about his genuineness.

In Berlin they were at last beginning to see the value of it all. Every courier plane carried fresh top secret British documents, documents so important that for a while even the private war between Ribbentrop and Kaltenbrunner took second place. Ribbentrop's personal attitude towards Operation Cicero seemed to be unchanged; at least he still preserved his haughty silence. He read the documents, but that was all. Presumably he still had doubts as to whether or not the whole business was a British trick. In any event, whether it was for that reason or because of personal enmity and spite, he never made the slightest effort to use the information he now possessed.

As for Cicero himself, he seemed a different man during that busy month of December. He was quite friendly now, even moderately talkative, and he seemed to have completely got over his original shyness and reserve. It was only when I asked him personal questions concerning his identity or his background that he closed up, making it quite clear that such matters were none of my business, and that I had better be satisfied with the goods he delivered without wanting any other information.

He was obviously very proud of his successes. What he really liked to talk about at our nocturnal meetings was his own future. He enjoyed thinking about the large house he was going to own in some pleasant country far away. I remember that he planned to have a great many servants. Sometimes his attitude reminded me of a child's exuberant excitement on Christmas Eve. He did not seem at all worried by the rapid worsening of Germany's position.

"I've made plans for every eventuality," he once told me in his lordly way. "I know exactly what I'll do if Germany loses the war."

But he never told me what those plans were.

He changed considerably in appearance as well. He now wore well-cut suits of the best English cloth and expensive shoes with thick crêpe soles. One day, when he appeared wearing a large and flamboyant gold wrist-watch, I thought it time I spoke to him.

"Don't you think your chief and other people might notice all your new and obviously expensive possessions? They might begin to wonder where the money to pay for them came from. Frankly, I think you're being a little rash. In fact, your behaviour strikes me as downright dangerous."

Cicero looked at me thoughtfully. I could see he was impressed. After a few moments he took off the wrist-watch and asked me to keep it for him until he had a chance to take it to Istanbul and store it there with his other jewellery.

He was very fond of jewels. On one occasion he asked me to give him his usual £15,000, not in English banknotes, but in the form of diamonds and other precious stones. He said he was afraid of arousing suspicion if he bought them himself.

I told him that it would seem equally suspicious if I were to go into a shop and buy £15,000 worth of diamonds. I did, however, finally agree to get him a couple of thousand pounds' worth. I felt that that was about the limit to which I could safely go in pretending I was buying presents for my wife.

Another noticeable change in Cicero's outward appearance was his finger nails. When I had first met him they had been bitten down to the quick. By now they were grown again. He had even had them manicured. And this was not the only evidence to show that his earlier nervousness had completely left him. He had given up peeping behind curtains and jerking open doors. He was entirely self-assured, and I was even afraid that he might become careless. Towards the middle of the month this cocksureness of his was to be rudely shaken, but that comes later in the story.

Meanwhile, shortly after the Allied conferences in Cairo and Teheran were over, Cicero rang up and asked for a meeting. I had to attend an official dinner that evening which I could not get out of at such short notice, so I asked him to meet me a little earlier than usual.

At eight o'clock I was at our established meeting-place, and with that curious, cat-like agility of his he jumped into the slow-moving car. He seemed to be in rather a hurry as, indeed, was I. I passed him a fat bundle of money which he stuffed right into his pocket while passing me two rolls of film. Later these turned out to be the most precious information that Cicero ever extracted from the Ambassador's safe. He said he would have some more for me in a few days' time, and at the next dark corner he slipped out of my car as quietly as he had entered it.

I did not want to be any later than necessary for the dinner party, so I drove straight there instead of first dropping the films at the Embassy.

It was not a particularly pleasant dinner, at least not for me. I could not stop myself from putting my hand in my pocket every two minutes to make sure my rolls of film were still there. I am afraid my worry and curiosity about Cicero's latest delivery made me a very poor conversationalist indeed, and I know that my bridge afterwards was shockingly bad.

As soon as I decently could I made some excuse, took my wife home, and went back to the Embassy. I had intended just to lock the films in the safe and leave the developing and so on till the morning. But holding them in my hand my curiosity was too strong and I decided to do the job at once.

I worked in the dark-room all night, finishing just as dawn was breaking. I found that I had in my possession complete minutes of the entire conferences both at Cairo and at Teheran.

I worked on all through the morning writing a provisional report for the Ambassador to forward to Berlin. Good old Schnürchen, when she came to my office at nine sharp, was probably surprised to see her chief at the typewriter, wearing a dinner jacket. Once again she showed her perfect diplomatic training; she made no comment either on my clothes or on the fact that I chose to type myself rather than to dictate to her.

With this delivery the sequence of events and development of Allied policy that was covered by the three recent meetings of Allied leaders became entirely clear to us. First there had been the Moscow Conference, called by Stalin and attended by Eden and Cordell Hull: then came the Cairo talks between Roosevelt, Churchill and Chiang Kai-shek: and finally there was the great Teheran Conference of the Big Three.

Sitting there all that morning, typing a résumé of what the batch of photographs on my desk told me, I realised with brutal clarity that what I was writing was nothing more nor less than a preview of Germany's destruction. The Moscow Conference had done the preparatory work: the Teheran Conference had put the finishing touches. Here a new world had been planned, whose premises were the utter blotting out of the Third Reich and the punishment of its guilty leaders. I never learned what effect these revelations had on the men whose personal fate had just been decided at Teheran. For myself I trembled with emotion at the spectacle of the vast historical perspective opened by these stolen documents.

I spent a very busy day drafting further long signals, each of which had to be approved by the Ambassador. That evening I met Cicero again. He had yet another roll of film for me. This one contained only a few exposures, but at least one of them was of vital importance. We immediately wired Berlin that the Head of the Turkish State had gone to Cairo to meet President Roosevelt and Prime Minister Churchill. Up to then none of us in Turkey, and certainly no one in Berlin, even suspected that President Ismet Inonu and the Turkish Foreign Minister had left Ankara.

Cicero now began to be more reckless. Every second or third day he produced fresh material. I had given him a brand new Leica sent from Berlin. I got him all the film he needed, which was also sent from Berlin, since it might have caused attention had he bought such quantities from the one photographic shop in Ankara.

We were still in the second week of December when he telephoned once again asking me to meet him that night. As usual we drove aimlessly through the dark streets and alleys of Ankara, while from the back he handed over a roll of film and I passed him his money. This time, though, he gave me a small package in addition to the roll of film.

"Open it later," he said. "They'll know what to do with it in Berlin."

I wondered what it contained and was about to ask him when I was blinded by the glaring headlights of another car reflected in my rear mirror.

I leaned out and saw a long, dark limousine, some twenty yards behind us. I remember congratulating myself that I had taken care of my back licence plate; it was bent and well coated with dried mud. Also the German origin of the Opel was not easily discernible at night; at a superficial glance that big, streamlined automobile looked like one of the many new American cars so plentiful in Ankara.

I drove on slowly waiting for the limousine to pass me, but it did not do so. I decided to draw in to the kerb until it had gone by. The great dark car behind me stopped too, still at a distance of about twenty yards. Now I really began to get worried. The other car's powerful headlights lit up the interior of the Opel. Cicero was still evidently unaware of what was going on. He seemed merely to be bothered by the light, as he drew the curtains of the back window. At that moment I heard the other car's horn and saw in my mirror that it was slowly creeping up towards us.

I became deadly frightened and drove off as fast as I could, putting on more and more speed, trying to shake off the car behind. I soon realised that it had at least as much speed as my Opel. Furthermore I could not go full out, since I did not dare take the risk of knocking down some pedestrian or crashing into something. An accident at this point would have been fatal. If we had been killed or even seriously injured, the Turkish police would have found the British Ambassador's valet, carrying a huge sum of money, in a car belonging to a German attaché who was carrying a roll of film . . . that is, if our pursuers let them find us at all.

Meanwhile the dark limousine kept close behind me, always at the same distance. Again I reduced speed to a mere crawl. So did the other car. I had no doubt in my own mind that Cicero had been shadowed, presumably since leaving the British Embassy, which would mean that they were aware of the valet being in a German diplomatic car.

I deliberately dismissed these thoughts. I was not going to give up before making one final attempt to get rid of them.

I went through a very narrow and dark alleyway. I took the corner rather slowly and then suddenly accelerated as heavily as I could, tearing around another corner and then another one. It was no good. In the mirror I could still see the reflection of the dark limousine, twenty yards behind me.

What could I do? Had it been daytime I might have tried to make a dash for the German Embassy, but at night it would take the porter at least a minute or two to open the heavy iron gates. Besides, even if the gates had been open, to go there would be to provide the people behind with absolute proof that Cicero was a German spy. I would have to think of something else.

While tearing around those street corners, I glanced at Cicero's reflection in the mirror. He was hunched in his corner, deadly white. He was aware that his life was at stake. A beam of light from the following car lit him up for a second, and I could see that he was sweating heavily. With his hands he clutched the back of the driving seat.

"Can't you go faster?" His voice was a hoarse whisper.

"Yes. But it wouldn't do any good."

It occurred to me to try and reach one of the great new motor-roads that radiated out from Ankara over the plains. On one of them I could drive my big car flat out and I might be able to shake off the limousine. I realised at once that this plan was useless. Once out of the town the roads were marvellous, but there were no turnings. Whoever left on one of them had to come back the same way. The British, if it were they, would not even have to bother to chase me. They could simply wait until I came back.

I had no gun. I never carried one while I was in Ankara. There seemed no point, since I would certainly never fire the first shot and the second shot would be too late. Besides, I have always thought that the mere carrying of a loaded gun is more dangerous than it is worth, since it gives a man a quite false feeling of security. It is always better to rely on one's brain, a far more useful weapon.

But Cicero had a revolver. By now he was palpably panic-struck, sitting hunched there, chewing on his finger nails. For him to have a loaded gun in his pocket was, I thought, extremely dangerous for everyone concerned. I wished at that moment that I could somehow get it out of his pocket.

Once again I tried the old trick. I crossed the intersection very slowly. So did my pursuers. Then I raced round the corner and round another one and round still a third. It was touch and go. I felt the car skidding on two wheels, screeching on the turns, and once we were within inches of grazing the near wall of a narrow alley. Back in the straight I got the car under control again. Doubling round two more corners, I reached the great central boulevard of Ankara, where I accelerated to sixty and then seventy and seventy-five. Looking round I saw to my intense relief that there was no one behind me. I kept my foot pressed down, the accelerator flat against the floor-boards. It was lucky that the boulevard, with its many crossings, was completely deserted at that hour of the night. We raced past the great iron gates of the German Embassy.

"Take me to the British Embassy," said the faint voice from the back seat.

XVII

GESTAPO METHODS IN P.O.W. CAMPS

from

THE IDOL OF SAN VITTORE

by Indro Montanelli

Translated and adapted by Erwin C. Lessner

(First published in the *Reader's Digest*, 1950)

Indro Montanelli, an Italian army captain at the time the Italian war machine was tottering, was taken prisoner by the Germans and sent to the notorious San Vittore prison for interrogation by Nazi intelligence officers.

This story has nothing to do with Montanelli but concerns a mysterious Italian General detained in a cell opposite his own. The captain narrates the moving and heroic adventure of that General who was massacred, together with sixty-five handcuffed Italian officers, on June 22nd, 1944, by his German captors.

★

My story begins on that day in March 1944 when His Excellency General Della Rovere, intimate of Marshal Badoglio and technical adviser to General Alexander, was brought to San Vittore Prison and put in the cell across from mine. The Italian underground was attempting, at that time, to disrupt the flow of German reserves to the fighting front in the south. The General, I learned, had been captured by the Germans in a northern province when he was put ashore by an Allied submarine to assume command of guerrilla operations there. I was impressed by his aristocratic bearing. Even Franz, the brutal German overseer of the prison, stood to attention before him.

Of all the German-operated "confession" factories in Italy, San Vittore was the worst. Captured Italian underground fighters who stood up under primary "routine" questioning were brought here. Then Gestapo Commissar Mueller and his bunch of picked S.S. men— by methods now celebrated in the annals of refined torture—usually squeezed desired information out of even the toughest customers.

Six months had passed since my own arrest. I had been "interrogated" several times, and I was exhausted and discouraged. I sometimes wondered how much longer I could hold out. Then, to my astonishment, one day Ceraso, one of the Italian guards, unlocked my cell door and told me that General Della Rovere wished to see me.

The General's door was unlocked, as always. Moreover, he had a
bed, whereas the rest of us slept on bare planks. Immaculately groomed,
monocle in his right eye, he greeted me courteously. "Captain Montanelli? I knew before I landed that you were here. His Majesty's
Government is keenly interested in your fate. We are confident that
even when you fall before a German firing squad you will fulfil your
duty, your most elementary duty as an officer. But make yourself
at ease, pray." Only then did I realise that I had been standing to
attention—heels touching, thumbs against trouser seams.

"We officers all lead provisional lives, do we not?" he asked. "An
officer is, so to speak, a bridegroom of the Goddess of Death; *novio de
la muerte*, the Spanish call it." He paused, polishing his monocle with
a white handkerchief, and it occurred to me that names often reflected the bearers' personality. Della Rovere means "of the oak."
Here, surely, was a man of solid timber.

"They have already sentenced me," he continued. "How about
you?"

"Not yet, Your Excellency," I replied, almost apologetically.

"They will," he said. "The Germans are rigorous when they expect
a confession, but they are also chivalrous in their esteem for those who
refuse to confess. You have not talked. Well done! That means that
you will be honoured by being shot through the chest, not through the
back. I urge you to persist in your silence. But should you undergo
torture—I don't mean to question your moral strength, but there are
limits to physical endurance—I suggest that you give them just one
name: mine. Tell them that, whatever you did, you were acting under
my orders. . . . By the way, what are the charges against you?"

I told him everything—unreservedly. His Excellency listened like a
father confessor. From time to time he nodded approvingly.

"Your case is as clear-cut as mine," he said when I had finished.
"We were both apprehended carrying out official orders. Our only
remaining duty is to die fighting on the field of honour. It should be
easy to die decently."

When Ceraso was locking me back in my cell I implored him to
send me a barber the following day. And that night I folded my
trousers and creased them on the window lattice before stretching
myself out on my plank to sleep.

During the following days I saw many prisoners visit the General's
cell. When they came out, they all seemed to hold themselves more
erectly, they no longer looked dejected.

Noise and disorder in our isolated sector abated. No. 215, who had
rent the air with cries for his wife and children, fell silent and showed

great composure when he was called for interrogation. Ceraso told me that after talking with the General almost everyone asked for the barber, and for a comb and soap. Prison guards began shaving daily and even tried to speak pure Italian instead of Neapolitan or Sicilian slang. Even Mueller, when he inspected the place, grudgingly commended the general improvement in discipline and dignity.

Best of all, the "confession factory" no longer produced confessions. The men persisted in a stubborn silence. From his own great store of courage, Della Rovere gave them strength to endure. From his own experiences under arrest, he gave them invaluable advice.

"The most dangerous hours are in the early afternoon," he would warn them. "The mere longing for distraction could make you confess." Or, "Don't stare at the walls. Close your eyes from time to time and the walls will lose their power to choke you." He reprimanded them for neglecting their appearance: "Neatness builds morale." He knew that the military formalities they observed with him strengthened their pride. And he never stopped reminding them of their duty towards Italy.

Someone cautiously inquired about His Excellency's personal reaction under questioning. The General laughed. "I was questioned by my old friend Field Marshal Kesselring," he said. "My task was easy, for Kesselring already knew all there was to know—except how I happened to be on a British submarine when I was picked up."

"Did you really trust the British?" Kesselring had asked.

"Why not?" was the General's retort. "We even trusted the Germans!" The General seemed to get a great deal of pleasure out of recalling this encounter.

After a while, a rumour began to sweep through the prison that the General was a counter-spy, a German stool-pigeon. The Italian guards, even though drawn from the dregs of Mussolini's old régime, felt there were limits to the humiliations they would take. They agreed among themselves to watch the General constantly; if he turned out to be a stool-pigeon, they were determined to strangle him.

Next morning Della Rovere received No. 203, a Major who was supposed to have more than the usual amount of information and who had not talked. Ceraso lingered near the cell door, and other Italian guards watched nearby.

"You will undergo extreme torture," they heard the General say to the Major. "You must confess nothing. Keep your mind blank, force yourself to believe that you know nothing. Even thinking of the secrets you are guarding might bring them to your lips." The Major listened, ashen-faced, as the General said to him what he had said to me: "If you are driven to speak, tell them that whatever you did you did on my orders."

That afternoon, an apologetic Ceraso brought His Excellency a few roses, a gift of the Italian prison guards. The General accepted the flowers graciously; he seemed not to have the slightest notion that he had been distrusted.

One morning the Germans came for Colonels P. and F. Before being led to the courtyard, the officers were granted one last wish—to say farewell to the General. I saw them at his cell door, standing to attention. I couldn't hear what the General said to them, but both officers smiled. He shook their hands—something I'd never seen him do before. Then, as if suddenly aware of the Germans present, he stiffened, raised his hand and saluted. The men returned the salute, turned on their heels and walked to their deaths. We learned later that both shouted "Long live the King!" as they faced the firing squad.

That afternoon I was questioned again. Commissar Mueller told me that my fate would depend on the results of this interrogation. If I were to persist in my silence . . . I stared at him with wide-open eyes, yet I could hear nothing; I couldn't even see him. I saw instead the pale, composed faces of Colonels P. and F., the smiling face of His Excellency. I heard a quiet, sedate voice in my ear: *novio de la muerte* . . . elementary duty as an officer . . . to die fighting on the field of honour. After the Germans had questioned me in vain for two hours, the interrogation came to an end. I was not tortured, but even if I had been, I think I would have been able to conceal everything. On my way back, I asked Ceraso to let me stop at His Excellency's cell.

The General put aside the book he was reading and looked at me searchingly as I stood to attention. Then, before I spoke, he said, "Yes, that's what I expected you to do; you couldn't have done differently." He rose. "I cannot put all I would say into words, Captain Montanelli, but since there is no one else to report on us, let this upright Italian guard be a witness to what we say in these our last days. Let him listen to every word. I am well satisfied, Captain. I am pleased indeed. Bravo!"

That night I was truly alone in this world. But my beloved country seemed nearer and dearer and more real than ever before.

I never saw the General again. Only after the liberation did I learn about his end. One of the survivors of Fossoli told me the story.

Fossoli was a notorious extermination camp where the ways of dying were intricate and of great variety. When General Della Rovere was transferred there by armoured train, together with hundreds of others, he maintained his dignity. Throughout the trip he sat on a heap of knapsacks the others had gathered to provide him with a couch. He refused to rise when a Gestapo officer inspected the train. Even when the officer slapped him across the face and shouted, "I know you, you swine, Bertoni," he remained unperturbed. Why should he explain to this blundering German that his name was not Bertoni, but Della Rovere, that he was a General of an Army Corps, intimate friend of Badoglio and technical adviser to Alexander? Unruffled, he picked up his monocle and squeezed it on again. The German walked away, cursing.

At Fossoli the General no longer enjoyed the privileges granted him in San Vittore. He was quartered with everyone else in a single barrack and, like everyone else, he was put to work. His fellow prisoners sought to spare him the lowliest chores, and took turns substituting for him. But he never tried to evade his tasks, difficult as they might be for a man who was no longer young. And at night he reminded his comrades that they were not convicts but officers. Facing his glaring monocle and listening to his voice, they stood a little straighter.

The massacre at Fossoli on June 22nd, 1944, may have been in reprisal for the Allied victories near Genoa. At any rate, on orders from Milan, sixty-five names were drawn from a total of four hundred inmates. As a Lieutenant Tito read the list, the doomed men had to step forward from the ranks. When he called the name Bertoni, nobody stepped forward. "Bertoni!" he roared, staring at Della Rovere. His Excellency did not budge.

Did Tito want to show indulgence to a doomed man? No one could say. In any case, he suddenly smiled. "All right, all right," he said. "Della Rovere, if you wish."

Everyone held his breath, watching the General. He pulled his monocle from his pocket and with a remarkably steady hand squeezed it against his right eye. "*General* Della Rovere, if you please," he said calmly as he joined the waiting group.

The sixty-five were handcuffed and led to the wall. All were blindfolded except His Excellency, who steadfastly refused, and they granted him his wish. While four machine guns were brought into firing position, His Excellency stepped forward, his bearing proud and determined. "Gentlemen, officers," he called in a firm, resounding voice. "As we face the ultimate sacrifice, may our thoughts turn faithfully towards our beloved country. *Long live the King!*"

Tito shouted "Fire!" and the machine guns rattled. They put the General in his coffin, still wearing his monocle.

.   .   .   .   .   .

The true story of General Della Rovere, which I learned after his death, is one of heroism and an impersonation almost beyond belief. For the idol of San Vittore was no general. Neither Badoglio nor Alexander had ever heard of him. And his name was not Della Rovere.

He was one Bertoni, a native of Genoa, a thief and confidence man with a long prison record. The Germans had arrested him for some petty crime and during the questioning had realised that the man was a superb natural actor. They believed that his unscrupulous outlook and his talent for acting would make him an excellent agent for tricking information out of guerrilla prisoners.

Bertoni was ready for a deal. He would do as requested in return for preferred treatment in prison and early release. The Germans invented the Della Rovere story and coached him in his part.

When Bertoni was sent to San Vittore he asked for and was granted a brief period during which he would gain the trust of the men he would later victimise. But Bertoni was shrewder than they knew; he was determined to trick no one but the Germans!

And then came the amazing transformation. Acting General Della Rovere's part, Bertoni *became* Della Rovere. He undertook a super-human task—to make San Vittore confession-proof and its inmates strong enough to meet their fate. And by his commanding presence, his impeccable grooming, his high courage and faith, he brought a new dignity and sense of personal worth to the poor devils who were incarcerated there.

But, finally, he knew his time was running out. Commissar Mueller grew more and more impatient with his delays: why weren't the confessions coming through? When "Della Rovere" spoke to me that last day in his cell and asked the guard to be a witness, he knew that it was all over, that this was the only way the outside world might learn his story, the only way that Italy might know he had kept his trust.

On June 22nd, 1945, the first anniversary of the massacre at Fossoli, I stood in the Cathedral of Milan and watched the Cardinal-Prince-Archbishop of that city consecrate the coffins of the heroes of Fossoli. The Cardinal knew whose body lay in the coffin marked Della Rovere. He knew, too, that no one had a better right to the title of General than the occupant of that coffin, the former thief and jailbird, Bertoni.

XVIII

ODETTE WILL NOT CONFESS

from

ODETTE

by JERRARD TICKELL

(Published by Chapman & Hall, London, 1949)

The part Odette Sansom (later Mrs. Peter Churchill, G.C., M.B.E.) played in the last war is less remarkable for sensational successes she achieved than for her heroism and spirit of self-sacrifice when captured by the enemy. There is no need to give a thumbnail sketch of this brave woman whose exploits are still vivid in the minds of the public.

Suffice it to say that this extraordinary Frenchwoman—British by adoption— responded to the call of duty during the darkest days of the war, and became a member of Buck's (Colonel Maurice Buckmaster) team in the French Section of the War Office. After months of strenuous training in the subtle art of sabotage, she was turned loose in France, for the purpose of putting into practice what she had been taught.

Together with Captain Peter Churchill, she was caught by the Germans after six months in Occupied France, and it was then that her heroism flowered forth. There is nothing fictitious about Major Tickell's account, who, having access to the official files, vividly describes the story of Odette from her early childhood in Picardy to her adventures in France and final capture by the Gestapo.

The editor apologises for the inclusion in this collection of the somewhat nauseating account of Odette's "interrogation" by the dreaded Gestapo torturers of 84 Avenue Foch, Paris, which he deemed necessary in order to convey Odette's steadfastness and moral fibre.

★

At about six o'clock on the morning of May 25th, an S.S. woman unlocked the door of Cell 108 and shouted "*Tribunal.*"

Odette's heart turned over and she drew a long, quivering breath. Though she had known that a summons to the commissars of the Gestapo was inevitable, though she had expected it every morning since her arrival in Fresnes more than a fortnight ago and she had steeled herself to accept it with composure, the knowledge that it had now come drained her momentarily of strength. Other women had been called to 84 Avenue Foch. Some of them had come back, but even those had never spoken about what had happened there. Most of them had not returned and a new occupant had come to their cells. Sitting on her bed, Odette tried coherently to run over the points of the story she had decided to tell, testing each lie for a possible flaw. Her *ersatz* coffee was slopped into her bowl and she drank it greedily, for her mouth was dry. She told Michèle in a whisper that she had been called to the *tribunal* at last, and Michèle said that she regretted for the first time in her life that she didn't believe in God. "If I believed, I would pray for you, Céline. . . . I shall be in fear for you all day."

Odette was taken out of the prison at eight o'clock. The sides of the *panier à salade*, the Black Maria, were windowless, but from each compartment one could look through a wire mesh into the centre passage. There was an iron grille in the back door and, by laying her cheek against the mesh, Odette could just see through the grille into the street. In a jumbled blur, she saw people walking on the pavements and once, in a traffic block, she saw for a static, poignant instant the sight of children playing. For no reason at all, she was reminded of her many journeys to Paddington when she had first tried to go to France and how remote she had felt then from the people on the pave- ments. She had stopped her taxi in the Edgware Road to buy a bunch of violets. "Good luck, miss," the man had said. "Good luck, miss. . . ."

The Black Maria stopped. Her compartment was unlocked and the back doors were flung open.

"H'raus, h'raus. Schnell, schnell. . . ."

Good luck, miss. Good luck.

·   ·   ·   ·   ·

She came back to Fresnes in the late afternoon. When the S.S. were out of hearing, she erected her improvised ladder and called softly down the *bouche de chaleur*.

" 'Allo, Michèle."

"Céline. You are back?"

"Yes. I'm back."

"Tell me what happened. Tell me everything. I have been in fear for you all day."

"It was not necessary—this time. We went in the *panier à salade* to the Avenue Foch and then I was taken upstairs to a small room and locked in. I waited there for two, three hours and then was given a

magnificent lunch, meat, potatoes and thick gravy." Michèle sighed.
"I knew the purpose of this feast—to make me sleepy before the interrogation, and I only ate half of it. I took a potato and hid it and I have
it here. I will send it down to you by the *Kahlfaktor*."
        "A potato! My God. . . ."
        "Then I was sent for by the commissar. He is a young man, very
clean and fair and correct. He smells of eau-de-Cologne. He asked
many questions. He was quite polite—in spite of the fact that after
two hours' questioning he had only been able to write three lines on a
very big sheet of paper. At the end he said that he and I would meet
again and I was locked up to wait for the Black Maria. That's all. I
had had meat and gravy for lunch—and all for nothing. Now I'm
going to my window to watch the sunset. I am a very lucky woman
to have been to the Avenue Foch and to come back as I am."

                  .   .   .   .   .

        "*Tribunal*."
        "But . . . but I went to the *tribunal* yesterday."
        "You go again today. *Tribunal, tribunal*."
        The door slammed. If going to the Avenue Foch only meant meat
and thick gravy and a stolen glance at free people walking the pavements she had little to fear. But she had a premonition that it was
going to mean a lot more than that. They had told her during her
training in England about these clean young commissars of the Gestapo
who lived in No. 84 Avenue Foch. They were the hand-picked inner
core of the Gestapo and their training in Himmler's No. 1 School was
long and thorough. They wore no uniform and they had nothing to
do with the ordinary bullies of the S.S. Their job was to make people
talk. To their impersonal eyes, the human body, male or female,
was merely so much raw material to be classified and sub-divided into
varying zones of articulate pain; in their eyes Odette or Lise or
Madame Chambrun or Madame Churchill was no longer a woman.
She was a subject, a number, a unit. She was a cipher from Fresnes, a
cipher with a tongue, vocal cords and a sensitive nervous system, the
laceration of which would cause the tongue to speak. These commissars
were very efficient young men and a credit to their master. It was rare
indeed that they took "no" for an answer while the subject of their
investigations continued to breathe. Sometimes, of course, death was
kind enough to intervene and then the commissars got a reprimand.
They were very healthy young men and lived in a sort of muscular
chastity with plenty of good music, P.T. and cold baths.

10

Odette told Michèle that she was going to the Gestapo again.

"*Oh là là*, that's not so good, two days running. I shall be anxious for you all day. If you get a chance, bring me back another potato, Céline."

"Somehow I don't think I shall be able to give my attention to potatoes today, Michèle. But if I can, I will."

"Try, Céline. The hunger in my belly is like a spear. *A ce soir*."

"*A ce soir*, Michèle."

Odette would far have preferred to stay in her cell all that day and rest.

It was not a good time for her, but the young gentlemen of the Gestapo could hardly be expected to take account of the feminine calendar. She drank her coffee and considered her pitiful wardrobe. She wore her coat and skirt—she had told Buck a very long time ago that it would be suitable for prison—a red blouse and her only silk stockings. A few minutes before eight, the guards came for her and she was marched out into the courtyard of the prison to the Black Maria. It was a lovely day and the courtyard was dappled with sunshine.

At 84 Avenue Foch there seemed to be rather more activity than yesterday. Odette was taken upstairs to a room on the third floor. This time, she was sent for almost at once and went into the same interrogation room where she had been yesterday. The same commissar sat at a table on which was spread his meagre notes. He looked very healthy and fresh, as if he had just come out of a cold bath, and she noticed again the faint not unpleasant scent of eau-de-Cologne. He indicated a chair and she sat down facing him, her back to the door. He said briskly, in very nearly perfect French:

"Lise, you wasted a great deal of my time yesterday. You will not be permitted to do this again. There are three questions to which I require the answers. The first is this. Where is your wireless operator, the man you call Arnaud?"

"I have nothing to say."

"We will see. It is known to us that you sent the British officer, Roger, from St. Jorioz to an address in the South of France. I want to know the address to which you sent him."

"I have nothing to say."

"Again, we will see. It is also known to us that you obtained from a French traitor a day or two before your arrest the layout of the docks of the *Vieux port* of Marseille. As it is impossible that you could have had time to send this to England, I want to know the whereabouts of this document or the name of the person in whose possession it is."

"I have nothing to say."

"Lise, there is a parrot-like quality about your conversation that I find most irritating. Here again are the three questions. Where is Arnaud, where is Roger and where is the Marseille dock layout? I propose to give you one minute to provide the answers."

He looked at his wrist-watch. It was one of those watches with a complicated dial that gave its owner a lot of trivial information about the sub-divisions of eternity. From the busy streets below, Odette could hear the *staccato* trumpeting of motor horns, as urgent and as strident as the hunting horns of the English shires.

"Well, Lise, I would now like the answers to my questions."

"I have nothing to say."

"It is very foolish of you. We have means of making you talk."

"I am aware of your methods. Do you think we come to France from England without knowledge of the sort of thing you can do to us? You must give us credit for something, monsieur."

There was another man in the room now. He had come in silently and he was standing immediately behind her chair. He caught her arms and held them behind the back of the chair. The fair man who smelt of cold water and eau-de-Cologne stood up and walked over to her and began leisurely to unbutton her blouse. She said:

"I resent your hands on me or on my clothes. If you tell me what you want me to do and release one hand I will do it."

"As you wish. Unbutton your blouse."

She undid the two top buttons. The man behind her drew her blouse back so that the corrugations of her spine were bare. On the third vertebra, he laid a red-hot poker. Odette lurched forward. The fair young man's mouth moved and his voice came from a long way away.

"Where is Arnaud?"

"I have nothing to say."

"You are more than foolish." He opened his cigarette case, offered it to her and snapped a lighter. From it sprang a small sedate flame, like an altar candle. Dumbly Odette shook her head. He said, smiling, "It's quite all right. I can assure you that the cigarette isn't poisoned. If you look, you will see that I am smoking one myself. Did they tell you that in your school for amateurs in the New Forest, to beware of poisoned cigarettes? You know the three questions. Are you now prepared to answer them—after the hors d'œuvre or do you want the full meal?"

"I have nothing to say."

He came over to her and stood there, half smiling. The cold bath and eau-de-Cologne smell was apparent. He said to her: "Perhaps you would prefer to take off your shoes and stockings yourself. If not, I can assure you that I am well experienced in the mechanism of feminine suspenders."

"I will do it myself."

To be tortured by this clean, soap-smelling, scented Nordic was one thing. To be touched by his hands was another. She slid her feet out of her shoes and unrolled her stockings. The wooden floor was warm and rough to her naked feet. She automatically adjusted her skirt over her knees.

"My colleague here, Lise, is going to pull out your toenails one by one, starting at the little toe of your left foot. In between each evulsion —to use the correct medical term—I propose to repeat my questions. You can bring the ceremony to an end at any moment by answering these questions. There are those who faint after the third or fourth toenail, but I don't think you are of the fainting kind. If you do faint, we can always revive you with brandy and the ceremony will continue. Now, before we begin, where is Arnaud?"

. . . clamor meus ad te veniat . . . .

A man knelt at her feet. He was a young man, under thirty, very good-looking in a dark, Mediterranean handsomeness, and he glanced up at her with blind, brown eyes. He did not see her as a woman but only as a living, sensitive adjunct to a naked foot. His impersonality was terrifying. He took her left foot in his left hand and settled the steel jaws of the pincers tightly around the tip of her nail. Then with a slow, muscular drag, he began to pull. A semicircle of blood started to the quick, oozed over the skin, flooded after the retreating nail. . . . He shook the pincers and her nail fell on the floor.

"Now would you care to tell me Arnaud's address?"

She tried to say the word "no" but no sound came from her mouth. She shook her head. *Clamor meus ad te veniat. . . .*

The commissar nodded to the kneeling man and sat on the edge of the table, swinging his legs. The pincers clasped the next nail, gripped hard, were slowly drawn back. The enclosing flesh ripped and yielded in agonising pain as the nail was dragged out. . . . The reiterated questions flew round her head like wasps as the agony leapt from toe to toe, from foot to foot. She gave no cry. After an eternity, her torturer stood up, his pincers in his hands. He looked at the commissar, waiting

obsequiously for more orders. Odette gazed incredulously at the bloody
furnace of her feet and at the red litter on the floor, litter of a diabolical
chiropody. The sound of motor horns below sounded thin in the
sunny air and she was aware of a subsidiary ache in the palms of
her hands.

"Well, Lise, I think you will find it convenient to walk on your
heels for some time. Now I would like to offer you a drink. A glass of
wine, a little brandy—or, better still, a cup of tea." He smiled. "In
England, the country of your adoption, a cup of tea is the cure for all
evils. I will order you some tea. You are a woman of surprising
endurance."

Sitting on a wooden chair, her body quivering, she drank her tea.
He talked to her easily and she hardly heard a word he was saying.
She felt as if she were drowning in recurring waves of nausea and she
tried desperately to reach the shore. The nausea passed and the walls
of the room took shape again and became solid. She leaned back in her
chair and shut her eyes. Though her lacerated toes were ten separate
hubs of pain, she was conscious of a sudden stab of elation. She was
Odette and she had kept silence. Now she had an almost irresistible
urge to talk freely and to laugh and to gabble with her mouth, anything to make sounds with her tongue. And then she recognised this
sense of triumph for the danger that it was. This was how the Gestapo
wanted her to feel. Her sense of relief and of triumph could easily be a
better weapon to their hands than a pair of pincers. The commissar
watched her like a cat, as if aware of every thought process of her mind.
She opened her eyes and looked at him. Just as he saw her as a mere
nervous system, she now saw him not as a commissar of the Gestapo
nor even as a man. She saw him for what he was, a creature from whom
human pity and human understanding had been deliberately drained
and the hollow filled with blasphemy. He half smiled.

"Well," he said, "how do you feel?"

"I have nothing to say."

"Conversationally we are becoming a bore to each other. I keep on
asking the same questions and you keep on making the same replies.
No doubt you see yourself as a heroine at this moment and me as a
monster. I am not. I am a servant of my Führer, Adolf Hitler, and I
have no regret for what I do. You should know that I shall stop at
nothing to get the information I require. Last night the charming
R.A.F. dropped two thousand tons of bombs on Dortmund. I do
not know how many good German men, women and children were
killed or maimed or burned. If mass murder by the R.A.F. is considered

to be a legitimate act of war, do you think I care for the sufferings of a single, obstinate, renegade Frenchwoman?"

"I am interested to see, monsieur, that you consider it necessary to defend what you have just done."

"Nothing of the sort. We Germans have no need to excuse ourselves to subject races." He stood angrily over her. "Are you going to answer my questions?"

"No."

"Then I shall now cause to be done to your finger-tips the same operation that has just been carried out on your feet."

Odette stared at her hands and the living pink nails on her fingers and the quick of the nails. Then her eyes travelled down to the red pulp of her toes and her stomach turned over in sickness. She heard the door open and the sound of steps in the room. The young commissar sprang to attention and snapped:

"Zur Befehl, Herr Major."

Another man in civilian clothes walked to the table glancing casually at the bloody débris on the floor. He said: "Wer ist das Weib?"

"Frau Churchill." He spoke rapidly, deferentially, in German and the other man shrugged, answered shortly and walked out of the room. The Commissar said:

"The Major says that I am wasting my time and that you will never talk. He has a higher opinion of the endurance of the French than I have. I do not agree with him, but he has ordered that you be taken upstairs. You are a very fortunate woman, Lise. I have no doubt that we shall meet again. One more thing. If you speak about what has happened to a living soul, you will be brought here again and worse things will happen to you." He gave an order, and the dark man laid the pincers on the table and spoke for the first time. Holding the door open he said in what Odette knew instantly and with horror to be his native tongue:

"Permettez-moi, madame."

She gathered up her shoes and stockings and stumbled in agony to the door.

. . . . . .

Cell 108, Fresnes.

Odette feebly tore her prison cloth into strips and wet them and bound her feet. Then she leaned back on her bed and lay without moving. She could hear Michèle calling and calling. She wanted to go to the window and say that she was back and alive and she was sorry she had no potato, but she couldn't summon the physical strength to stir a muscle. The sun's rays turned from yellow to orange and greyness came into her cell. Sometime in the space between dusk and darkness, her door was unlocked and an S.S. woman brought a bowl of soup to her bedside. She was too weak to sit up and eat and it stayed on the floor untouched. Though she had kept silent, she was filled with sickness and fear for she had heard of some of the other things that the Gestapo could do to women's bodies and, alone in the darkness of Fresnes, she was afraid lest her strength might give way.

XIX

COLONEL BUCKMASTER TELLS THE STORY

from

SPECIALLY EMPLOYED

by Maurice Buckmaster

(Published by The Batchworth Press, London, 1952)

The great achievement of Colonel Buckmaster, head of the French Section of the War Office since its inception, was to organise and co-ordinate the subversive warfare in which Britain was engaged in Occupied France.

He had to start from scratch, in March 1941, with ten men in training for work in France, and there were never more than five hundred; but they were all hand-picked, both men and women, all of them accomplished linguists, quick-witted, reliable, courageous, trained in the subtle art of murder, sabotage and destruction.

Every one of the team was a volunteer, acting as British liaison officer between London and the members of the Resistance movement in France. Some of them were captured by the German counter-espionage service and subjected to fiendish tortures; some were executed; others died in the notorious concentration camps of Dachau, Buchenwald, Belsen and Ravensbrück. Colonel Buckmaster could do nothing for those of his agents who fell into the hands of the enemy. The story of Odette, also a member of the Buckmaster outfit, is told elsewhere in this book.

The following excerpt from the Colonel's book deals with adventures of Prosper, an agent sent to Paris in 1942, to organise sabotage acts against the Nazis in the French capital. He, too, was caught in the end and had to face the Nazi firing squad.

★

Not unnaturally, Paris was for us a most important centre and, obviously enough, a very difficult and dangerous place in which to work. In the summer of 1941, Lucas had established there some useful contacts, but for various reasons we were not satisfied that we had in these the wide connections that we needed. It was clearly essential to start up a new *réseau* there.

An ideal candidate was in training in the middle of 1942, one Prosper, a barrister of very high intelligence, whose knowledge of France was good and, more important still, whose personality was such as to create instant confidence in his powers of leadership.

Prosper was calm, conscientious and of a logical mind. It was a joy to brief him, so quick and thorough was his assimilation of the necessary facts. The whole of the Paris region was short of arms, for parachute deliveries could perforce only be made to the country areas well away from the suburbs, and we found that, in most cases, once the reception committee had taken delivery, it was extremely difficult to induce them to pass on their precious weapons to any other group. This was where Prosper's force of character showed itself. His decision was final, and, when he was established at the beginning of 1943, arms and ammunition began to flow to the different groups in a satisfactory manner. The greatest difficulty was thus overcome.

Prosper, equipped with identity papers describing him as a traveller in agricultural products, spent much of his time visiting farms in the Ile de France, generally accompanied by the courier Denise, whom we had assigned to him, and whose papers made her out to be his sister. If Denise did most of the talking (for Prosper could not conceal a very slight trace of British accent) that fact caused no comment in a society where the women have generally done all the bargaining. Denise was invaluable, she shunned no risk if she thought that by taking it the business would be done more quickly and effectively.

What a strange life for a man of Prosper's background. He was continually in danger of meeting someone who had known him when he lived in France before the war, someone whose joy at seeing him again might outrun discretion. Some members of his family were still living in the north, but he dared not let them know of his presence in France, for fear of their possibly over-enthusiastic welcome. This was, in fact, often a very serious risk for our men and women. So greatly coveted was the honour of being in touch with a British officer that it became sometimes a subject for idle boast with dire results. There was also the danger of denunciation by a Pétainiste, in whose mind the struggle between patriotism and obedience to the official head of the State produced turmoil which could only be exorcised by an open avowal.

The caretaker of a flat in Paris where Prosper was staying suffered from twinges of conscience: he had reason to suspect some of Prosper's activities and, although he had no proof, he deemed it wise to un-burden his soul to an acquaintance. The latter, frankly a collaborator, hastened to the *Feldkommandantur*.

One evening, as Prosper was returning to the flat, he noticed out of the corner of his eye a lurking form in front of the tobacconist's shop on the corner. Acting on the principle that needless risks should never be run, Prosper strolled unconcernedly past, never to return to the flat. Instead he found, with Denise's help, a lodging in a more humble part of the city.

At that time—the spring of 1943—Paris was rife with denunciations. You never knew if the young lady at the grocer's, who smiled so sweetly as she detached the coupon from your (imitation) ration book, was about to inform the security police of her suspicion as soon as your back was turned. A knock on the door in the evening set your heart thumping.

Prosper was as prudent as he possibly could be. But such prudence undeniably slowed down the work, and Prosper realised that he had much to accomplish, that he was working against time. Between the suspicious informers and the over-enthusiastic would-be colleagues (whose zeal he found misplaced) Prosper had to walk a tight-rope. He was continually on the move. If a parachute operation miscarried, he had generally to make inquiries on the spot as to the reason for failure. That involved questioning the reception committee, for if the lack of success was attributable to remissness on their part they would have to wait a long time for a second chance. If it was the fault of the pilot or due to mechanical trouble or bad weather, Prosper took it upon himself to reassure the doubters that the operation would soon be tried again.

Four months after his arrival in France, Prosper sent us a detailed report. He had built up excellent relationships with the big Parisian resistance groups, and the co-ordination of their activities was far advanced. Most of the parachute operations for which he had asked had been carried out successfully. Between Beauvais and Tours, and between Chartres and Melun, he had formed dozens of small groups, totalling perhaps ten thousand men and women (for the most part, of course, unarmed as yet), who welcomed his assistance with gratitude and relied on his radio link with London. The moment had come, Prosper added, to show the boys what we had in mind as regards sabotage.

At that time, stocks of petrol were considered as targets of high priority. The R.A.F. were continually attacking petrol dumps in Germany. Prosper proposed to carry on the good work in France.

St. Ouen l'Aumonier provided an excellent target. Here, large stores of petrol were very lightly guarded and seemed to offer a remunerative objective. But it is extremely difficult to destroy petrol in bulk. You don't do it by dropping a match and running. Prosper had had instruction in the art of destroying petrol in bulk and he therefore insisted that he should personally carry out this operation.

We told him he might do so, exceptionally.

A fortnight later we received his report in London. According to the report the whole operation was "perfectly simple," but such phrases as "I was obliged to seize and silence a German guard" or "When the alarm was given we felt very naked lying on the railway track between the wagons," made us realise that Prosper was toning down the risk for our benefit.

Railway cranes, turntables, locomotive depots and shunting points were the next objectives. German morale fell as that of the Prosper groups rose. As early as April 1943, the rumour ran like wildfire that the Allies were about to land in France. The patriotic upsurge of enthusiasm was dangerous. It had to be quelled. Prosper himself did not know whether the rumour was founded on fact or not. For reasons of security, we could not tell him by radio.

We decided that we must bring Prosper back to London.

A Lysander fetched him, without incident. Indeed the whole operation seemed ridiculously simple. Within two and a half hours of the machine taking off from an aerodrome in the South of England on the way out, I saw its cheerfully flashing signal as it came in to land: "Mission accomplished." Two minutes later I was shaking Prosper's hand.

His detailed report was extremely encouraging. It was clear that the Allies, when they landed, would be assured of magnificent support from French patriots. But the Allies were not ready to return to the Continent in the summer of 1943, as so many Frenchmen confidently hoped. The fires of enthusiasm would have to be damped down, without, however, being extinguished. Only a first-class man like Prosper could convey that message successfully. Prosper would have to return as soon as possible.

Indeed, after a week in England, he was begging us to let him pursue his mission, for he realised that each day's delay was dangerous. Within ten days he was back in Paris, on June 20th, 1943. His radio operator announced his safe arrival. And then there was silence. We became uneasy, and finally desperate. Not for several months did we learn just what had happened.

Prosper, returning from a parachute operation which had taken place near Pontoise, had been arrested at the Gare St. Lazare in Paris. He had been searched and held on a vague suspicion. Finally he had been confronted by another officer of the service, previously arrested. A very intelligent corporal of the German security police penetrated the secret.

The Germans were mightily pleased at the arrest of Prosper. They allowed themselves to crow a little too loudly, for they boasted that, with his arrest, there remained no "Buchmeister [sic] boys" in France. . . . They were only wrong to the extent of some hundred and fifty officers and thirty-five different réseaux.

Denise, also, was arrested, but, through the complicity of a French wardress, managed to get information to us about herself and Prosper. Both of them were taken to Germany, and both were shot, in 1945, shortly before the prison camp was liberated.

In the forest of Fontainebleau stands today a monument in souvenir of the members of Prosper's groups who lost their lives. It is sited on the ground where the first parachute operation for the Paris region was organised by Prosper in 1942. His loss was very grievous. We missed him sorely, for his judgment, his enthusiasm and his capacity for leadership were quite irreplaceable.

XX

THE TRAITOR OF ARNHEM

from

SPY CATCHER

by Lieutenant-Colonel Oreste Pinto
(Published by Werner Laurie, London, 1952)

Lieutenant-Colonel Pinto's chief preoccupation has always been the catching of spies. During the last war, when he was head of the Dutch intelligence service, he had the satisfaction of running to earth a heavy bag of Nazi spies; some of them were small fry but some were really big fish.

The biggest fish he ever caught was Lindemans, the traitor of Arnhem, known to members of the Dutch underground as King Kong. The disaster of Arnhem, in which thousands of British and Allied soldiers perished, was entirely due to the treachery of Lindemans, and to have laid his hands on him, albeit belatedly, was solely to the credit of the astute Netherlands colonel.

Oddly enough, at a time when spies were summarily executed on capture, Lindemans eluded the firing squad, due to certain machinations which are still shrouded in mystery. One explanation that has been given is that Lindemans, considered a hero at the time of his capture, could not have been shot without causing a tremendous stir in Holland, though he fully confessed his betrayal. Some attempts were made, in fact, to whitewash him. Lindemans was found dead in his cell eighteen months after his capture, having committed suicide two days before his trial.

Colonel Pinto claims that the world has never learned the full extent of Lindemans's treachery, as a result of which seven thousand gallant "Red Devils" lost their lives. In Spy Catcher he relates how, following up a first intuition, he managed, step by step, to get King Kong into his net. The excerpt we have selected describes the actual capture of the traitor.

★

Meanwhile, although I was very busy on other cases, I had not shelved the Lindemans case. The report which I had sent up to S.H.A.E.F. had no doubt been neatly filed in a pigeonhole somewhere in that enormous headquarters. The intelligence branch had many different problems to consider and this would only be one of them. In any case, most senior officers who had to rely for their information on what was reported to them on paper would be likely to dismiss my suspicions as being utterly fantastic. To accuse the famous Resistance leader of one of our Allies of being a traitor was not only absurd but was really in doubtful taste. Such a charge could easily have serious political and diplomatic repercussions. No soldier likes to be mixed up in politics or diplomacy in the middle of the greatest war yet known to mankind. All his instincts would be on the side of shelving such a nasty problem, if he could be persuaded for one moment to believe in the gravity of the charges. So nothing further occurred. Whenever I met my opposite number in the British Counter-Intelligence attached to S.H.A.E.F., a brilliant man who has subsequently occupied some of the most important political positions in the land, I tackled him on the subject of Lindemans. He was always courteous but I could see that he was not impressed with my deductions. If such a clever man with direct experience of counter-intelligence work felt no confidence in my claims, it was all the less likely that the "chair-borne" officers in S.H.A.E.F. with many diverse problems of immediate urgency to overcome would follow up my suggestions.

So for six weeks no results came from my efforts to have Lindemans arrested. Thus far there was no absolute evidence of his guilt but only circumstantial evidence supported by deductions. Then one evening the additional proof arrived dramatically. The Allied advance had continued, although since the tragic failure of Arnhem the armies had had to fight for every foot of ground they gained. I was in Eindhoven, which had now been taken, and was just concluding an interrogation which had lasted for nearly three hours. I had by this time been denuded of my assistants and also of my personal transport. I was working alone and had to act as interrogator, judge and jailer where my suspect was concerned.

He was a young Dutchman named Cornelis Verloop. I had finally trapped him into admitting he was a spy. He was at his wit's end with fear.

I stood up and stretched myself, dusting cigarette ash off my uniform. He watched me closely.

"Am I to be shot?" he whispered. His throat was too dry to allow him to speak normally.

I shrugged without answering. It seemed obvious that he was going to be shot. He was a spy.

."I have a young wife in Amsterdam, sir, a good Dutch girl. She is innocent, I swear it."

"So? We do not propose to shoot your wife. We are not like your German masters."

Desperately he tried another tack. "I will give you valuable information, sir—in return for my life."

"You fool," I said. "Any information you have can be extracted from you before you are shot. It is a simple and painless process."

He gave a wan but sly smile. "You can make me tell what you think I should know but you cannot find out those facts which you do not suspect I know."

"Well, my young philosopher, what do you know?" There was an edge of contempt to my tone.

Verloop leaned forward eagerly and, squeezing his fists together to aid his memory, recited the names and descriptions of all my intelligence headquarters staff. Even many G.H.Q. staff officers did not know the identities of some of the men whose names Verloop rattled off.

"Also, your chief agent in Brussels is Paul Leuven and in Amsterdam a man named Dampreny, and . . ." He sat there at the table and glibly recited the main network of our counter-espionage system in Belgium and the Netherlands.

I was worried for the sake of those agents still behind the German lines. If this traitor knew so much, then perhaps his masters knew more. I kept my voice level and asked in as casual a tone as I could muster. "Who told you all this?"

He was alert, hope was beginning to trickle back into his veins. "Colonel Kiesewetter of the Abwehr told me. In the Abwehr headquarters at Driebergen. But who told Colonel Kiesewetter is my secret. Do you wish to make a bargain, sir?"

I was tired and for the moment sick to death of the human degradation confronting me. I had seen many men fight for their lives like cornered rats, prepared to sacrifice employers, country or friends to save their own skins, but somehow I could not stomach this last case of sordid bargaining. Having no assistants and no transport, I had to march Verloop back in person to the military prison at the other end of the town. The night was dark and I did not want him to make a break for his life on the journey. So I drew my pistol and looking at him balefully, said, "Come along, Verloop. I have had enough of your scheming. You are a traitor and you are not going to add to your treachery by bargaining with me. Your Nazi friends made the rules for this game. I didn't. So let us play the game their way. Who told those facts to Colonel Kiesewetter?"

The hopeful smile faded. "In exchange for my life, sir. . . ." He made a despairing gesture.

I jerked the pistol forward. "Get up." A night of wakeful thought in jail would soon bring him to his senses.

But Verloop, that astute spy, misread my gesture. He thought I was about to shoot him. "Wait," he gasped, "I'll tell you. Don't shoot! It was Chris Lindemans—King Kong. He told Colonel Kiesewetter."

So here, unexpectedly, was the last link that made my chain of

evidence against Lindemans complete. I leaned forward and prodded
Verloop with the muzzle of my pistol. He went white with fear and
gulped. "Did King Kong betray Arnhem to the Nazis?" I asked.

Verloop nodded. He could not speak until he had slipped his tongue
over his dry lips and then the words came tumbling from him. "Yes,
he told Colonel Kiesewetter on September 15th, when he called at
Abwehr headquarters. He said that British and American troops were
to be dropped."

"Did he say where?"

"Ja. He said that a British airborne division was waiting to be dropped
on Sunday morning beyond Eindhoven."

I lowered my pistol-hand and looked thoughtfully at Verloop. It
seemed certain that this miserable coward had pushed the last piece of
my jigsaw puzzle into place. He misunderstood the pause and falling
on his knees said, "You won't shoot me now, will you? I've told you
what I know."

"I won't shoot you myself," I said, "but I can't speak for the Army.
A court-martial will decide your fate. Now stand up and let's go."

My years of training in counter-espionage work had taught me that
giving vent to personal emotions could be a dangerous luxury. But for
once I could not control myself. I trembled with a white-hot anger that
left me speechless for the moment. Notwithstanding my frequent
warnings, King Kong had been allowed to go on a secret mission
behind the enemy lines where he could do most damage to the Allied
cause. Before I had only suspected the truth. Now I knew it, thanks to
the shameless traitor Verloop. Nothing could undo the tragedy of
Arnhem but at least a summary end could be put to Lindemans's
treachery.

Once Verloop was safely in his prison cell, I rushed, still seething
with rage, to Dutch Intelligence Headquarters. I burst into the officers'
mess. The sight of my fellow countrymen, lolling in their soft arm-
chairs with drinks in their hands, listening to some hurdy-gurdy tune
on the radio, made my anger leap to its full tension. I stood there,
speechless with fury.

One of my acquaintances looked round. "What's up, Pinto?" he
asked. "You look as white as a sheet."

That mild inquiry did it. My anger boiled over. "Turn that damned
thing off!" I shouted. I crashed my fist on the table and, as the
radio crackled into silence, they all looked at me in surprise. For a
second I hated those open-mouthed moon-faces turned to mine in
astonishment.

"God damn it!" I roared. "It's high time you lot realised that when

I say a man is a suspect, I mean it. And what do you do? Straight away
you send him behind the enemy lines with the most vital message of
the war!"

"What do you mean?" someone blurted out.

"Lindemans—King Kong. Two of you will go by car to Castle
Wittouck at once and arrest him."

"Arrest Lindemans—you must be crazy! Why, with his bare hands
he could smash a couple of men like rag dolls. Besides, he's always
armed to the teeth. It would be sheer suicide."

One of the senior officers spoke. "In any case, Pinto, what are your
grounds for arresting Lindemans? Do you realise the public scandal
there would be?"

Rapidly I gave my reasons. Something in my manner must have
shown them my sincerity. But there still remained the problem of
carrying out the arrest without risking the lives of the escort. And then,
as sometimes happens when one is keyed up with excitement, the
answer came to me in a flash.

"I have it," I cried. "Two of you—you and you—will go to Castle
Wittouck and interview Lindemans. Tell him he is to be decorated for
his gallant services. That should appeal to his colossal ego. Persuade
him to disarm, put on a clean shirt and brush his hair. Then take him
into a private room. In the meantime I will have sent a message by
teleprinter to S.H.A.E.F. asking for ten military policemen to be sent to
the castle. When Lindemans enters the room they will overpower him
and arrest him. Understood?"

The two officers I had selected grinned and got to their feet.
"Fair enough," one said as he buckled on his pistol-belt. "I hope ten
will be enough for him. Tell S.H.A.E.F. to pick the biggest they've
got."

That was the plan—and it worked. As I had suspected, King Kong's
vanity was easily assailed. As soon as he heard that he was to be
"decorated," lamblike he allowed himself to be shorn of his weapons
and, having smartened himself up, was shepherded to a private room
set aside for the purpose.

Then, swaggering into the private room ahead of his "guard of
honour," King Kong advanced to receive his award. It arrived in the
shape of the ten military policemen who overwhelmed him and, after
a struggle, secured him. There were no handcuffs in Holland big
enough to clamp round his mighty wrists so instead his arms were
lashed with steel-cored rope. When he was brought on to the R.A.F.
airfield at Antwerp I ordered his legs to be bound as well. It was just
possible that with the brute strength in his legs he could smash a hole

through the thin walls of the aircraft and to plunge to his death from mid-air might be a spectacular last gesture that would appeal to the vanity of King Kong.

When the aircraft touched down in England, Lindemans was rushed to a private country house outside London. It was staffed by the British Counter-Intelligence whose interrogators were possibly the most skilled in the world at extracting a full confession without resorting to any form of physical torture. They were expert at assessing the psychological strength and weakness of their suspects and at breaking down the mental obstacles that held back the truth. For two weeks they kept Lindemans under cross-examination. When he was flown back to Holland, this time pinioned with a pair of Scotland Yard's special adjustable ratchet handcuffs, and lodged in Breda Prison, I escorted him to his cell. I looked at him carefully. Gone was the swagger and the truculence, but there was not a bruise nor a wound on his massive body, no puncture marks where a hypodermic needle had been plunged in. His eyes were lowered but there were no tell-tale signs around them to show that he had been violently frightened or kept awake for days on end. But with him came a full and detailed confession covering twenty-four pages of closely typed foolscap. Without resorting to any kind of torture the experts had sucked King Kong's mind dry of all the self-incriminating facts it contained.

I took the top-secret confession to my office and sat down to study it. It was more exciting than any detective story and it was satisfying to read the confirmation of much guess-work and deduction. The story of Lindemans's treachery began in 1943 when he was at the height of his fame as a Resistance leader of the Dutch Interior Forces. He had always been promiscuous in his sexual tastes and with it vastly extravagant. Running short of funds for lavishing presents on his numerous girl friends, he hit on an ingenious method for supplying his private exchequer. He persuaded rich women, some of them physically attracted by him, to part with their best jewels to provide fighting funds for the "underground" escape route through Belgium and Holland into Occupied France and thence into Portugal. Many of these women whose friends and relatives were only too often languishing in Nazi concentration camps and whose fine houses were billeting German officers were eager to oblige the romantic Resistance hero.

Lindemans had sold many of the jewels thus collected but the proceeds never augmented the Resistance funds. They were spent in taverns and night clubs in drunken orgies and in buying the favours of girls whose virtue needed dazzling with gold before they would agree to endure the bear-like caresses of the great man. Those jewels which he did not sell he gave away to his mistresses, boasting that they were part of the loot he had taken from the Nazis by force.

Thus far Lindemans had descended to embezzling but he was still an honest man where his country was concerned. Yet although he may not have realised it he was driving down a one-way route. Sooner or later he would have to account for the jewels he had embezzled, unless he could make sufficient money by other means to pay their value into Resistance funds. Already one or two of the other Resistance leaders were growing suspicious of his extravagant way of living. It was not an easy matter in Occupied Europe to acquire large sums of money suddenly by any honest means and Lindemans began to wonder how he could set about making good his fraud without giving up the extravagance he loved.

Then in February, 1944, an event occurred which must have precipitated the crisis. His youngest brother and a French cabaret dancer named Veronica were captured by the Gestapo in a raid on a house which was a hostel on the secret escape route. In an amorous career which featured hundreds of girls, sometimes as many as three or four during the one orgy, she had been the only constant factor. However often he strayed, he always returned to her in the end. If there were room in Lindemans's massive frame for love of anyone but himself, then Veronica occupied that place.

One of the worst moments in any man's life is to know that his dearest friends are in the hands of torturers like the Nazis and, worse, that he can do nothing to rescue them. But it happened every day to one Resistance man or the other. All they could do was to clench their teeth and go about their job of revenge with a savage coolness. The good Resistance man could not indulge his feelings by a reckless and desperate gesture which might risk the lives of even more of his friends and relatives.

But after ten days Lindemans proved to be weaker in moral calibre than his lesser-known colleagues. Frantic with worry over the fate of Veronica and his brother and sensing the growing suspicions of other Resistance leaders who were beginning to wonder aloud about the fate of the jewels and money entrusted to him, Lindemans decided to make a deal with the enemy. He knew two Dutchmen living in Brussels who were in the pay of the Nazis. One was Anthony Damen, the other Cornelis Verloop, my "friend" of Eindhoven. He arranged to meet them privately in the café of the Hotel des Grands Boulevards on the Place Rogier in Brussels. There, over a cup of coffee, Lindemans offered his services to the Nazis on two conditions: one, the instant release of Veronica and his youngest brother; two, big money payments. Verloop went off at once to discuss the matter with Colonel Giskes, then head of the German Abwehr. Giskes must have realised that here was a golden opportunity of exchanging two minnows for a whale. Two days later he met Lindemans secretly in a house in the suburbs of Brussels where they talked together for a long time.

The bargain was sealed and next day the Germans kept their end of it. Veronica and the youngest Lindemans were pulled out of their dark, damp cells, made to sign certificates to the effect that they had been well treated and were then thrust to freedom in the spring sunlight of the Rotterdam streets. Their joy at the unexpected release could not have been marred by any foreknowledge that this was the first step in a series of events which culminated a few months afterwards in the deaths through disease and famine of twenty-five thousand citizens of Rotterdam in the terrible "black winter" of Holland.

King Kong, having taken the decisive step into infamy, revelled for a time in the immediate results. He spent the first instalments of his traitor's pay in a new burst of revelry, drinking, wenching and fighting tavern brawls with more zest then ever before.

But, as I had suspected during my earlier investigations into his career, his employers, the Abwehr (the German Intelligence), either through a sense of rivalry or because they dared not spread the news too wide, had failed to inform the other security branches, the Gestapo and the security police, that Lindemans was now in their pay. One day the security police raided another Rotterdam Resistance headquarters. They burst into the cellar with guns levelled. Lindemans was among the Resistance men there!

It was a bad moment for him. He could either give himself away as a traitor in the full view of his Dutch comrades or else risk sudden death at the hands of the S.D. police. He hesitated for a second and then took the coward's choice. He moved one hand in a certain secret gesture to let the S.D. men know that he was on their side. But before their commander could rasp out the order for his men to avert their rifles, one of them misinterpreted the gesture. Already "trigger-happy" at the great bulk and fierce appearance of King Kong, he thought that the big man was reaching for a revolver. He fired and the bullet hit King Kong in the chest, piercing one lung.

He was rushed off to a Gestapo hospital for the S.D. commander realised that here was no ordinary Resistance man. The wound would have proved fatal to many humans of average physique but the jungle strength of King Kong brought him through the crisis into convalescence within three weeks. The head of the Abwehr visited him in hospital to make plans for him to "escape" and return to his own side where he could continue to be a valuable agent of the Abwehr. The idea was to arrange a plausible "escape" but Lindemans himself had an ingeniously savage suggestion which made even the hard-headed colonel gape. It was Lindemans himself who suggested that his own Resistance men should attempt the rescue, so that they would walk into an ambush and be killed while he got away. The plan was put into effect and unluckily worked only too well. Forty-seven of his gallant colleagues gave up their lives to rescue their treacherous leader.

For the next few months Lindemans earned his German pay by betraying several groups of agents. One such British group, which included women as well as men, had been working in the part of Belgium still occupied by the Germans. They were arrested, flung into Scheveningen Prison and there suffered exquisite agony until death mercifully ended their torture. Scheveningen Prison near The Hague contained weirdly ingenious instruments of torture of modern design, beside which the medieval thumbscrew and rack seemed like play-things. There were, for example, steel helmets which were screwed down over the victim's head and eye-balls and then electrified, so that the shock would pierce most keenly to the very nerve-centres of the head. When the Germans evacuated the prison they were in too much of a hurry to remove these damning signs of their vicious ingenuity. When I first saw their instruments of torture, contraptions which any sane men could hardly imagine, let alone manufacture and use, my blood ran cold at the sight. And yet Lindemans, who could not bear to think of his brother and girl friend being in German hands, cheerfully betrayed whole groups of agents for cash. When I read the list of names, many of whom were known to me and some indeed being my great friends, I vowed that I should not rest until Lindemans had met his deserts.

The climax of his confession was, of course, the betrayal of Arnhem. When he was attached to the Canadian First Army and given the job of alerting the Resistance movement in the Eindhoven area so that they could aid the forthcoming airborne landings, he realised at once that this was a golden opportunity for bigger and better treachery. He completed his Eindhoven mission—not without difficulty for the local Resistance leader was suspicious of him and had him arrested. In fact, with supreme irony, as it turned out, the Canadians had to send an intelligence officer to "bail out" Lindemans and vouch for his integrity before the Eindhoven Resistance men would listen to his proposals. Even this setback did not deter him from his traitorous course. He met Colonel Kiesewetter of the Abwehr at Driebergen on September 15th, two days before the landings were to take place, and told him all the secret facts with which he had been entrusted. It is true that Lindemans did not mention the word "Arnhem." A certain section of the Dutch Press subsequently tried to make much of this and claimed that Lindemans could not have betrayed Arnhem because he did not know the exact area of the landings.

This argument is puerile nonsense. Lindemans may not have mentioned the actual name of Arnhem but he did tell Colonel Kiesewetter that the landings were to take place north of Eindhoven. He said as much in his signed confession. Now every large-scale parachute landing, as any amateur tactician should know, is made with the object of seizing some vital area and holding it for a limited length of time. Paratroops, the *élite* of the Army, are too valuable to be scattered aimlessly over the countryside in penny packets. One glance at the map would suffice to tell the German military experts what points these airborne troops would be concentrated on "north of Eindhoven." There was no valuable objective in the open fields. No! the obvious targets were the bridges at Grave, Nijmegen and Arnhem. If these could be seized and held long enough for the main body to link up with the paratroops, then a dangerous bridgehead aimed at the heart of Germany would be developed.

So Lindemans's infamy can never be whitewashed. When he told Colonel Kiesewetter of the top-secret plan to land airborne forces "north of Eindhoven" in two days' time, he betrayed the Battle of Arnhem.

XXI

THE CRIME OF THE CENTURY

from

THE CRIME OF THE CENTURY

by J. EDGAR HOOVER

(Published in the *Reader's Digest*, 1951)

In this thrilling account J. Edgar Hoover, of F.B.I. fame, reveals the case histories of Klaus Emil Julius Fuchs and Harry Gold, condensed from the secret files of the Federal Bureau of Investigation, of which he has been the head for a number of years.

He reconstructs with consummate skill the first meeting between Fuchs and Harry Gold at a street corner on New York City's lower East Side, and then goes on to give a step-by-step account of subsequent developments that eventually led to the apprehension and arrest of Harry Gold.

★

LONG afterwards the Federal Bureau of Investigation learned that the basic facts of nuclear fission had been stolen. The source of that disheartening discovery cannot be told; security and human lives are involved. The most that I can say is that conclusive information was laid on my desk—*the secrets of atom-bomb construction had been acquired by a foreign power.* It was the responsibility of the F.B.I. to find the guilty men; to this end we immediately mobilised every resource known to us.

When we started, we had no reason to suspect Dr. Fuchs. Investigation at home and abroad, however, led us to the conclusion that the inside man was most probably a trusted member of a foreign scientific group. Day by day, as our researches continued, the finger of suspicion pointed more and more directly at a shy, brilliant young physicist and mathematician, Klaus Fuchs. Careful as he had been, he had left some clues in the United States—clues which cannot be disclosed but which were to betray him. In time we became certain that, after fleeing from the totalitarian fury of Hitlerite Germany, this son of a minister had accepted the hospitality and shelter of English democracy and then, with cynical disdain, had stolen the free world's most important secrets to aid a still greater tyranny than Hitler's, that of the U.S.S.R.

By this time Fuchs had returned to England, where he was stationed at Harwell, the atomic-research plant. Data developed by the F.B.I. about him was promptly given to the English authorities, and under the direction of the very competent Sir Percy Sillitoe, British security officials took up the investigation.

By January 1950 Fuchs was identified beyond all reasonable doubt as the principal culprit. After prolonged interviews he confessed. But with his confession we realised that our real search had just begun. For Fuchs, while indicting himself, implicated no one else by name.

He admitted to English officials that, in the years before Hitler's rise to power in Germany, he had been a member of the German Communist Party and had engaged in underground work. After entering atomic research in England he had, on his own initiative, approached the Soviet espionage apparatus and had volunteered to furnish information. He had been in touch with several agents in England prior to his arrival in America and, after his return to the British Isles, he had continued to give secret information to the Communists until early 1949.

Dr. Fuchs disclosed that while in the United States he had dealt with one Soviet agent only. The man's name? Fuchs had never known the agent's name. The man appeared to know chemistry and engineering but was not a nuclear physicist. Fuchs thought he was probably not an employee of an atomic-energy installation.

What did the man look like? Well, he was from forty to forty-five years of age, possibly five feet ten inches tall, broad built, round face, most probably a first-generation American. A description which might fit millions of men!

Where did he live? Dr. Fuchs had never known. Fuchs had carried a tennis ball to their first rendezvous and met a man with a pair of gloves and a book with a green binding. How many times had he met this person? Several times in New York City, once in Cambridge, Massachusetts, and twice in Santa Fé, New Mexico. When? The New York meetings were in 1944; the last contact, Fuchs believed, was in the autumn of 1945. That was about all he could tell.

A flimsy fabric from which to find the identity of a spy who remained at large in the United States, obedient to the Soviets!

.   .   .   .   .

In all the history of the F.B.I. there was never a more important problem than this one, never another case where we felt under such pressure. The unknown man simply had to be found. And the job was all the more difficult because of the necessity for absolute secrecy; only a few top American officials shared with me the full details and widespread ramifications of the investigation. I doubt whether it will ever be possible to disclose publicly all the factors involved.

But the time has arrived to tell what can be released without violating security or needlessly placing human lives in jeopardy.

At the start, the quest was utterly unlike the pursuit of a bank robber who had left fingerprints on a safe door; unlike the investigations of a "hot car" ring where photographs, detailed identifying descriptions and long criminal records often facilitate the job. In this man-hunt the wanted person could be almost any man in the United States.

Our starting place was Cambridge, because Fuchs had admitted meeting the agent there, and because it was the home of Fuchs's sister, Mrs. Kristel Heineman. We already knew that the scientist had visited her there. Did Mrs. Heineman know anything about the agent Fuchs had mentioned?

Well, Mrs. Heineman recalled a man about forty years old, stocky and with dark-brown hair, who had called at her home three times. On his first visit he had introduced himself as a friend of her brother, and said he was a chemist. He said he had worked with Dr. Fuchs and was anxious to see him. (This was at the time Fuchs disappeared from New York.) She could not remember his name. No, he had no accent.

The second call occurred when Fuchs was visiting the Heinemans after Christmas. It was clear to the sister that the two men had met before when they greeted each other in her living-room, but though present in the room a part of the time, she had not followed their conversation. When the visitor left, her brother told her nothing. The Heineman children liked him, however—he brought them sweets.

Some time later—a few weeks or months—the unknown had again appeared at the Heineman house, and had stayed for lunch. Mrs. Heineman thought he might have mentioned that he had a wife and two small children.

The shadow seemed to be taking a semblance of form—a man of about forty, stocky, with dark-brown hair; a chemist; a friendly, genial man who liked children; he was probably married with youngsters of his own; he talked without an accent. Part of this, as you see, was right, and part of it was very wrong.

Robert Heineman, Kristel's husband, offered some more details— he had seen the stranger at the time of the third visit, having come home from his classes at Harvard for lunch. He recalled that the visitor had mentioned Philadelphia, and he was of the opinion that the man had arrived in Boston by train.

Another avenue opened: a friend of the Heineman family, who had been present during one of the visits, remembered that the man discussed vitamins. From this conversation he obtained the impression that the stranger was a bacteriologist, perhaps connected in some way with a New York wholesale grocery company.

And then Mrs. Heineman recalled that on the third visit the stranger had promised her son a chemistry set. The youngster, then aged six, now eleven, was questioned by his father, but he could remember nothing. Nor could his little sister.

Suddenly Mr. Heineman remembered another clue. He thought the stranger's first name might have been "James," with his last name starting with the letters, let us say, "D-a-v." "James Dav . . ."—that was the best that Mr. Heineman could recollect.

. . . . . .

Was there a "James Dav . . ." in New York City, Santa Fé or Philadelphia, possible residential districts for the shadow? As a starting point on this lead, the F.B.I. undertook to sift its own files, a tedious and time-consuming process, but no possibility could be overlooked.

Soon, during this file check, one name stood out above all others— an individual whom we shall call James Davidson, an engineer residing in New York City. He met the general physical and background requirements, and his employment records showed that he was absent from his job during Fuchs's visit to Cambridge. Moreover, James Davidson could have been available at other meetings.

A group of photographs was flown to England and laid before Dr. Fuchs in Wormwood Scrubs Prison. These were photographs of many different individuals, each a possible suspect.

Dr. Fuchs rejected all except one—a picture of the man we call James Davidson.

He examined that photograph for a long while, his delicate fingers tapping the table, his forehead wrinkling in deep furrows. "There is something familiar about this man," he murmured, then covered the forehead of the picture to simulate a hat, and added, "I cannot swear, but I am pretty sure this is the man. "

The interrogator requested the German scientist to try to visualise his American contact, just as he saw him at their first meeting in Manhattan, then look again at the photograph. Fuchs complied, staring long and hard. Then he nodded his head and said again: "I think it is the man."

But, obviously, no investigation can be allowed to rest exclusively on evidence of this nature. There had to be corroboration; the charges were too serious for any possibility of error. The next persons to be shown the pictures would be the Heinemans in Cambridge. If they, too, should happen to select Davidson's photograph from the others, Fuchs's identification would be greatly strengthened.

The Heinemans looked carefully at the pictures, then shook their heads. No, they had never seen any of these men before. Later, Robert Heineman was given an opportunity to observe the real James Davidson in person, a test far more accurate than a photograph. And now he was even more positive that James Davidson had never visited his home.

Who was right—Fuchs or his sister and brother-in-law?

For the very same reasons that Davidson could not be arrested on the basis of Fuchs's identification, he could not now be dismissed on the Heinemans' rejections. The investigation still had a long way to go.

Since Fuchs and the Heinemans seemed fairly certain that Fuchs's contact had been a chemist, the F.B.I. had immediately instituted a systematic review of all Bureau cases in which chemists had been involved. In our Washington headquarters and in each of our fifty-two field offices we were looking for a chemist who would possess the other identifying factors.

Soon we had numerous suspects, some tallying in virtually all the identifying details, others in some of them, and a few in only one item. Each was thoroughly considered, and more and more photographs were shown to the Heinemans in Cambridge, then flown across the Atlantic for Dr. Fuchs to observe.

In some photographs the Heinemans saw familiar characteristics; Dr. Fuchs saw familiar points in others. But nowhere, among the fifteen hundred-odd photographs which were exhibited to them, did the Heinemans feel they saw the face of the man who had called at their home. Thus far, only in Fuchs's tentative identification of James Davidson had any recognition been obtained.

By now the F.B.I.'s investigation was many-pronged. Here are some of the forms it took:

Agents set out to talk with all the tenants who had lived in the New York City apartment house at 128 West 77th Street when Fuchs was a resident there. Naturally, the years had scattered many of them into distant places, but they were found and interviewed. But could any of them furnish any information? No!

Former members of the British Mission and former employees of the Manhattan Engineer Project were also interviewed. All remembered Fuchs as a brilliant scientist, not given to social mixing or chatty conversation—and they knew nothing important about his friends. Did they know or suspect anything about his espionage activities? Nothing! Not a thing. In fact, Fuchs's arrest had been deeply shocking.

In Santa Fé agents made inquiries at bus, air-travel and railway ticket offices. Hotel registrations were analysed. But no information appeared which seemed to tie in with any suspects.

Could the chemical laboratories in New York City offer any leads? As an indication of the scope of such an undertaking, seventy-five thousand licensing permits had been issued to chemical firms by the city of New York in 1945 alone.

The principal result of these widespread inquiries was definitely to eliminate James Davidson as a suspect. Undoubtedly, Davidson had had some association with Communist activities, but we knew from some of the evidence on him that he could not have been Fuchs's accomplice.

There was also a long-term benefit: we had gathered masses of new background material about Communist affairs. Such data, now a part of the F.B.I.'s files, will remain as a valuable reserve for future investigations.

And meanwhile we were coming closer to our man. As suspect after suspect was eliminated, the field had narrowed from fifteen hundred possibilities to only about a score. And in this final handful one suspect was beginning to stand out. He was around forty, brown-haired and stocky, while not a first-generation American, he had come to the United States as a small child and might easily be mistaken for a native. He was a chemist, he lived in Philadelphia and he had taken many trips to New York City.

His name was Harry Gold.

However, there were points of discrepancy. Gold was single; the Heinemans thought the stranger was married and had children. Mr. Heineman believed the chemist's name had been "James Dav . . ."; this in no way sounded like "Harry Gold."

Nevertheless, for one important reason, we began to concentrate on this man. The reason was that in 1947 the F.B.I. had found it necessary, in a different Communist inquiry, to question him.

Harry Gold first came to the attention of the F.B.I. in May 1947, as the result of an F.B.I. interview with one Abraham Brothman, a chemical engineer in New York City. The investigation of Brothman had grown out of information furnished by Miss Elizabeth T. Bentley —self-confessed Communist courier—which indicated a relationship between Brothman and Jacob Golos, a known New York Communist who was a Soviet spy master in 1940.

During approximately ten meetings with Brothman during the summer and autumn of 1940, Brothman had furnished Miss Bentley with blueprints of various chemical processes, which she transmitted to

Golos. Some time in the autumn of 1940 Golos told Miss Bentley that he was becoming disgusted with Brothman and was turning him over to a new courier. Brothman told the F.B.I., during his 1947 interview, that Miss Bentley—whom he knew only as "Helen"—was succeeded by Harry Gold.

It happened that, in 1947, Gold was working as a chemist in Brothman's Long Island laboratory. So Gold was interviewed. He candidly admitted that he had been introduced to Golos in October 1940, during a meeting of the American Chemical Society at the Franklin Institute in Philadelphia. After the meeting Golos confided to Gold that he had connections with Abraham Brothman, who occasionally turned over to him certain types of blueprints in the chemical field. Golos proposed that Gold pick up these blueprints from Brothman and analyse them from a chemist's point of view.

Gold said he had agreed, and that several days later he had telephoned Brothman for an appointment. Each time they met, he said, Brothman furnished more plans, more blueprints, more information about chemical processes, which, however, Golos never bothered to pick up. Gold claimed he had later destroyed the various papers. Anyway, Gold and Brothman insisted these were all simple and legitimate transactions. And when our agents interviewed Gold in 1947 Golos was already dead, so there was no one to contradict the story.

Later in 1947 Gold had been subpœnaed to testify before the Special Federal Grand Jury in New York, called to hear evidence of possible violations of espionage and other federal statutes by persons implicated by Miss Bentley. The Grand Jury's investigation of the charges resulted in "no bill." This established that their passing of blueprints and information did not come within the technical definition of the espionage statutes. Harry Gold was not indicted, but the F.B.I.'s investigation had developed some highly useful information about him.

We knew that *some* chemist had worked with Dr. Fuchs. And Harry Gold was a chemist who seemed to fit the general pattern in many other particulars.

. . . . . .

Our hopes were high as photographs of Gold were flown across the Atlantic to Dr. Fuchs. The wan prisoner squinted at the American's round face and bushy hair. Then he shook his head. No, he declared, Harry Gold was not his American confederate.

Was the great search back again at the starting point? Such heart-breaking setbacks are not unusual in investigation work. To start all over again on another approach and try to construct success out of the rubble of defeat is more or less routine. But we were still not entirely convinced that Gold was cleared.

The question always existed—were Fuchs and the Heinemans telling the truth? Did the relatives fear that if their shadowy guest were identified and brought to justice they themselves might be implicated? On the other hand, they had tried, seemingly, to be as helpful as they could, and the passage of time might understandably have dimmed their recollections. So, too, with Dr. Fuchs: in his agitated state of mind, he might honestly believe Gold was not the man.

But one fact we could not ignore. Not only was Gold the one suspect, among the final twenty, who most closely fitted the description, but he had been associated, one way or another, with Golos, a known Russian spy.

We decided to dig deeper for more data about Harry Gold. We would talk with associates of Gold and Brothman. Perhaps they would be able to clarify the character and career of this Philadelphia chemist. The most minute clue might open untold avenues of investigation.

In this process a provocative detail came to light. A former associate of Brothman, in discussing that individual, stated that he remembered a certain man by the name of Frank Keppler who was a friend of Brothman. He hadn't seen Keppler for years, but he felt that Keppler might be in the same line of business as Brothman—chemistry.

Could he pick out Keppler from a group of pictures? Looking at a large number of photographs, he pointed unhesitatingly to one and said, "That is Frank Keppler."

But he was indicating a picture of Harry Gold!

Why had Gold used an alias in meeting an associate of Brothman? Something was peculiar. Larger than ever, in the spring of 1950, Harry Gold loomed as our most likely candidate.

. . . . . .

It was May 15th, 1950, when two special agents of the F.B.I. entered the Philadelphia General Hospital and asked for Harry Gold, who held the responsible position of chemist in charge of biological research at the hospital's heart station. They wanted to interview him. Gold was busy. Would the agents kindly come back a little later? Yes, they would.

That evening, declaring he was glad to co-operate, Harry Gold consented to be interviewed. He had been questioned before by the F.B.I. What did they want to know now?

The discussion centred first on Gold's general background. Then a picture of Dr. Fuchs was shown to him. Gold frowned at it a moment, then surprised the agents by exclaiming: "This is a very unusual picture. He is that English spy!"

It was a tense moment. The agents spoke with meticulous care. Had Gold ever known Fuchs? Certainly not. Had he ever seen Fuchs? No; he recognised the picture merely because it had been published in the newspapers.

Gold readily gave details regarding his life and employment—facts which the F.B.I. already knew, intimately. But where had he gone on holidays and special leaves in 1944 and 1945? Gold asserted that he had never in his life been west of the Mississippi River, nor had he made any trips to New England.

These were points of significance, because Fuchs's partner had undoubtedly been in both Cambridge and New Mexico. For a moment the agents changed the subject.

How about Abraham Brothman? Yes, they had been good friends. He had talked with the F.B.I. about Brothman in 1947. He had stopped working for him in 1948 because the business enterprise in which they were associated had fared badly; Gold wasn't being paid, so he left. He liked his job in the Philadelphia General Hospital much better.

Next a vital question: Why had Gold used the alias of Frank Keppler when he was introduced to an associate of Abraham Brothman? Honest individuals don't need to masquerade under false names.

Gold had a ready answer. While he was still employed at the Pennsylvania Sugar Company he was conducting laboratory experiments for Brothman and he had not wanted his Philadelphia boss to know of this unethical practice. But this defence was weak—and by now Gold's eyes looked troubled.

Then came another discrepancy. Why had Gold told Miriam Moskowitz, Brothman's secretary, that he was married, the father of two children, and further that his brother had been a paratrooper and had been killed in action? Gold denied ever making the statements, but the agents knew better.

Next, they showed him pictures of the Heinemans. Could he identify them? Positively not. Who were those people? He had never seen them in his life.

Now a still more delicate matter: Would Gold allow moving pictures to be taken of himself? Of course! Why not? Take as many as you want. And the agents took moving pictures. Much earlier, however, unknown to Gold, the F.B.I. had already obtained other motion pictures of him, and these secret films had already been flown to Dr. Fuchs in Wormwood Scrubs.

Gold was interviewed on several occasions in the next few days. He was always most polite and offered his co-operation. But, he kept saying, he didn't have much to tell. His life was that of any ordinary citizen. He had never been prominent, received a high salary, or worked in plants possessing confidential or restricted contracts.

Now, to prove beyond any doubt that he had nothing to conceal, he offered to allow the F.B.I. to search his rooms. He readily signed a written consent.

The search of Gold's dwelling, a comfortable, two-story brick and stone row house at 6823 Kindred Street in Philadelphia's north-east section, was conducted by two F.B.I. agents in Gold's presence on the morning of May 22nd. The chemist suggested they start in the bedroom, where he kept most of his personal possessions, papers, books, chemical journals.

The agents proceeded methodically. Whenever an item of interest was found, Gold was ready to give an explanation. He was supremely confident. He had an answer for every question. Almost!

Suddenly an agent dredged up from behind a bookcase a yellow folder marked "Santa Fé, the Capital City." This brochure, issued by the Chamber of Commerce, contained a detailed map, showing a complete layout of streets, public buildings, churches and hotels, Silently Gold was shown the folder.

A startled gleam flashed through his eyes, his mouth fell open and he seemed momentarily to freeze. The map that he had obtained in the Santa Fé museum, so that he could find the way to the bridge without asking questions! The shock of seeing the Chamber of Commerce folder was profound; it unmanned him, shattered the habitual, impregnable poise of an accomplished deceiver.

In a sleep-walker's voice, Gold finally asked, "Where did that thing come from?"

An agent intoned: "You said you had never been west of the Mississippi. Or have you?"

The question seemed to pound with resistless force upon the stunned mind of Harry Gold, a man who had lived for years behind a front of lies and fantasy. There was a pause. Gold said nothing. Then the other agent prodded: "About this map, Mr. Gold. Would you like to tell the whole truth?"

Then, abruptly, Gold blurted out, "I . . . I am the man to whom Klaus Fuchs gave his information."

With these words the mysterious shadow we had been seeking became a living, breathing prisoner—Harry Gold. And, quite by coincidence, less than an hour after the confession a cable from London was received at F.B.I. headquarters in Washington, saying that Dr. Fuchs, after seeing the secretly taken films, had identified Harry Gold as his American partner. Two days later, after viewing the films made with Gold's co-operation, Fuchs was positive this was the man.

.   .   .   .   .   .

Had Harry Gold, at any time in his espionage career, ever tried to withdraw from his Soviet entanglement? We could find no evidence, even from Gold himself, that he had. In promoting the Red cause, he had been almost morbidly self-sacrificial. Denying himself luxuries, spending hard-earned money, wasting holiday periods, making long trips, suffering loss of sleep, enduring the nervous pressure of illegal activities, he gave everything he had, including his honour. Even after he had confessed, he continued for a while to fabricate. To his credit, however, I must say that ultimately he poured out the whole story.

Then he ransacked his memory for names, dates and incidents, and provided the F.B.I. with a wealth of information which will be of value in pending and future investigations. That was his only way of making restitution.

Although too late, he had come at last to see that Communism had robbed him of the conscience of a free American, completely paralysing his power of moral resistance. No spiritual force was left within him to stay his deeds of treason.

And what had it all brought him except disgrace and the certain prospect of long years in prison? The Soviets, to be sure, had "honoured" Harry Gold. He told us how, one evening, his espionage superior had announced to him that they were going to celebrate that night. Gold had been awarded the Order of the Red Star for his outstanding work on behalf of the U.S.S.R. The Russian displayed the written order but for obvious reasons could not give him the document or the medal. But he did reveal that one of the privileges of the award was free bus rides in the city of Moscow!

.   .   .   .   .   .

Standing in the Federal Court in Philadelphia on December 9th, 1950, Gold confessed his "terrible mistake" to Judge McGranery.

"There is a puny inadequacy about any words telling how deep and horrible is my remorse," he declared. He thanked the Court for a fair trial, and commended the F.B.I. and other agencies of the Department of Justice and the prison authorities for good treatment.

"Most certainly," he asserted, "this could never have happened in the Soviet Union or in any of the countries dominated by it."

And then the Judge pronounced the sentence: "Thirty years."

The moon-faced prisoner nodded, and United States deputy marshals led him out of the courtroom. Harry Gold had sacrificed his life and hazarded the security of his nation for "free bus rides in Moscow"—a privilege which fate was never to allow him to enjoy.

XXII

THE DEFECTION OF ALLAN NUNN MAY

from

THE ATOM SPIES

by Oliver Pilat

(Published by W. H. Allen, London, 1954)

In the same category as Klaus Fuchs and Bruno Pontecorvo, who betrayed vital atomic secrets to Soviet Russia during and after the last war, belongs Allan Nunn May, with the difference, however, that whereas the former were British subjects by naturalisation only, the latter was a native son of England.

His innate intelligence and quick grasp of scientific data distinguished him as one of the luminaries in the field of atomic research, and by the time he was thirty years old, in 1944, he had reached an important position in the most secret of war services. About the same time he was lured by the Communist ideal into divulging to the Russians vital information to which he had access. The secrets he thus conveyed to the Soviets rank with, and perhaps surpass in importance, those which Klaus Fuchs betrayed.

He was able to carry on his treacherous activities undisturbed for over two years. When he was at last suspected by the chiefs of the British security service, they had no need to coax him into a confession, which he made readily enough. Tried by jury on May 1st, 1946, he was sentenced to ten years' penal servitude.

★

Formal and informal appraisals of Allan Nunn May are now available from Canadian, American and British sources. Not unnaturally, each country has been somewhat reluctant to stress the full extent of his penetration of secrets in its area. Cross-checking of the accounts lengthens May's shadow beyond any doubt. It seems logical to believe that he had a relation to the mysterious acrostic of the four Gs. He may well have been the Soviet superior, or director in espionage, of Fuchs himself.

May was a native of England, born in 1912, which meant that he reached manhood in the early 'thirties, that period of turmoil and depression which helped to fashion Gold and Fuchs. He became a Communist in youth, then a secret Communist, presumably a Soviet agent, since the Canadian Report said he was "known" in Moscow before he left England. A physicist, with a Ph.D. from Trinity College, Cambridge, he was recruited in May 1942 for early research on the hush-hush Tube Alloy Project. Under the direction of Sir Wallace

Akers, various teams of experts were then following separate leads at different university and industrial laboratories. May's team was using the Cavendish laboratory in Cambridge.

The first biographical reference to May in the Canadian Report read as follows:

"In July 1944 Dr. Cockcroft, who holds the chair of Jacksonian Professor of Natural Philosophy at Cambridge, England, and who is a scientist of international reputation, had been made director of Atomic Energy Project, Montreal and Chalk River, and worked in collaboration with Canadian scientists at the Montreal Laboratory of the National Research Council. Dr. Allan Nunn May, a British temporary civil servant, formed part of the research group that came over to Canada and was at the Montreal Laboratory as a group leader under Dr. Cockcroft."

From this, one might infer that May did not reach Canada until the summer of 1944. Actually, he arrived in January 1943, with a contingent of British scientists under Dr. Halban, Joliot-Curie's former colleague, who resigned eighteen months later and was succeeded by Dr. Cockcroft. "Not long after his arrival," according to the Canadian Report, May was claimed by Zabotin's military intelligence outfit in Ottawa, on specific instruction from the Spy Centre in Moscow. This meant that May was spying in the Western Hemisphere eleven months before Fuchs showed up, and did not follow Fuchs across the Atlantic, as many persons assumed. It provided a long undisturbed interval for May to build up an atomic spy net.

The earliest references to May in the documents stolen from the Soviet Embassy at Ottawa by Gouzenko are dated 1945. They show May, then using the cover name of Alek, providing a steady flow of atomic information for Lieutenant Angelov, one of Zabotin's assistants, who was given the cover name of Baxter.

Long before 1945, May had established himself as an authority on the United States phases of the nuclear fission research. He had some claim to do so as senior in the nuclear physics division of the British effort at Montreal, and as a member of two highly important Allied committees. With a dozen other British scientists, he made his first visit to the Metallurgical Laboratory at the University of Chicago in January 1944. It was during this visit that he met and impressed Major-General Leslie R. Groves, who had just been put in charge of the entire Manhattan District Project. Groves later recalled May as a reliable scientist (reliable because cleared by British Intelligence) and a mature one, around forty, though May was almost ten years younger than that.

For two weeks in April 1944 May worked on a minor experiment at the Argonne Laboratory in Chicago where the original atomic pile using graphite was located, as well as a later pile using heavy water as a slowing-down material. Towards the end of August, May conferred for three days with officials of the Chicago laboratory on setting up of the Montreal pile.

During his fourth visit to the United States, from September 25th to October 30th, 1944, May carried on extensive research with American scientists "in a highly secret and important new field"—so secret, apparently, that even now the details are not available. During his earlier visits, May stayed at an hotel in Chicago. This time he lived in the Argonne dormitory, except for weekends which he spent with an American scientist in the apartment of another scientist who was temporarily out of town.

In a letter sent to Senator Hickenlooper (R-Iowa) in 1946, and later read on the Senate floor, General Groves revealed he had a hunch about May in 1945, before May was exposed. "May had spent more time and acquired more knowledge at the Argonne than any other British physicist," the General wrote. "Although I had no reason to suspect him, I did not like to have him acquire such a wide knowledge of later developments. It is for that reason that in the Spring of 1945 I declined to approve a proposed fourth [Note: really fifth] visit of one month's duration. May never returned to the Chicago laboratory and never visited any other Manhattan District installation."

General Groves added a perfect example of retroactive wishful thinking. "It is very doubtful if May has anything but a general knowledge of the construction of the atomic bomb. He would not have been able to secure any such knowledge through legitimate channels. . . ."

It is true that the bomb assembly was handled in Los Alamos, yet the freemasonry among scientists, noticeable even under strictest rules of secrecy, might well have operated in the Argonne dormitory and at that weekend hangout of the scientists. Anyway, why should a spy worry about legitimate channels?

On August 9th, 1945, two days after President Truman announced the dropping of the mushroom on Hiroshima, Zabotin wired the Director of the Centre in Moscow, describing, among other things, the rate at which the Americans were turning out plutonium, or $U235$, at the Clinton Engineer Works (Oak Ridge) in the Tennessee Valley and at the larger Hanford Engineer Works on the Columbia River in the state of Washington. The telegram read in part:

"FACTS GIVEN BY ALEK: (1) THE TEST OF THE ATOMIC BOMB WAS
CONDUCTED IN NEW MEXICO (WITH '49,' '94-239'). THE BOMB DROPPED
ON JAPAN WAS MADE OF URANIUM 235. IT IS KNOWN THAT THE OUTPUT
OF URANIUM 235 AMOUNTS TO 400 GRAMS DAILY AT THE MAGNETIC
SEPARATION PLANT AT CLINTON. THE OUTPUT OF '49' IS LIKELY TWO
TIMES GREATER (SOME GRAPHITE UNITS ARE PLANNED FOR 250 MEGA
WATTS, I.E. 250 GRAMS A DAY. . . . (2) ALEK HANDED OVER TO US A
PLATINUM WITH 162 MICROGRAMS OF URANIUM 233 IN THE FORM OF
OXIDE IN A THIN LAMINA. . . ."

This was not the first souvenir acquired by May. Back in April of
that year, according to a handwritten entry by Angelov in a notebook
taken by Gouzenko, May handed over a sample of plutonium, and
was rewarded by two hundred dollars and two bottles of whisky.
He got five hundred dollars for the second sample. Both samples were
flown immediately to Moscow. Where did they come from? The
Canadian Report refused to guess. The samples might have come
from Montreal. General Groves conceded they might more easily
have come from Chicago.

According to the Smyth Report, the Metallurgical Laboratory in
Chicago contributed more towards the eventual bomb than any
other United States installation. Its rôle was to prepare plans for
the large-scale production of plutonium, and the use of plutonium
in bombs. This required (a) finding a system using normal uranium
in which a chain reaction would occur; (b) showing that in such a
chain reaction plutonium could be separated chemically from other
material; and (c) figuring how to manage an explosive chain reaction
using U235 or plutonium. May's 1945 report on production was so
accurate that when Life magazine, in 1951, wanted to make a chart of
fissionable materials production, it used May's figures as a base. By
extension, May must have found ways to dig out other basic secrets
in Chicago.

Masterminding a net from an adjoining country is an axiom of
Soviet espionage, Alexander Foote pointed out in his authoritative
Handbook for Spies, which describes his actual experiences. This principle assures "the maximum degree of efficiency with the minimum
danger of compromise," he noted. Assuming that as resident director
in Canada for Soviet military intelligence, Zabotin was concentrating
on the United States, what was surprising was the way he cleaned out
the atomic kitchen and pantry in Canada itself. He may have felt that
the rules did not need to be followed too closely in a case of improvised
wartime spying against allies.

Back in 1944, a site was selected on the Chalk River, near Petawawa, Ontario, for the construction of a pilot plant, or small-scale atomic pile taking advantage of Canadian supplies of uranium and using heavy water from the United States as a slowing-down medium. This important and in some ways unique installation grew rapidly. Since it was guided from Montreal, May had no trouble insinuating himself there. Zabotin was sufficiently impressed by hush-hush reports about Petawawa to pay a social visit, in the summer of 1945, to a friend living near Chalk River, and subsequently to cruise along the river in a motor-boat with the sole purpose of wiring the Director of the Spy Centre in Moscow a description of what the plant looked like from the outside.

As atomic research reached its climax, Soviet espionage worried over developing new links at the Chalk River plant, in Montreal, and elsewhere as soon as May was ordered back to England. A wire from Zabotin to the Director in Moscow, dated August 9th, 1945, conveyed excellently the implication, running through their correcpondence, that May possessed a rare degree of autonomy among spies. It read:

"ALEK REPORTED TO US THAT HE HAS MET NORMAN V . . . (HE WAS AT HIS HOME). V . . . WORKS IN THE LABORATORY OF THE MONTREAL BRANCH OF THE SCIENTIFIC RESEARCH COUNCIL. . . . HE ASKED THE OPINION OF ALEK: IS IT WORTH WHILE FOR HIM (V . . .) TO HAND OVER INFORMATION ON THE ATOMIC BOMB. ALEK EXPRESSED HIMSELF IN THE NEGATIVE. ALEK STATED THAT V . . . OCCUPIES A FAIRLY LOW POSITION AND KNOWS VERY LITTLE. . . ."

After they have been cultivated with cash and established (in the sense that rose bushes are established), Soviet spies are directed here and there, and may be ordered to switch jobs, if necessary. May, however, was always handled with deference. On one occasion in 1945, the Director in Moscow wired Resident Director Zabotin in Ottawa:

"DISCUSS WITH HIM (ALEK): DOES HE THINK IT EXPEDIENT FOR OUR UNDERTAKING TO STAY ON THE SPOT; WILL HE BE ABLE TO DO THAT OR IS IT MORE USEFUL FOR HIM AND NECESSARY TO DEPART FOR LONDON?"

After the dropping of an actual bomb, Canadian and British contributions to the joint atomic project began to dwindle. Zabotin replied:

"HE CANNOT REMAIN IN CANADA. AT THE BEGINNING OF SEPTEMBER HE MUST FLY TO LONDON. BEFORE HIS DEPARTURE HE WILL GO TO THE URANIUM PLANT IN THE PETAWAWA DISTRICT WHERE HE WILL BE FOR ABOUT TWO WEEKS. HE SAID HE MUST COME NEXT YEAR FOR A MONTH TO CANADA."

May appears to have been visiting Petawawa when Gouzenko strolled from the Soviet Embassy. Like Zabotin; like Carr, the spy recruiter; like Nikolai Khevinov, the Tass correspondent who played a considerable rôle in the ring under the cover name of Martin; May wasted no time in leaving Canada.

Long before he left, May arranged, through Zabotin, about meeting a new contact in London. He was to walk in a specified direction in front of the British Museum at a specified time on October 17th, carrying *The Times* under his left arm. His new contact would approach, holding the *Picture Post* in his left hand, and say, "What is the shortest way to the Strand?" May would reply, "Well, come along, I am going that way," and after an interval, "Best regards from Michael."

British counter-intelligence may or may not have been alerted soon enough to post an observer outside the British Museum on October 17th, because considerable time and patience were required to interpret, classify and check the Gouzenko documents. The Canadian Report declared: "The evidence before us does not reveal whether the contact . . . was made."

Dr. May had five months to prepare. (In the Zabotin wires it had been specified that he would be lecturing in physics again at King's College, and that he could be reached there by phone in case of an emergency; one of the first steps to repair the dikes broken by Gouzenko must have been to make such a phone call.)

On February 15th, 1946, the same day on which the general round-up of Gouzenko suspects began in Canada, Lieutenant-Colonel Burt, counter-intelligence head at Scotland Yard, came around to see Dr. May at Shell-Mex House in London, where he was working. Colonel Burt inquired whether there had been any leaks in nuclear matters during May's period in Canada. "That's the first I heard of it," said May, with some brusqueness. May denied he had been approached by Soviet agents in Canada, and refused to answer further questions.

Five days of close surveillance followed. May betrayed nothing. Additional information from Canada having been received during this interval, Colonel Burt came around again. The counter-espionage chief said he knew May had been supposed to meet somebody near the British Museum, but had failed to keep his appointment. This was true, May agreed. "I decided to wash my hands of the whole business," he said.

Before anybody could arrest him, May said he wanted to confess. He quickly wrote out a statement and signed it. Like the fairy tale produced by Harry Gold for the beguilement of the 1947 New York Grand Jury investigating subversion, May's statement had the effect of sweetening up any facts which could not be denied, and of avoiding any new revelations. Presumably by this time Soviet Intelligence had figured out what was missing from the Ottawa files, and had decided that May could not be salvaged. In any event, here is how the confession went:

"About a year ago whilst in Canada, I was contacted by an individual whose identity I decline to divulge. He called on me at my private apartment in Swail Av., Montreal. He apparently knew I was employed by the Montreal laboratory and he sought information from me concerning atomic research.

"I gave and had given very careful consideration to correctness of making sure that development of atomic energy was not confined to U.S.A. I took the very painful decision that it was necessary to convey general information on atomic energy and make sure it was taken seriously. For this reason I decided to entertain propositions made to me by the individual who called on me.

"After this preliminary meeting I met the individual on several subsequent occasions whilst in Canada. He made specific requests for information, which were just nonsense to me—I mean by this that they were difficult for me to comprehend. But he did request samples of uranium from me and information generally on atomic energy. At one meeting I gave the man microscopic amounts of U233 and U235 (one of each). The U235 was a slightly enriched sample and was in a small glass tube and consisted of about a milligram of oxide. The U233 was about a tenth of a milligram and was a very thin deposit on a platinum foil and was wrapped in a piece of paper. I also gave the man a written report on atomic research as known to me. The information was mostly of a character which has since been published or is about to be published. The man also asked me for information about the U.S. electronically-controlled A.A. shells. I knew very little about these and so could give only very little information.

"He also asked me for introductions to people employed in the laboratory including a man named V . . . but I advised against contacting him. The man gave me some dollars (I forget how many) in a bottle of whisky and I accepted them against my will.

"Before I left Canada it was arranged that on my return to London I was to keep an appointment with somebody I did not know. I was given precise details as to making contact but I forget them now. I did not keep the appointment because I had decided that this clandestine procedure was no longer appropriate in view of the official release of information and the possibility of satisfactory international control of atomic energy."

From this unapologetic apology, Allan Nunn May emerged "as a man of honour who had only done what he believed to be right," his lawyer argued later in court. Actually, the statement was a tissue of evasions and distortions, starting with the fact that May received seven hundred dollars *and* two bottles of whisky, not an unknown number of greenbacks *in* a bottle.

The new anti-aircraft shells developed by the U.S. Navy for use against Jap suicide flyers in the Pacific were so secret at the time when Dr. May dug out the details for his Soviet superior that they had not yet been shared with the British. May had to make some admission in this field, because of references in the Gouzenko documents, even though the admission riddled his pious talk about spying solely to safeguard humanity against A-bombs. In point of time, the anti-aircraft spying indulged by May followed publication of the Smyth Report on atomic energy which he claimed dissolved his own intentions of espionage.

One continuing Soviet objective in atomic matters has been to sow suspicion among the three nations which created the bomb. Dr. May contributed to this by subtle appeals to anti-American prejudice in England. To insiders, his admission about a precisely arranged rendezvous with a stranger on another continent, his careful forgetfulness as to who did the arranging, and how, his whole procedure, in fact, suggested a disciplined agent acting under orders. So did his statement, which protected Russia, Soviet officials in Canada, Communist parties in three countries, and then himself, almost in that order.

Quite transparently, the statement was an exercise in counter-espionage, designed to protect the exposed Soviet apparatus in the Western Hemisphere. It could have been, perhaps was, worked out at Znamensky 19, Red Army General Intelligence Headquarters, in Moscow.

The prosecution of Allan Nunn May proceeded in an atmosphere of offhand vagueness which later characterised the trial of Klaus Fuchs. At the arraignment on March 20th, 1946, Gerald Gardiner, Dr. May's lawyer, asserted that Commander Burt had told the physicist there was a lot of information about his spying and that he was thoroughly implicated. Commander, or Colonel Burt replied he had not been in any position on March 20th to accuse May of anything. The counter-intelligence chief did say he appreciated May had not done his spying for money, Gardiner insisted. "Oh, no," said Burt. "That was contrary to my instructions, which were that the question of gain had entered into it."

Taking full advantage of the protections of Anglo-Saxon law which do not prevail in the country for which he did his spying, May demanded a trial by jury. He got it on May 1st, 1946. After the trial began, May pleaded guilty, thus getting maximum leverage out of his supposed confession and avoiding a presentation of the evidence against him.

When defence counsel Gardiner remarked that May had told him the person to whom he gave information was a Russian, the Attorney General, Sir Hartley Shawcross, replied in a shocked tone, "There is no kind of suggestion that the Russians are enemies or potential enemies. The court has already decided that this offence consists in communicating information to unauthorised persons."

Justice Oliver, in imposing sentence, told May, "Whether money was the object of what you did, in fact you did get money for what you did. It is a very bad case indeed. The sentence upon you is one of ten years' penal servitude."

This sentence was four years longer than any other imposed on a member of the Soviet underground in America exposed by the Gouzenko documents. The Association of Scientific Workers of Great Britain protested vehemently and sent copies of its protest to similar bodies in the Western Hemisphere, arguing that the punishment was out of proportion to the offence. However, if Allan Nunn May failed to earn fully his decade of incarceration in Wakefield Prison in Yorkshire by his espionage work in the United States and Canada before exposure, he certainly earned it by his performance after exposure.

XXIII

IGOR GOUZENKO SEEKS ASYLUM IN CANADA

from

THE SOVIET SPIES

by RICHARD HIRSCH

(Published by Nicholas Kaye, London, 1947)

Ideology is one of the strangest twentieth-century phenomena that causes otherwise sane and perfectly intelligent people to commit the most outrageous acts, including treachery and, not unfrequently, murder. The cases of the Fuchses, the Nunn Mays, the Pontecorvos, Rosenbergs, et al., are typical examples of the effects of this modern virus.

But the reader should not run away with the idea that the scientists of the "Free Western World" are the only ones who go over to the enemy camp; for every Englishman and American who have succumbed to the attraction of Communism, there is at least one Communist going over to the West. The Kravchenkos and Alekseevs, the Krivitskys and Petrovs, are sufficient proof that all isn't lovely in the garden behind the Iron Curtain.

This is the story of Igor Gouzenko, code clerk at the Soviet Embassy at Ottawa, who, seduced by the easy atmosphere of Western democracy, severed his ties with Soviet Russia and betrayed important Intelligence secrets to the Canadians; he supplied one hundred authentic documents to the Canadian Government agencies, which later revealed the activities of Soviet espionage in Canada and in the United States.

★

MRS. JOUBARNE was a loyal public servant. She was also a human being. When Mrs. Gouzenko began to cry softly and hug her child to her bosom, she realised what it would mean if the code clerk and his family were to be turned back to the Embassy.

Accordingly, after consulting with Crown Attorney Raoul Mercier, she began to make a series of telephone calls. She kept at it until late afternoon. Everywhere it was the same story—Gouzenko and his documents were too hot to handle. One by one the Government offices began to close for the day and finally Mrs. Joubarne was forced to admit failure.

Gouzenko thanked her. "You have been so kind—you were the only one who would talk to us," he said. "We will never forget you."

Then they left the Justice Building. Although Gouzenko knew that his absence must have raised an alarm at the Embassy, he decided to bring his wife and child back to Somerset Street.

They went into the house by the back entrance. When they reached their flat Gouzenko stepped to the window. Concealing himself in the shadow, he looked towards the park across the street. Seated on a bench opposite he saw what he had feared—two men wearing loose-fitting brown trenchcoats and hats with brims too small for their high cheekbones and square faces. They sat with their hands in their pockets and looked up towards his windows.

As he watched they put their heads together. Then one got up and came across the street.

The code clerk stepped back, motioned for silence. Footsteps were heard in the corridor, and a moment later there was a knock on the door.

"Gouzenko—*otcroite dwer*. [Open the door.]" It was Under-Lieutenant Lavrientev of the Embassy staff.

Both the cipher clerk and his wife held their breath. Little Andrei had run across the floor towards a toy teddy bear. He tripped, stumbled against the door.

Gouzenko picked up the child, went to the kitchen of his flat, and out of the back door leading to the rear balcony shared in common with Apartment 5 on the second floor.

Here were seated an R.C.A.F. sergeant and his wife. The man was smoking a pipe and reading the evening paper, while his wife was sewing.

"Excuse me," interrupted Gouzenko. "May I speak with you?"

The sergeant looked up in surprise. There was something about Gouzenko's appearance that told him this was no ordinary social call.

"Sure, man. What is it?"

"Please to take my little boy with you tonight—something maybe happen to my wife and me."

"What's going to happen?"

"Get killed," was the laconic reply.

"So about that time," the sergeant related later, "I figured that maybe we should go inside. We went into our flat and he said he figured that the Russians were going to try to kill him and his wife. He wanted to be sure that somebody would look after his little boy if anything should happen to them.

"After a bit of a conference my wife and I decided that we didn't want to see him stuck with nobody to look after him."

Meanwhile Under-Lieutenant Lavrientev must have been sorely puzzled. He had heard sounds of movement inside the flat, yet no one had answered his knock. Only a flimsy brass tumbler and thin veneer panel separated him—an official of the U.S.S.R.—from the code clerk and his family. Yet his instructions had said nothing about breaking down doors. He had merely been told to watch for Gouzenko and report back to the Embassy if and when he or his family were seen. He left the floor, went downstairs, and began to circle the house from the rear to see if Gouzenko had gone out through the back entrance.

Gouzenko and the R.C.A.F. sergeant were standing on the balcony when they saw Lavrientev walking down the lane. The code clerk paled. "There he is," he whispered. "Perhaps you had better take my wife in your apartment as well."

As they were talking a motherly-looking housewife who lived in Apartment 6 on the same floor appeared. Hearing the story, she said, "I am alone in my flat. I have plenty of room for all of your family, including yourself, Mr. Gouzenko. I will be very happy to give you shelter as long as you require it."

"That settles it," said the sergeant. "You go along with her. I'll get my bike and go for the police. Those fellows will not dare break into the house of a Canadian citizen."

That was at seven o'clock. At half past seven Constables Tom Walsh and J. B. McCullough responded to the call.

In Apartment 6 they found Gouzenko, his wife and child. The code clerk identified himself as a member of the Soviet Embassy staff, said that he had information of extreme importance to the Canadian Government, and requested protection.

The constables listened without committing themselves. They assured him, however, that they would watch the block of flats. "Keep the light on in the bathroom. We can see it from the park. If you need us, put out the light."

In Apartment 6, Mrs. Gouzenko prepared their child for bed. Her husband sat in a living-room chair listening for a sound of movement in the corridor outside.

At ten o'clock his hostess urged him to lie down on the couch and get some sleep. He thanked her but said that he thought it would be better if he remained awake. "Something will happen tonight. I know those people too well. I am sure they are planning a raid."

With each passing hour his alertness sharpened. He could picture only too clearly what was happening at the Embassy—all lights burning, the code rooms in a turmoil, the staff trying to discover if anything was missing from the files. The code name for the N.K.V.D. was "the Neighbours." He wondered particularly what their reaction would be.

13

As it was, four men left the Embassy at eleven o'clock. They were Vitali G. Pavlov, Second Secretary and Consul and secret head of the N.K.V.D. in Canada; Lieutenant-Colonel Rogov, Military Air Attaché of the Red Air Force; Lieutenant Angelov; and Alexander Farafotnov, a cipher clerk who occupied the office next door to Gouzenko, and who had specialised in N.K.V.D. communications. As they crossed the pavement to their car they looked like a guard detail, minus the prisoner in the centre.

At eleven-thirty they were at 511 Somerset Street. They went at once to Gouzenko's flat, knocked on the door. The R.C.A.F. sergeant in Apartment 5 thought that it was the police returning for a further inquiry. He opened his door and looked out.

Seeing the three men in plain clothes and one in uniform with Red Star insignia, he realised his error. Before he could close his door, however, one of the men ran up to him.

"Where is Gouzenko?"

The R.C.A.F. sergeant gave him a blank look. "You got me, buddy," he said, and shut the door tight.

There was a conference in the hall, and the four men started to leave. They went downstairs; then they came back with a rush. They knocked once on Apartment 4, put their shoulders to the door, and pushed. The lock gave way with a snap.

From Apartment 6 Gouzenko watched the proceedings through the keyhole. He got up, went to the bathroom, switched out the light.

In the park the police constables caught the signal. They ran to the block of flats and went up the stairs at the double. In Apartment 4 they found all of the lights on and all of the closet doors open. Pavlov was in one and Colonel Rogov was in another.

"What are you people doing here?" demanded Walsh.

Pavlov motioned his companions to be quiet. He produced a card identifying himself as the Soviet Second Secretary. He said that all present were members of the Embassy staff, who were looking for certain official papers.

"The man who owns this flat has left town, but we have his permission to enter and get what we need."

Walsh pointed to the broken lock, part of which still lay on the floor. "For people that have permission to enter a flat you certainly chose a funny way to get in." He picked up the lock from the floor. "This doesn't look as if it had been done with a key. You must have used a bit of pressure to get in. From what I've seen of the door you didn't open it with your fingers."

Pavlov shrugged. "We lost the key," he replied. "There is something in here which we have to get. This is Soviet property, and we can do as we wish. You will please leave."

The constables shook their heads. "Not until an inspector arrives," they replied.

Detective Inspector Duncan Macdonald, a rugged, ruddy-cheeked man, arrived within a quarter of an hour after Walsh called headquarters. After sizing up the situation he asked Pavlov and the others to accompany him to the police station.

Pavlov claimed diplomatic immunity for himself, his associates and the flat. He refused to budge. The Inspector, realising that he had stumbled on what he later called a "delicate" situation, told Walsh and McCullough to remain while he went to headquarters to clarify the diplomatic status.

When he had gone, Consul Pavlov held a conference with his group. After further poking about in the closets he decided to call it a night. The police made no effort to detain them, and they went back to the Soviet Embassy. What happened there has not been disclosed.

For the rest of the night the Gouzenkos remained in Apartment 6 under the watchful care of the city police. Towards dawn there was another caller at Apartment 4. He knocked and tried the door but the police had padlocked it, and after a while he went away. Shortly after daybreak on September 7th, the Gouzenkos and their documents were moved from Somerset Street to the headquarters of the Royal Canadian Mounted Police. Since the Prime Minister had already turned down the code clerk's original offer, Commissioner S. T. Wood personally notified Mackenzie King of the events of the preceding evening and the protection being accorded by his force.

Again the Prime Minister pointed out the need for proceeding with caution. "I felt that the situation with which we were confronted could not be viewed too circumspectly. I felt that we must make sure what type of person Gouzenko was, and what the motive was that prompted his action. . . . One had to consider other nations as well as one's own before taking a step that might be considered premature."[1]

The inquiry proceeded in the order outlined by the Prime Minister. Gouzenko told Commissioner Wood and his Deputy, H. A. Gagnon, that he would be glad to explain his decision to leave the Soviet Embassy. His statement is reproduced below for whatever light it may shed on his motives:

"I, Igor Gouzenko, wish to make the following statement of my own will:

[1] House of Commons Debates, March 18th, 1946. Pages 48, 50.

"Having arrived in Canada two years ago I was surprised during the first days by the complete freedom of the individual which exists in Canada but does not exist in Russia. The false representations about the democratic countries which are increasingly propagated in Russia were dissipated daily, as no lying propaganda can stand up against facts.

"During two years of life in Canada, I saw evidence of what a free people can do. What the Canadian people have accomplished and are accomplishing here under conditions of complete freedom the Russian people, under the conditions of the Soviet régime of violence and suppression of all freedom, cannot accomplish even at the cost of tremendous sacrifices, blood and tears.

"The last elections which took place recently in Canada especially surprised me. In comparison with them the system of elections in Russia appears as a mockery of the conception of free elections. For example, the fact that in elections in the Soviet Union one candidate is put forward, so that the possibilities of choice are eliminated, speaks for itself.

"While creating a false picture of the conditions of life in these countries, the Soviet Government at the same time is taking all measures to prevent the peoples of democratic countries from knowing about the conditions of life in Russia. The facts about the brutal suppression of the freedom of speech, the mockery of the real religious feelings of the people, cannot penetrate into the democratic countries.

"Having imposed its Communist régime on the people, the Government of the Soviet Union asserts that the Russian people have, as it were, their own particular understanding of freedom and democracy, different from that which prevails among the peoples of the western democracies. *This is a lie.*[1] The Russian peoples have the same understanding of freedom as all the peoples of the world. However, the Russian people cannot realise their dream of freedom and a democratic government on account of cruel terror and persecution.

"Holding forth at international conferences with voluble statements about peace and security, the Soviet Government is simultaneously preparing secretly for the third world war. To meet this war, the Soviet Government is creating in democratic countries, including Canada, *a fifth column*[1] in the organisation of which even the diplomatic representatives of the Soviet Government take part.

"The announcement of the dissolution of the Comintern was

[1] Underlined in original document.

probably the greatest farce of the Communists in recent years. Only the name was liquidated, with the object of reassuring the public opinion in the democratic countries. Actually the Comintern exists and continues its work, because the Soviet leaders have never relinquished the idea of establishing a Communist dictatorship throughout the world.

"Taking into account least of all that this advantageous idea will cost millions of Russian lives, the Communists are engendering hatred in the Russian people towards everything foreign.

"To many Soviet people here abroad, *it is clear that the Communist Party in democratic countries has changed long ago from a political party into an agency net of the Soviet Government, into a fifth column in these countries to meet a war*, into an instrument in the hands of the Soviet Government for creating artificial unrest, provocation, etc.

"Through numerous party agitators the Soviet Government stirs up the Russian people in every possible way against the peoples of the democratic countries, preparing the ground for the third world war.

"During my residence in Canada I have seen how the Canadian people and their Government, sincerely wishing to help the Soviet people, sent supplies to the Soviet Union, collected money for the welfare of the Russian people, sacrificing the lives of their sons in the delivery of these supplies across the ocean, and instead of gratitude for the help rendered, the Soviet Government is developing espionage activity in Canada, preparing to deliver a stab in the back of Canada—all this without the knowledge of the Russian people.

"Convinced that such double-faced politics of the Soviet Government towards the democratic countries do not conform with the interests of the Russian people and endanger the security of civilisation, I decided to break away from the Soviet régime and to announce my decision openly.

"I am glad that I found the strength within myself to take this step and to warn Canada and the other democratic countries of the danger which hangs over them.

(*signed*) GOUZENKO.

"I have read the foregoing translation which was made from my original statement in Russian, and have found it to be correct.
"October 10, 1945   (*signed*) GOUZENKO."

In conversation with the Commissioners, Gouzenko added that in the Embassy the fact that the Soviet Union was preparing for a third world war was freely discussed. He said that there were two schools of thought on the matter. Those who were not really tied in with the Communist Party feared another world war. Those who were ardent members of the party and its subsidiary organisations really wished for it because they considered it to be a part of the process leading to a general world upheaval resulting in the establishment of Communism.

Meanwhile, the Soviet Embassy was not idle. To the Canadian Department of External Affairs it addressed a note, dated September 7th.

"The Embassy of the U.S.S.R. in Canada presents its compliments and has the honour to inform the Department of External Affairs of the following:

"A colleague of the Embassy, Igor Sergeievitch Gouzenko, living at 511 Somerset Street, failed to report to work at the proper time on September 6th.

"In connection with this and for the purpose of clarifying the reasons for the failure of I. Gouzenko's reporting for work Consul V. G. Pavlov and two other colleagues of the Embassy visited the apartment of I. Gouzenko at 11.30 on September 6th.

"When Mr. Pavlov knocked at the door of Gouzenko's apartment no one answered. After this the apartment was opened by the above-mentioned colleagues of the Embassy with Gouzenko's duplicate key, when it was discovered that neither Gouzenko, nor his wife, Svetlana Borisovna Gouzenko, nor their son Andrei, were in the apartment.

"It was later established that I. Gouzenko had robbed some money belonging to the Embassy and had hidden himself together with his family.

"At the time when Consul Pavlov and two other colleagues of the Embassy were in Gouzenko's apartment, i.e. about 11.30 p.m., Constable Walsh of the Ottawa City Police appeared together with another policeman and tried in a rude manner to detain the diplomatic colleagues of the Embassy, in spite of the explanations given by Consul Pavlov and the showing of diplomatic cards.

"As a result of the protest expressed by Mr. Pavlov, Walsh called Inspector of the City Police Macdonald, who appeared at the Gouzenko apartment in fifteen minutes, and also in a rude manner demanded that Consul V. G. Pavlov and the other diplomatic colleagues of the Embassy go with him to the police station, refusing to recognise the diplomatic card shown by Consul Pavlov.

"Upon the refusal of Mr. V. G. Pavlov to go to the police station,

Mr. Macdonald went away, leaving a policeman in the Gouzenko apartment with the colleagues of the Embassy, for the alleged purpose of finding out who it was who had notified the police of the forced entry into the Gouzenko apartment.

"Consul V. G. Pavlov and the other two colleagues of the Embassy, after waiting for Mr. Macdonald to return for fifteen minutes, left, having locked the Gouzenko apartment.

"The Embassy of the U.S.S.R. asks the Department of External Affairs to take urgent measures to seek and arrest I. Gouzenko and to hand him over for deportation as a capital criminal who has stolen money belonging to the Embassy.

"In addition the Embassy brings to the attention of the Department of External Affairs the rude treatment accorded to the diplomatic colleagues of the Embassy by Constable Walsh and Inspector of the City Police Macdonald, and expresses its confidence that the Department will investigate this incident and will make those guilty answerable for their actions.

"The Embassy asks the Department that it should be informed of action taken in relation to the above.

                          "Ottawa, September 7th, 1945."

The Department of External Affairs was very much interested in that note, especially the portion designating Gouzenko as a "capital criminal who has stolen money belonging to the Embassy." In its reply, the Department asked for particulars concerning the funds and their theft. The Embassy made no answer. Instead, on September 14th, it sent a second note. Pitched to a higher degree of urgency, it read:

"Confirming its communication in the Note No. 35 of September 7th, of the fact that Gouzenko had robbed public funds, the Embassy, upon instructions from the Government of the U.S.S.R., repeats its request to the Government of Canada to apprehend Gouzenko and his wife, and without trial to hand them over to the Embassy for deportation to the Soviet Union.

"The Soviet Government expresses the hope that the Government of Canada will fulfil its request."

By that time, however, matters had gone too far. The hundred documents were telling their story and the Government of Canada had no intention of handing Gouzenko over to anyone.

XXIV

PONTECORVO SEEKS ASYLUM IN SOVIETLAND

from

THE ATOM SPIES

by OLIVER PILAT

(Published by W. H. Allen, London, 1954)

Italian-born Bruno Pontecorvo, believed by some to be an even more brilliant nuclear physicist than Fuchs, accepted in 1942 a British offer to do some atomic research work in the United States. His competence and startling successes made him rise rapidly in the hierarchy of nuclear fission scientists, and in 1948 he received British citizenship in recognition of his valuable work.

There is no evidence that Pontecorvo ever did any spying for Russia. But it has been established that he had always been flirting with the opposite camp; despite the most stringent security tests, he had been able to conceal his sympathies for Russia and the Communist régime. Only after he had been transferred to Harwell as a senior principal scientific officer were the suspicions of the security service aroused.

However, long before those suspicions were sufficiently strong to warrant his arrest, he managed to leave the country. As in the case of Guy Burgess and Donald Maclean, his movements were shrouded in mystery and could not at first be ascertained with any degree of certainty. Not until he was long overdue to assume his duties as Professor of Experimental Physics at the University of Liverpool, a job he had accepted on leaving Harwell, did it transpire that he had vanished—in the direction of Moscow.

★

IN the April 1935 *Proceedings* of the Society of London an article appeared entitled, "Artificial Radioactivity Produced by Neutron Bombardment," which became famous in later years because of what it foreshadowed in atomic development. Its six authors, all connected with the University of Rome, included Pontecorvo's physics professor, Enrico Fermi; Pontecorvo himself; Emilio Segre, later with the University of California Radiation Laboratory; and Franco Rasetti, subsequently with Johns Hopkins University.

Just as Pontecorvo took his first step upward on the ladder of scientific achievement, Mussolini began grinding the Jews, to please his fellow dictator, Adolf Hitler. As a Jew, Pontecorvo saw his future foreclosed in his native country. Through friends, he wangled a Government fellowship in 1936 for study with Professor Frédéric

Joliot-Curie, the Communist physicist in Paris. The fellowship was renewed for a second year, and a third, with financial help from French sources. During this period, Pontecorvo ran with a mixed international set of Leftists and anti-Fascists who vied to see who could hurl the worst insults at Hitler and Mussolini. When hostilities began, the Communists in this group turned lukewarm to the war effort, or actually sabotaged French defence. Those young scientists who had firmly replaced the paternal picture in their minds with Stalin, and had substituted Stalinism for their original religion, found at hand plausible explanations for the deceptive tactics of the party. They were instructed to continue their scientific education elsewhere, in whatever way they or the party could arrange, in preparation for the day when they would assume Soviet scientific leadership in their native country.

While in Paris, Pontecorvo met and married a Swedish girl named Mariana Nordblom, and had a boy named Gil by her. When the Nazi troops neared Paris, in June 1940, the Pontecorvos left by bicycle for Bordeaux, taking turns carrying their two-year-old son in baskets attached to their machines. Early the next year, the family moved to the United States. The Italian scientist's first job in America was radiographic oil-well logging for the Wells Survey Inc., in Tulsa, Oklahoma. It was characteristic of the man's technical competence that he soon developed an improved method of doing the work.

Pontecorvo decided to become an American citizen. He took out first papers, and to protect his standing, continued to pay taxes to the United States Internal Revenue Bureau after moving to Canada.

In the autumn of 1942, Pontecorvo received an offer, which he promptly accepted, to join the contingent of British nuclear physicists heading for the United States to take part in a tremendous allied research problem of military significance. According to Canadian sources, he was recommended initially by American scientists for a rôle in this joint effort. He worked briefly in New York, then shifted to Montreal, as part of the Anglo-American-British atomic team being formed under Dr. H. H. Halban.

Allan Nunn May arrived in Canada early in 1943, and became friendly, though not ostentatiously so, with Pontecorvo. They were both members of the British group of scientists which visited the Metallurgical Project in Chicago for secret talks with United States physicists in January 1944. Subsequently Pontecorvo concentrated on experiments for setting up the Canadian heavy-water atomic pile at the Chalk River plant near Petawawa, Ontario.

This Chalk River plant was the one which aroused such intense interest in Colonel Zabotin and the other spies operating out of the Soviet Embassy in Ottawa during the war. It still houses the reactor of most advanced design and performance in North America. The Pontecorvos moved to Chalk River in 1944 to be close to the work, and he made important nuclear contributions there.

From 1943 to 1949, Pontecorvo travelled regularly to scientific gatherings in Canada and the United States. In addition to his secret work at Chalk River, which could not be discussed, he made a speciality of cosmic rays, the great Russian wartime field of exploration. Since cosmic rays—particles which bomb the earth from somewhere in outer space with energy factors thousands of times greater than man has been able to produce artificially—were unclassified, Pontecorvo could, and would, if encouraged, talk about them at length. In this field alone, he could certainly have been of great help to Russia. More importantly, his latest studies at Chalk River involved ultra-secret work on tritium, a substance intimately related to the hydrogen bomb.

Despite his earlier European record, and some hints of Communist party agitation in Oklahoma, no substantial suspicion seems to have caught up with Pontecorvo during the war. He didn't look like a spy, any more than Selzinger, who furnished the Russians with a daily, up-to-date report on the line-up of the Nazi armies in the East during World War II, or Judy Coplon, the little Brooklyn girl who provided the Soviet with tips on the United States exposure of Russian spies in the postwar period so they could be replaced with minimum damage to the apparatus. What successful spy ever did look like a spy, for that matter?

Pontecorvo did not act secretively. He and his wife (who seems to have been non-political) acquired two more sons during this period: Tiro (named after the Yugoslav partisan leader) in 1944, and Antonio, in 1945. Unlike May and Fuchs, those gentle bachelors, Pontecorvo was a good family man and a fond father. Unlike May and Fuchs, who were socially reserved and shy, Pontecorvo revelled in social affairs, hearty laughter and outdoor exercise. Acquaintances from this period recall no hint of Communism in his reading, talk or behaviour.

Bruno Pontecorvo may have still hoped to become an American citizen. Early in 1946, he visited the General Electric plant in Schenectady, looking for a job, without success. He returned to Canada to his old job at Chalk River, which had been taken over by the British Ministry of Supply, Atomic Energy Division. In 1948, Pontecorvo visited the University of California Radiation Laboratory, which still maintained a key atomic rôle, as may be judged from a significant

paragraph in a publicity release that year from England on the building
of a cyclotron at Harwell:

"The machine will permit the breaking-up of the nuclei of most
atoms, and will also provide new types of nuclei which even the
piles cannot produce. It will also make possible experiments in
nuclear physics which can only be carried out at present in one
place in the world—in the Radiation Laboratory of the University
of California."

Pontecorvo's ostensible purpose for visiting the Radiation Laboratory
was to look for a job. If that was his real purpose, he failed to connect.
Later in 1948, the Italian refugee scientist received British citizenship
in absentia for his valuable war work. Early the following year he
crossed to England to take a five thousand five hundred dollar-a-year
job as a senior principal scientific officer in the nuclear physics division
at Harwell, a notch higher in rank and pay than Fuchs ever achieved.
He and Fuchs became acquainted, inevitably, but they were not
particularly close friends.

In June 1950 Pontecorvo agreed to accept a professorship of experimental physics at Liverpool University starting January 1951. Deputy
Director Skinner of the Harwell installation was going to Liverpool
to expand its scientific programme, and he was looking for brilliant
assistants. Pontecorvo's professional qualifications, particularly in
cosmic rays, could not be denied. He declared, and nobody then
doubted his sincerity, that he was accepting the job because it promised
a wider research opportunity rather than because of the improved
status, and salary.

If Pontecorvo had any dream of eventual wealth at this time it was
probably anchored to America, where a patent had been applied for in
1935 on behalf of the six University of Rome scientists, including
Fermi and himself, who had written the famous paper on neutron-
bombardment. In 1940, United States Patent No. 2,206,634 was granted
to the scientific sextet. A later suit in their names for ten million
dollars against the United States Government for infringing on the
patent during and after the war—which if successful would have netted
Pontecorvo at least one and a half million dollars—was pending when
he disappeared behind the Iron Curtain.

Many aspects of the Pontecorvo disappearance were puzzling. If he
were under any suspicion at all, why was he allowed out of the country?
Apparently the answer was that, short of arrest, the British did not
then restrict the international movement of their citizens. Supply
Minister Strauss, during a House of Commons debate in October

1950, hinted that a tightening-up of security rules at Harwell had played a rôle in Pontecorvo's decision to go to Liverpool. "As he was the holder of a British passport," added Strauss, in relation to Pontecorvo's Continental trip, "there was no means of retaining him in this country."

Were the Pontecorvos under surveillance by the British in Europe? The delay in learning what happened to him suggested the contrary. Certainly there was nothing harried, or hurried, about the way the Pontecorvos took their own car from England to France, and drove south through France to Italy for a visit, as it turned out, to one of Bruno's sisters, who had married an important Communist official in Italy. Emilio Sereni, a member of the Italian Politburo, was a cousin of Bruno Pontecorvo, it developed later. At least one of Bruno's brothers was said to be an Italian Communist of some standing. Friends of the family insisted that the parents, Bruno's brother Guido, a professor in eugenics at Edinburgh University in Scotland, and another brother, unnamed, doing radar work in the United States, were not associated with the party.

After he reached his decision at Lake Como, Bruno Pontecorvo began accumulating luggage. He had been travelling light, but by the time he started north he had twelve suitcases. Did these contain scientific material accumulated with an eye towards a possible, eventual migration?

To cover his escape, Pontecorvo wrote a letter to Harwell on August 31st, the last day of his leave, explaining that he had trouble with his car, which was true enough, but that he hoped to be back in time, which was apparently untrue, for an important mid-September scientific conference in England. Simultaneously a letter went to him from Harwell suggesting that he attend an important European conference on cosmic rays in Switzerland, on the way home. If this were designed to suggest continued confidence, to put him off his guard, like the promotion of Klaus Fuchs after he fell under suspicion, it failed in its purpose. That same day, the Pontecorvos started on the road to Russia. Because of uncertainty about the scientist's plans, embodied in these cross-communications, no inquiries about his movements were initiated by the Harwell authorities until September 21st. By then, the Pontecorvo family had been in Russia at least two weeks.

Abandoning his ailing auto, Pontecorvo took his wife and three boys on the regular passenger plane from Rome to Copenhagen on August 31st. They left the plane there, "for fear of being followed," and travelled by express train to Stockholm. The night of September 1st they stayed at the Soviet Embassy in Stockholm. Next morning, they did not visit, or even phone, Mr. and Mrs. Hans Nordblom, Mrs. Pontecorvo's parents, living nearby in Stockholm. At 11 a.m., they arrived in a Soviet Embassy car at the Bromma Airport, Stockholm, with all their bulging suitcases. During the plane trip to Helsinki, their youngest boy, Antonio, told one of the other passengers, "We are going to Russia." Later the boy noticed land under the plane, and asked, "Is that Russia?"

Bruno Pontecorvo chatted with Finland's Interior Minister, Johannes Virulainen, during the plane trip to Helsinki, and upon arrival handed Virulainen his British passport, saying he had no further use for it. Mrs. Virulainen noticed Mrs. Pontecorvo because the latter was "conspicuously nervous, pale and haggard," she said. Mrs. Virulainen's recollection was that the Pontecorvos travelled to Helsinki with the other passengers in an airlines bus. Enrico Altavilla, the Stockholm correspondent of *Il Tempo*, a Rome newspaper, who happened also to make the trip, declared that the Pontecorvos did not travel in the airlines bus, but waited at the airport for a car from the Soviet Legation, which took them and their precious suitcases to the harbour. The Soviet ship *Byelostrov*, scheduled to sail at 10.40 that morning, was waiting with steam up. When the scientist and his family came on board at 5 p.m., the gangplank was immediately raised, lines cast off, and the voyage to Leningrad begun. The *Byelostrov* reached Russia September 5th.

When the Pontecorvo story broke in Rome on October 20th, a wild orgy of speculation developed. Some experts contended that the scientist had been kidnapped by the Russians. Others asserted he was insane. A few analytical minds deduced that the scientist had been lured to the Soviet by some fake offer, under the illusion that he could serve as an intermediary between the scientists of the West and the scientists of the East. There did not seem to be any supporting evidence for these assorted assertions and beliefs. The stark fact remained that Pontecorvo had followed the standard escape route for British agents of the U.S.S.R., after the circulation of reports that another important atomic spy at Harwell was in jeopardy.

Ostensibly on the basis of Swedish intelligence reports, Victor Riesel, an American labour columnist, declared on April 16th, 1951, that Pontecorvo's assignment in Russia was to develop, by June 1952, an air-defence system based on cosmic rays which would destroy America's ability to deliver atomic or hydrogen bombs. Riesel said Pontecorvo was expected to help in the accelerated production of A-bombs, and to work on a rocket capable of accurate guidance between distant continents.

On September 24th, Kenneth de Courcy, editor of the *Intelligence Digest* in London, said the Russians expected to explode an H-bomb under the guidance of Pontecorvo by June 1952. An earlier deadline of October 1952, said De Courcy, had been moved up to June by Stalin personally. De Courcy, who did not reveal any particular understanding of atomic energy, said his tips came from anti-Soviet persons behind the Iron Curtain who had access to classified material. He declared Pontecorvo was working at a main Soviet H-bomb research centre in the extreme south of Asiatic Russia.

Issa Yusuf Bey Aliptekin, former Secretary-General of Sinkiang province in China, declared in Cairo on November 11th, 1951, that Pontecorvo was working in a huge atomic stronghold in Sinkiang centring around a new octopus-shaped city at Kualja, not far from Urumchi, the capital. Issa Bey traced his information to refugees from Sinkiang as well as to Soviet broadcasts over Radio Turkestan. Two or three days later, the *China Union Press*, from Taihoku, reported that Wang Wen-Hao, a famed geologist and former National Premier, had joined Pontecorvo in Sinkiang on H-bomb work.

United States scientists were inclined to dismiss the Sinkiang rumours, on two grounds: (1) that the sources did not seem reliable enough, and (2) that atomic energy plants needed connections with sources of supplies and machinery, and well-developed communications, which would not be available in Sinkiang. Riesel's tip was considered more to the point, though no verification of a June 1952 deadline, or any Soviet deadline, had reached United States atomic leaders.

Towards the end of November 1951, two newspapers in Rome, *Il Tempo* and *Momento Sera*, quoted unidentified Russian sources in Stockholm to the effect that Bruno Pontecorvo had been jailed in Russia on suspicion of being an American atomic spy. These sensational yarns asserted that Stalin had come to the conclusion that Pontecorvo had been slipping data about the Russian atomic explosions to President Truman. The British did not seem impressed. "It is intriguing," said one Ministry of Supply official in London, "that such news, if true, should have percolated through the Iron Curtain." Reliable Western listening posts in Finland and elsewhere did not seem to have picked up any reports of Pontecorvo's arrest. Furthermore, President Truman's first announcement about a Soviet atomic blast came on September 23rd, 1949, a full year before Pontecorvo left England. The second and third White House announcements on the subject were dated October 3rd and October 29th, 1950, which did not allow Pontecorvo much more than a month, after his arrival, to start spying, which seemed silly on the face of it. Towards the end of December 1951, some slight evidence developed that could be interpreted as suggesting an improved scientific status for Pontecorvo in the Soviet Union, rather than arrest. The Alichanian brothers, who had received a Stalin prize three years previously for discovering varitrons, were repudiated by the leading Soviet scientific journals, according to a dispatch in the *New York Times*. Since Pontecorvo was one of the foreign physicists who had doubted the existence of varitrons, this could have meant a victory for him of a personal sort.

Nothing surpasses spy fiction, of course, and occasionally spy fact. All sorts of elaborations were possible on the basis of the Pontecorvo rumours. In a country like Russia, where officially sponsored suspicion of anybody who had ever been abroad had sharpened almost into mania, and where the ordinary intellectual impatience over restraint was not given any leeway, it was conceivable that Bruno Pontecorvo, despite his past services, could have been arrested on some pretext or other. It was conceivable that Mrs. Pontecorvo had gotten fed up with life in Russia, and wished she were back in England again, only to find, as thousands of others had found before her, that it was easier to get in than to get out of Russia.

All these suppositions did not actually add up to much in the way of fact. Why should the Soviets antagonise Pontecorvo, his wife, or any of the little Pontecorvos? What greater appeal could there be to any scientist than responsibility for a research programme as broad as some of the reports suggested? Some American students of espionage wondered whether the stories could involve an effort to force disclosure of Bruno Pontecorvo's whereabouts and activities. If so, they did not succeed. No flaw appeared in the monolithic secrecy imposed by the Kremlin in scientific matters.

XXV

TRAITORS IN THE FOREIGN OFFICE

from

THE MISSING DIPLOMATS

by CYRIL CONNOLLY

(The Queen Anne Press, London, 1952)

Reams have been written about Guy Burgess and Donald Maclean, the two officials of the Foreign Office who, on May 25th, 1951, left England and mysteriously vanished into thin air. Public interest in their disappearance stimulated the official and unofficial hunt of the missing diplomats both in England and on the Continent, but nothing definite came to light, though it was surmised that they had fled to Russia.

Thanks to the revelations of Vladimir Petrov, the Soviet official who sought political asylum in Australia, we now know for certain that the two are actually in Russia, but little light has been shed on the reasons that motivated their flight.

Cyril Connolly, who knew both Burgess and Maclean personally, and who, in fact, had lunch with Maclean on the very day of his disappearance, analyses in his little brochure, The Missing Diplomats, *the characters of the two protagonists in the mystery.*

★

So many explanations of their disappearance have been put forward that it is best to deal with a few of them like chess-openings.

1(a). NON-POLITICAL. *The two disappeared on an alcoholic fugue, to wander about like Verlaine and Rimbaud and to start a new life together.*

This fits in with Donald's character. He is said to have disappeared once for a few days from a party in Switzerland and been found living quietly in the next village. Again, he once remarked to a friend that he wished he could start a new life as a docker in the East End or as a carpenter, but that ration books and identity cards now made it impossible. Burgess also had a reputation for vanishing, but there would be much less reason for him to give up the kind of existence to which he was addicted. Neither could have a lasting attraction for the other, the force which united them would also drive them apart and the wanderers would certainly have been heard of again, for where they were in company incidents would be bound to arise. The element of anti-social aggression in such a flight would have caused them to leave behind some kind of statement.

1(b). VOLUNTARY BUT POLITICAL. *Like Hess in reverse, Burgess and*

Maclean decided to go to Russia to make a personal appeal for the ending of the war in Korea.

This also fits in with the expiatory side of their characters, and would clear up Donald's guilty feelings about himself and the state of the world, while satisfying the "Brigadier Brilliant" aspect of Burgess. I do not find this idea altogether ridiculous. Donald minded terribly about the war in Korea and had submitted a paper on it to the Foreign Office of his own free will, and Guy had worked in the Far-Eastern Department and attempted a "mission to Moscow" in '42. Although the hue-and-cry would to the Russians demonstrate the spontaneity of their visit, one would have expected Donald to drop some reassuring hint to his superiors and certainly to have chosen a better moment, for domestic reasons. Yet we cannot entirely dismiss this theory.

2(a). THEORIES WHICH IMPLY A FORCED MOVE. "*A twitch upon the thread.*"

The argument is that Burgess and Maclean were both Communist agents. The Cambridge dose of Marxism had, in fact, been lethal—as it was for Maclean's fellow scholar at Trinity Hall, Dr. Nunn May, or Burgess's Etonian convert to Marxism who became one of the Californian Communist leaders and died there. Maclean (or both) was growing indiscreet and unreliable, and so they were recalled before one (or both) could give away others who were more secret and more important; they were then immediately imprisoned or even liquidated and may have got no farther than an uncertain address in Paris. If they had refused to go, they would be exposed to the British and bring disgrace on their families. Even so, it is doubtful if two such experienced diplomats, aged thirty-eight and forty, would sign their own death-warrants without a murmur and depart without a farewell.

2(b) *They both (or Maclean alone) had given information to the Russians at some time, perhaps on one occasion only, and this was preying on Donald's conscience.*

If the information was given in Washington, it might have been valuable and the leak would have taken a long time to trace. Burgess might have had wind in Washington of this investigation and even got himself sent home through his erratic behaviour in order to warn Maclean on his return. A beautiful gesture; a knight's tour. According to a newspaper report Burgess spoke of "a young married friend of mine in trouble, serious trouble," and he might perhaps have been a kind of private commissar to Maclean for some time. After his carefree luncheon, then, on that last Friday, Maclean was somehow tipped off that exposure was imminent. He might have received the warning at his club or it may indeed have come earlier in the week and thus resulted in Burgess taking the tickets on Wednesday with the American as a piece of window dressing, like Maclean's last luncheon party.

This theory bristles with difficulties, but is the only one to explain the sudden departure and is consistent with the recent rumours of money being sent to him from behind the Iron Curtain. And yet, it conflicts with Maclean's character. As one who worked long and closely with Donald puts it, "I could not conceive of his choosing to be a traitor." He might, however, have compromised himself through his indiscretions in Washington, though it may be mentioned that he made no attempt to see secret papers, to which he could have access, while in charge of the American division. Was Burgess his evil genius or his saviour? Or both? One more fact. He had often expressed an inclination to suicide, only his love for his children kept him from it. This love was the one emotion which he felt without ambivalence and he would not have taken any drastic step unless he had been convinced that as far as their happiness was concerned it was the lesser of two evils.

Perhaps the two divided personalities are at least completely integrated through contact with that mysterious elixir, the Proletariat. But, as Maclean said, what matters most is people, and that is what makes his case essentially tragic. Guy Burgess always enjoyed being himself, and for a while he lived his own dream, a realistic example of the "new type of diplomat" who is always demanded in wartime. But Donald Maclean, were it not for his lack of balance and emotional security, had the qualities of a great public servant. Yet with all his admiration for people, he betrayed those who loved him, humiliated those who trusted him, and discredited those who thought like him. . . . But once again we are condemning them unheard.

At this point I feel I should offer a solution of my own, had my judgment not been worn away by the balancing of opposites. In the beginning I was as convinced of their innocence as I was apprehensive of their fate but, as I went on with these "variations," I experienced more and more uncertainty about the one and less and less alarm about the other. Somewhere, I feel sure, the comic genius of Burgess is standing sentinel over the tragic propensities of Maclean. I believe the telegrams to be genuine, though dictated, and if they are genuine and freely given then they were sent by two people who well knew what they were doing and who had found it essential to take violent evasive action. Why they thought this necessary we do not know. Ever since his return from Washington Burgess was in an increasingly disturbed condition, he seemed almost to have an hallucination about the evil intentions of America, for he told a stranger whom he met while going round Winchester College that America was deliberately forcing privations upon us by not permitting trade with China. I believe he may have worked up Maclean with his Hiss complex into the belief that war was imminent and that Senator MacCarthy was after their blood, thus causing them to seek refuge from an imaginary danger perhaps through diplomatic connections behind the Iron Curtain. One would like to know much more about Burgess's contacts with the foreign Press from 1944 to '46 and about Maclean's Washington life from 1944 to '48 and also about all their movements a full week before their departure. Since they knew each other well enough to run away together a relationship must have existed and was therefore concealed, presumably for political reasons. By the evening of the twenty-fifth Maclean is involved in deception. How can we be certain that at lunchtime he was any more truthful? The special leave for Saturday morning, the false name, the tourist boat where they would be unlikely to be recognised, the suitcases left behind to suggest that they were coming back to the cabin, the taxi engaged after all the other passengers were scattered—all these suggest a careful plan to gain as much time as possible (from Friday night to Monday morning) before they would be missed. By travelling from Rennes in separate carriages they would attract less notice. They could either change at Le Mans, catch the fast train to Tours and link up eventually with some night *rapide* like the Bordeaux-Milan or go on to Paris and catch the Arlberg express. (Even this summer I found myself looking for them—it's infectious—in Zürich, Feldkirch, Liechtenstein.) By Sunday evening they could be almost anywhere in Europe by train or plane, for not until the following Monday was Maclean's absence from work noticed and a week elapsed before the French were warned to watch the frontiers.

XXVI

THE PETROV STORY

from

THE PETROV STORY

by MICHAEL BIALOGUSKI

(Published by Heinemann Ltd., London, 1955)

Perhaps the most sensational espionage episode of recent years, one that made for banner headlines and acted like a camphor injection on the circulation of the world's popular Press, was enacted in far-off Australia. Everybody knows the Petrov story, so there is no need to expatiate on its details.

Vladimir Petrov, a high M.V.D. official attached to the Russian Embassy in Canberra, became the central figure of the greatest diplomatic scandal of recent history when, on April 3rd, 1954, he left his Embassy and applied to the Common-wealth authorities for political asylum in Australia. What led up to the defection of this Soviet dignitary is aptly told in The Petrov Story, *by Michael Bialoguski, a medical doctor of Polish extraction, who had lived in Australia for over fourteen years, and who did some secret service work for Australia in his spare time.*

The Soviet system of making hostages expiate the "crimes" of their nationals can only affect citizens with a family behind the Iron Curtain. It so happened that Petrov's wife, Dusya, was held at the Soviet Canberra Embassy at the time of the M.V.D. man's defection, and thus liable to be transported to Russia for expiatory punishment.

Her rescue by the Australian security service was one of the outstanding features of the Petrov case. Escorted by a couple of Soviet gorillas on her plane ride from Canberra to Darwin, which aroused great public indignation, she was separated from her armed companions on landing at Darwin by Australian security men. The excerpt we reprint from Bialoguski's thrilling book describes that incident.

★

I DID not have to keep up my pretence of searching for Petrov for long. Within a week his defection became public knowledge.

During my manœuvring I had been seeing him every few days. Most of our talk had been about Dusya; apparently he had accepted that nothing could be done, for the time being at least, about Jack.

There was no doubt now that Dusya was being held in the Embassy. This had a most distressing influence on Petrov. It was now certain that he wanted her to stay; he needed somebody who had been close

to him. To some degree I supplied moral support and comfort, but he
needed more, which in these circumstances, at least, could come only
from his wife.

He was in no state of mind to face his problems alone. Now that he
had crossed the line, he lived almost entirely under the direction of
Security, and being the man he was, he had no real trust in them.
He had a persistent fear of violence, not only from his former colleagues, but from Security. The M.V.D. method, he knew, would
be to use a man in his position until the desired purpose had been served,
and then to dispose of him. He saw no reason why Security should not
do the same thing; in his eyes, in fact, it would be the reasonable thing
for them to do.

This line of thought produced in him a subconscious urge to share his
fears, and who better to share them with than his wife?

He talked to me almost interminably about her. On all his visits—
and they were frequent—the conversation inevitably came round to
Dusya. Petrov was persistently pessimistic; he always took the gloomy
view that he would remain in Australia alone.

"It's her family," he would say. "But for that she would have been
here with me. She was as sick of it all as I was, I know it. She told me
that many times." Then after pausing for a moment his voice would
drop despondently: "But she'll go back. I'm sure she will."

I never accepted that view. My argument, which I pressed unceasingly
on Petrov, was that Dusya was a sensible, practical woman, and her
inclination now was to stay. Right, the only obstacle was her family.
Now, what good would she do by going back? Would she save her
family by doing so? It seemed to me she would not, and that after
some thought she herself would almost certainly come to the same
conclusion.

"You know yourself, Vladimir," I would say, "that once you de-
fected, Dusya would, according to Soviet practice, bear equal responsibility with you. And it goes further than that, as you also know. Anyone
even remotely connected with you will be persecuted whether Dusya
is here or in Russia. Her whereabouts doesn't matter."

That did not end my argument. Vladimir had based his opinion on
the attitude Dusya had adopted months before his defection.

I told him: "You must realise that circumstances now are entirely
different for her. I don't think she ever took your complaints as an
indication that you might walk out of the Embassy. Now you have
done so, and Dusya is confronted with a *fait accompli*. I say she is
sensible enough to perceive that she now has no choice but to stay,
if only to save herself."

Petrov would agree with all I had to say, but still was not convinced. He would shake his head mournfully: "She'll still go back. I know her. She's a determined woman."

This kind of talk could not but prompt other forms of speculation about Dusya. What was she thinking? What was she doing? Was she miserable and blaming Petrov? Was she being ill-treated? What would be her fate if she got back to Russia?

I found it hard to resist the emotional undercurrents of the situation, which tended to thrust into the background the practical questions of what was best from a security point of view. I found myself caught up in the human elements of the drama, and no longer able to preserve the impersonal approach with which an agent must go about his work. I had brought this drama to its climax, and what was to happen to Dusya was in a large measure my responsibility. No longer was she a cipher in the game; she had become a human being.

My discomfort of mind was increased by my helplessness to do anything. Whatever Security was planning—if they were planning anything—I was excluded from their deliberations.

I was unsettled and uneasy, and pondering what could be done, when one Saturday evening, two weeks after his defection, Petrov visited me with Richards at a new flat I had taken at Lindfield. Petrov's anxiety and distress had left their mark on him. He was pale and drawn, and his cropped hair, shorter than usual, accentuated the puffiness of his cheeks and gave him an unhealthy appearance.

None of us had much to say. We all knew now that Dusya would be taken back to Russia soon.

Petrov brought up the subject that was on all our minds. "If only I could speak to her," he said, "I could persuade her to stay."

"Well," said Richards, "we are making arrangements for you to talk to her."

"How are you going to do that?" I asked.

"We'll see that Vladimir meets her when she's about to leave Sydney."

From what Richards went on to say I gathered that the plan was for Petrov to appear before his wife at the last moment and urge her to stay. I said nothing, but the more I thought about the proposal the less I liked it; the risk of failure was too great. I decided that whether Security heeded my advice or not, I should point out my objections and submit an alternative. I knew I must act at once—before their plan had reached the operative stage—if I were to get a hearing.

On the Sunday morning I rang East and arranged to meet him that day. I told him of Richards's visit and of his plan to keep Mrs. Petrov here.

"I don't think it will work," I said.

"The idea is suddenly to confront Dusya with her husband. You must remember that Dusya will be coming direct from the Embassy and she will have an escort. By now, I'm sure, she will have been reduced to a bundle of nerves, and subjected to an incessant schooling in behaviour and attitude to the outside world. This treatment will have had an effect on her mind, already made susceptible by her own thinking. She could not have helped blaming Petrov in her mind for her troubles.

"You must also remember that she still is very much a Soviet woman. For the truth of that we have a record of my conversation with her.

"All these factors would combine to create in her a highly emotional state. Her reaction to any sudden and unusual situation would be dictated by emotion, not by reason. What do you think is likely to happen if she is suddenly confronted by Petrov?

"Knowing her as I do, I believe she might see him merely as the person who was the cause of it all, and burst out with some irrevocable attack before she had time to think. If she did that, she would commit herself and there would be no retreat for her."

I paused for a moment to marshal my thoughts. Then I went on, trying to hammer home every point.

"But if you concede a chance of success to your plan, you must, by the same token, concede a greater chance to my alternative.

"My proposal is: Don't make any approach, direct or indirect, to Mrs. Petrov in Sydney. Keep Petrov away and let her go. There will be other opportunities before she is outside British jurisdiction.

"Once she is aboard the ship or plane, whichever it might be, she will feel that now there is no turning back. Then she will begin to think about what is in store for her in Russia. With years of service in the M.V.D. she knows the answer—probably a labour camp for the rest of her days. Isn't she more likely to listen to you then than she would have been before the journey began?"

I went on to discuss the technicalities of the approach—how best, in my view, it could be made. "You must create circumstances which would make it appear to the Soviet officials that Mrs. Petrov is not staying voluntarily. That would, for the moment, allay her fears for her relatives in Russia. It would also save face for her with the escorts. I feel strongly about this. I have been close to Mrs. Petrov personally, and think I can predict better than anybody else her likely reactions in a given situation. I would be glad if Security would consult me before it makes any future moves with the Petrovs."

East took a note of all I had to say, and assured me he would place my ideas before Richards immediately.

.　.　.　.　.

The time came when we all knew that Dusya was to leave for Russia the next day, and I had heard nothing from Security. I thought a great deal about Dusya that last night and speculated on what her thoughts must be.

By now, I felt, she must have come to realise that she had the choice of two courses.

She could stay in Australia whereby she might sign the death-warrant of her family, or she could go back to Russia and forfeit her personal freedom, perhaps her life. Then there was the further entirely unknown factor; if she went back would this save her parents, sister and brother? Most unlikely, but perhaps it might help.

Suppose she decided to stay here, how would she go about it? She would be sure to be watched. If only she knew where Vladimir was and what had actually happened to him!

The longer she thinks the more confused she becomes. Each doubt raises a question which in turn creates a new doubt.

The morning has come. What does the future hold? All she knows is that she is miserable, bewildered and scared.

.　.　.　.　.

The Russians, with astounding ineptitude, had thrust Mrs. Petrov into the world spotlight and kept her there for days. If public interest showed any sign of slackening, they immediately revived it by some clumsy manœuvre which restored her to the centre of the stage.

Even at the last minute, they acted in a manner calculated to preserve a note of high drama. Instead of travelling to Sydney openly, they attempted to shroud Mrs. Petrov's movements in mystery in so obvious a manner that even a "hick" reporter could not have failed to be on their heels.

Just as in a dime detective story, the sleek, powerful black limousine moved off from the Embassy at high speed, with all the appearance of a gangster car taking a victim "for a ride."

Reporters excitedly noted that in the front seat were the driver and Second Secretary Kislitsyn, while in the back a shrouded female figure—presumably Mrs. Petrov—sat between two powerful diploma-tic couriers—Zharkov and Karpinsky, who whatever their personal qualities had the appearance of a couple of mobsters from a third-rate gangster film.

The Russians could hardly have found two more provocative-looking characters for the job.

One glance at Zharkov and Karpinsky was quite enough to provoke the mob assembled at Mascot to wild excitement and mad rage. The two men looked bad, and when they laid hands on Mrs. Petrov, the demonstrators were convinced they were bad. Mrs. Petrov immediately became the world's sweetheart in the grip of evil, an image that was confirmed in the fairy-tale tradition when, bustled by her two oafish escorts, she cast a shoe!

The clumsiness of the Russians was never more strikingly manifest. Nothing could have been more calculated to precipitate a crowd already infuriated to the point of riot.

As Mrs. Petrov, confused and bewildered, uncertain whether the crowd was hostile to her or to her escorts, was literally dragged up the gangway to the plane by the now panic-stricken Russians, groups of people rushed forward menacingly, aiming blows at the party.

Throughout this wild scene, in which violence repeatedly seemed imminent, Security men on the spot remained inactive. There could be only one explanation, I thought, why Security remained aloof. They had been given orders not to intervene. This, I thought, could mean only that they had dropped their plan of producing Petrov at the last minute, and intended to act somewhere along the route her plane must follow. I could draw only one conclusion: they had adopted my plan.

The demonstration could have become really serious if civil police and members of the air crew had not intervened. With Security lying low because it had other plans in view, one of the main reasons for public hostility towards the authorities was the latter's apparent in-difference to Mrs. Petrov's fate. People believed that the final act had been played, and Mrs. Petrov abandoned.

Even as the plane took off at 10 p.m.—right on schedule—the mob was still seething around the airport, and for some time police were kept on the alert by the threat of trouble.

But my thoughts were now on the immediate future. What would happen? I had gambled! Was the gamble going to succeed? In what-ever way I looked at it, I could not help but feel that the responsibility was mine. Had Dusya's last chance gone and was she now on her way back to her death?

THE PETROV STORY 207

Security, however, still had cards in their hand; one of their men was on the plane and would play a part next day in the historic scene at Darwin.

Meanwhile, her journey begun, Mrs. Petrov appeared too shaken by her recent ordeal to give thought to the major problem which still confronted her.

According to a special *Sydney Morning Herald* reporter who travelled on the plane, she lay back in her seat, looking pale and exhausted.

He records how, just before the plane took off, Mrs. Petrov had burst into tears; her make-up smudged and her face glistening with perspiration.

She spoke to a steward, evidently asking for permission to smoke. Although this was refused, she lit a cigarette, and none of the crew passing up and down the aisle made any attempt to tell her to put it out.

Mrs. Petrov sat next to Kislitsyn, with the two couriers, Karpinsky and Zharkov, sitting behind.

As the plane took off, she appeared to quieten and looked fixedly out of the window as the aircraft gained height over the myriad lights of Sydney.

Then again she was overcome by emotion, and broke down crying for a few minutes. Meanwhile Kislitsyn sat upright in his seat, paying no attention.

As the journey wore on, all the Russians were on edge, but Mrs. Petrov was particularly unsettled. Repeatedly she picked up the afternoon's papers in which Petrov had made an appeal to her to remain in Australia. Each time she picked up a paper, she would read for a minute or two, put it down and appear to be deep in reflection. In the early morning she was ill, apparently from emotional strain, for the plane was quite steady.

Several times during the night Mrs. Petrov made trips to the back of the plane—apparently to visit the toilet. Actually she talked with stewardess Joyce Bull, who was, unofficially, an emissary of Security.

Shortly after the plane had taken off, Security had contacted Captain J. Davys by radio and asked that he should have three questions put to Mrs. Petrov:

What was the state of her health?
Whether she was in fear?
Whether she wished to remain in Australia?
By the time Miss Bull, at Captain Davys's instruction, contrived an

opportunity to put the questions, the plane was approaching Darwin, and Mrs. Petrov's chances of retreat were becoming slimmer.

But apparently Mrs. Petrov had by now become fully seized with her situation.

She was afraid, she told Miss Bull. The couriers, she said, were armed and would, if need be, use force. She would like to stay in Australia, but she was scared.

This was the tense atmosphere in which the plane made its landing at Darwin—the last Australian airport—at 5.15 a.m. on April 19th, 1954.

In contrast with their immobility in Sydney, Security acted promptly, and surrounded the Russian party immediately the Constellation touched down.

Police quickly separated the couriers from Kislitsyn and Mrs. Petrov.

They asked the couriers to surrender their weapons, but both refused, and in a struggle that followed, six police disarmed them, taking .32 Walther automatics from each man. Karpinsky was carrying his gun on the hip, and Zharkov had his in a shoulder holster.

Meanwhile, Mrs. Petrov was separated from Kislitsyn and questioned by Mr. R. Leydin, the senior Government officer in the Northern Territory, representing the absent Administrator.

He had been asked to meet Mrs. Petrov and to find out whether she wished to remain in Australia. If she said yes, he was to accept her on behalf of the Commonwealth. He was authorised to use police officers to protect Mrs. Petrov if any attempt were made to restrain her.

It was obvious at this stage that Mrs. Petrov was not prepared to commit herself, because, officials reported later, she was still scared of what might happen to her.

Then, two hours later, there came a dramatic development; Mrs. Petrov was called to the Customs office. She was told that her husband was on the phone, and that he wanted to make a final appeal to her to stay in Australia with him.

It was revealed later, by the Prime Minister, Mr. Menzies, that until then Mrs. Petrov had believed her husband to be dead. She had not heard from him since he had sought political asylum, and his efforts to arrange a meeting with her had been frustrated by the Russian Embassy.

As Mrs. Petrov picked up the receiver, her three Russian companions and Australian Security and police officials clustered around. Mrs. Petrov spoke in Russian, and nobody made any attempt to interfere.

At first her voice was very low, and for long periods she listened intently without speaking. Then, as she started to speak again, she raised her voice saying "Nyet, nyet!" (No, no!)

When the four-minute call ended, she looked depressed and tired. She shook her head and shrugged her shoulders when Mr. Leydin spoke to her.

Then, twenty minutes before the plane was due to leave Darwin for Singapore, Mr. Leydin came forward again.

Kislitsyn intervened, but Mrs. Petrov said in English "No, I go with him." She and Leydin walked into the airport office and closed the door, with police and officials standing guard outside.

The two "gorillas," Karpinsky and Zharkov, sat stolidly on a bench in the terminal hall staring vacantly into space. Kislitsyn was still protesting about Mrs. Petrov's disappearance when the Commonwealth Law Officer in Darwin, Mr. K. Edmunds, approached him. "Mrs. Petrov and Mr. Leydin have gone to Government House by car."

"For what?" shouted Kislitsyn.

"She wants to have a rest in Australia," Edmunds replied.

Kislitsyn became extremely agitated. "It's a provocation," he shouted, "she's been kidnapped."

. . . . . .

These final words of Kislitsyn—"She's been kidnapped"—the last he uttered in Australia, meant a great deal to me. It seemed that I could claim, without presumption, that all my calculations and deductions had been confirmed.

It will be recalled that when I saw East to oppose Security's plan to confront Mrs. Petrov with her hysband at Mascot, I argued that it was both premature and dangerous because it could provoke in her a hostile reaction, and commit her to a course from which she could not retreat.

I proposed that the best psychological approach was to await the point where Mrs. Petrov was confronted realistically with the dangers of her situation, and then to give her the chance to create in the minds of the Russians the impression that she had been kidnapped.

With Kislitsyn's cry "She's been kidnapped," my ideas were confirmed down to the last detail. Security had succeeded with an efficiently applied plan based on those ideas.

. . . . . .

Meanwhile I had spent a sleepless night and was in the city early next morning. The day wore on, but I didn't feel tired. Dusya must be in Darwin now. The crucial moment had come and maybe passed. I wandered aimlessly along Pitt Street, through the shopping crowds. I should know soon; the papers would be out in a few minutes. On the corner of King Street I paused and looked up as a van passed. On its side was a poster: SHE STAYS.

I knew I would not need a paper.